Anonymous

Report of the Committee appointed to revise the Soldiers' Record

Anonymous

Report of the Committee appointed to revise the Soldiers' Record

ISBN/EAN: 9783337134235

Printed in Europe, USA, Canada, Australia, Japan

Cover: Foto ©ninafisch / pixelio.de

More available books at **www.hansebooks.com**

OF THE

COMMITTEE

APPOINTED

TO REVISE THE SOLDIERS' RECORD.

DANVERS:
PUBLISHED BY THE TOWN.

PRINTED BY
NEWCOMB & GAUSS,
SALEM, MASS.

CONTENTS.

Illustrations:

The boulder on the Old Training Field,	frontispiece
The Lexington monument,	opposite page 88
The Rebellion monument.	
Report of committee,	v
Rebellion records,	
Military service,	1
Naval service,	68
Additional records,	74, 86
Character and behaviour of discharged soldiers,	note, 79
Regimental histories,	81
The monument erected to the soldiers and sailors of Danvers who fell in the late war.	88

APPENDIX.

Early military organizations and service,	91
King Philip's War,	93
Bloody Brook,	94
French Wars,	96
Soldiers in French and Indian War, 1756-1763,	100, note 112*
Militia organizations, 1763-1775,	108
The Lexington Alarm, 19 April, 1775,	
Company of Capt. John Putnam,	110
" " " Jere. Page,	110
" " " Edmund Putnam,	111
" " " Asa Prince,	111
" " " Samuel Flint,	111
" " " Samuel Eppes,	112
" " " Israel Hutchinson,	112
" " " Caleb Lowe,	112*
Militia organizations during the Revolution,	113*
Gen. Gage in Danvers, 1774,	115*
Privateers and privateersmen from Danvers,	115*, 136

CONTENTS.

List of Revolutionary Soldiers.	113
Militia Officers.	136
Shay's Rebellion. 1786.	137
Soldiers of the War of 1812,	138
Soldiers of the Mexican War,	141
Militia companies of Danvers. 1796-1817.	142
Danvers Light Infantry, M. M., 1818-1850.	143
Danvers Light Infantry, M. V. M.,	144
Proceedings of the Danvers Historical Society. 20 April, 1891,	146
What the Danvers men did, by Ezra D. Hines, Esq.,	147
The Putnams at Lexington fight, by Eben Putnam,	154
The Old Training Field,	162
The Lexington Monument,	163
List of soldiers and sailors buried in Danvers.	164

REPORT.

The task of compiling a complete and accurate account of the Soldiers of Danvers, is an impossible one, but careful and effective work has been attempted by your committee in the hope that their report will be received as a fair testimonial of their services, and as a lasting memorial to the brave men who have claimed Danvers as their home.

That two years should be needed to prepare a report such as this is, is not to be wondered at, when it is considered that nearly if not quite one thousand letters of varying character have been mailed, that but a very small percentage of the persons addressed have paid any attention to the questions of the committee, and, that in the records of the State and National Departments exist errors innumerable.

The records of the town have been carefully consulted for information leading to any suggestions of error on the records of the adjutant-general's department* at the State House, and whenever such have been found, from any source, that department has willingly and promptly requested information from Washington, which has as promptly been supplied. By these means many errors and omissions have been corrected at both those offices. That mistakes should have occurred was unavoidable. It is strange that they were not found in greater number. That there are numerous instances in the report we make to you is probable. Cases will be found where men were credited to towns entirely without their knowledge, and so erroneous is the record of bounties that the committee have omitted that item entirely in the printed report, but the amounts can be examined by any proper person, in the original manuscript.

---

*Thanks are especially due to Mr. John Baker of that department, whose acquaintance with the various records in his charge is remarkable.

The greater part of the expense contracted by your committee is, of course, accounted for by this report, and we pride ourselves that it has been so slight, considering the variety, remoteness and miscellaneous character of the records consulted.

The committee has held twelve regular meetings at each of which except upon rare occasions, all of the members have been present. Several informal gatherings of the committee have been held, and throughout our existence as a committee the utmost harmony and combined effort has prevailed. The greater part of the labor of preparing the record has fallen upon the chairman, who from his profession and knowledge of the sources of information was selected to collect and arrange the material, which, however, has been carefully inspected in detail by the several members of the committee.

It was thought best to add as an appendix some account of the soldiers of Danvers in other than our late war*, and we have endeavored to present a record of our men in the Indian and French wars, the Revolution, the War of 1812, Mexican war, and some account of our early and present militia organizations.

A feature of this report is the preservation of the family records of our soldiers. Here we may have made some errors and crave your indulgence, but that in the generations to come, the same honor and veneration will be paid to the men of 1861 as is now paid to the heroes of 1775 is undoubted, and our descendants and successors will thank us for placing on record some account, however fragmentary, of the families and lives of the soldiers.

It is earnestly hoped that every person having knowledge of any

---

*The number of enlistments in the Union Army was 666, of whom 552 were native born. The places of nativity of the men as far as can be ascertained are as follows: Danvers, 125, of whom four were of Irish parentage; other towns in Essex, 98, of whom one was of Irish parentage; other places in Massachusetts, 39, of whom three were of German parentage; New Hampshire, 43; Maine, 45; United States, 202, of whom eight were negroes, and thirty-five of Irish parentage (probably many in this division are Danvers born); Canada, 30, of whom twenty-seven came from the Maritime provinces; England, 15; Scotland, 13; Ireland, 47; Germany 9.

There were at least thirty-seven Danvers men in the naval service, and forty-nine additional records are appended, of men who have lived or died in Danvers. Thus the records of 796 separate individuals, who served in the Rebellion are printed.

We have gathered information relating to 139 French war soldiers in addition to the names given in the historical sketch; and some 300 Revolutionary soldiers in addition to an equal number of Lexington Alarm men. Mention will also be found of others who were probably in the service for longer or shorter periods.

Over 1800 names of soldiers or sailors born or resident at some period in Danvers are printed in this report.

soldier born in or credited to Danvers will inspect this report, will note the various records, and send to your committee, or to the town clerk, all corrections and omissions, however gross or slight, that, as nearly as possible, a correct record may in time be obtained by the town.

We cordially extend to all of the many persons who have contributed aid and information, our grateful acknowledgments; to the great interest exhibited by a few, is, indeed, due the accomplishment of our task.

Danvers has had in the past a great history and has given birth to a race of warriors. She has had no occasion to be ashamed of her men; an intensely military and patriotic spirit has always influenced her citizens, as the record will show. It behooves us to place upon record both in print, and on stone and brass, memorials to those of her citizens who have fought for and guarded the nation.

Respectfully submitted,
EBEN PUTNAM,
WALTER S. LOVEJOY,
JOHN W. PORTER,
MALCOLM SILLARS,
ANDREW NICHOLS.

DANVERS, March, 1895.

MILITARY SERVICE.

ABBOTT.

George H.,
m. 5 July, 1861, Co. I, 1st H. A.; dis. 8 July, 1864, ex. term.

Æt. 21 at enl.; lives in Peabody.

Henry G.,
m. 23 Feb., 1864. Co. H, 3d H. A.; dis. 18 Sept., 1865, ex. term.

b. Shapleigh, Me., 1841, son of John and Lydia Bean Abbott; m. 27 Nov., 1862, Elizb. A. Coffin. Ch.: Henry Grover, b. 14 Sept., 1863. Jessie Esther, b. 7 May, 1867. Bertha Hanson, b. 3 Dec., 1868; Inf. 1 Nov., 1870. Mary Elizb., b. 9 June, 1872. Wm. Sherman, b. 29 Jan., 1878. Lives in Danvers.

Richard C.,
m. 29 July, 1863, Co. B, 2d H. A.; dis. 3 Sept., 1865, ex. term.

b. in Shapleigh, Me., æt. 25 at enl., son of John H. and Lydia H. Abbott; m. 27 Aug., 1863, Theresa Hill; m., 2d, 8 Dec., 1877, Lizzie Leach of Malden. Ch.: b. in Danvers: Mabel, b. 22 Sept., 1878.
Lives in Danvers.

ACTON.

John M.,
m. 25 Dec., 1863, Co. B, 17th Inf.; dis. 11 July, 1865, ex. term from Co. C. Credited to South Danvers.

b. Ireland, 1833; m. Bridget Banni. Ch.: William Edward, b. 10 Mar., 1851. Mary Ellen, b. 22 Mar., 1859.
Lives in Danvers.

ADAMS.

Charles H. jr.,
m. 6 July, 1861. Co. I, 1st H. A., 1st Lt., resign. 20 Sept., 1861; m. 22 Dec., 1863, Co. K, 2d H. A., sergt. Com. 2d Lt., 3 June, 1865; dis. 3 Sept., 1865, ex. term.

b. Georgetown, 1838; died in Danvers; son of Charles H. and Elizb. (Moore) Adams; m. 26 May, 1858, Elizb. P., dau. of Timothy and Mary Hawkes. Ch.: Alice Putnam, b. 18 June, 1860; d. 3 Sept., 1879. Family now reside in Lynn.

Henry P.,
m. 19 July, 1861. Co. H, 13th Inf.; dis. 11 Feb., 1863, disability.

b. New Boston, N. H., 1839; son of Marshall and L. G. Adams; m. Frances B. Petterson, b. Amherst, N. H., 3 July, 1861.

William I. (J.),
m. 11 Sept., 1861, 2d Co. S. S.; dis. 18 Feb., 1863, disability.

b. Buxton, Me.; æt. 34 at enl.; m. Mary L. Mayberry, b. Windham, Me. Ch.: Hattie L., b. 19 Jan., 1856. Alfred Royce, b. 8 Sept., 1859. Cora Belle, b. 13 July, 1864. All b. in Danvers.

AIKEN.

Hector A.,
m. 5 July, 1861, Co. I, 1st H. A., reenl. 9 Dec., 1863, same; dis. 16 June, 1864; died at Washington of wounds received at Petersburg, Va.

(Aiken Continued.)

b. Hardwick, Vt., 8 June, 1827; d. 3 June, 1864, City Point Hosp., Va.: m. Abby Ann Titus, b. in Boston; Ch.: Edwin Augustus, b. 28 Mar., 1853. Emma Josephine, b. 4 June, 1854. Charles F., b. 28 June, 1855. Arabella F., b. 11 Dec., 1857. Arthur Augustus, b. 22 Dec., 1858. Elvira A., b. 22 Dec., 1860.

ALLEN.

Albert G.,

m. 1 Oct., 1862, Co. K, 8th Inf., Capt.; dis. 7 Aug., 1863, at ex. term.

b. Shapleigh, Me., Apr., 1818, son of Samuel and Abigail (Pray) Allen; m. Stonington, Ct., 4 June, 1847, Martha Lamson of Beverly. Ch.: Etta Lamson, 3 Apr., 1848. Annie G., b. 23 Dec., 1850. Augustus L., b. 14 July, 1852. Albert C., b. 3 Apr., 1854. Albert G., 15 June, 1865. All b. Danvers. Lives in Danvers.

Charles W.,

m. 1 May, 1861, Co. A, 5th Inf.; dis. 31 July, 1861, ex. term; reenl. m. 1 Oct., 1862; Co. K, 8th Inf., 1st serg.; dis. 7 Aug., 1863, ex. of term.

b. Shapleigh, Me., 1841, brother of Albert G.
Lives in Philadelphia; firm of Allen & Marvin.

George W.,

m. 7 Dec., 1863, Co. I, 1st H. A.; dis. 29 Oct., 1864, died of wounds at Petersburg, Va. Credited to Pelham.

Æt. 44 at enl., and married.

Henry F.,

m. 22 Dec., 1863, Co. K, 2d H. A.; dis. 13 Aug., 1864; died Portsmouth, Va.

b. New Hampshire.

AMBROSE.

John,

m. 22 Aug., 1864, Co. A, 4th H. A.; dis. 17 June, 1865, ex. term.

(Ambrose Continued.)

b. Ireland, 1842, son of Michael and Julia (Ahern) Ambrose; m. 10 Nov., 1870, Mary King. Ch.: Julia, b. 2 Oct., 1871. Michael, b. 7 Feb., 1875. Mary A., b. 11 Feb., 1876.
Lives in Danvers.

ANNABLE.

Charles,

m. 1 Nov., 1861, Co. K, 2 Inf.; dis. 5 Apr., 1864, disability.

b. Hamilton, 27 Oct., 1827; m. 18 July, 1852, Rebecca Adams, b. Buxton, Me., 21 Sept., 1828. Ch. b. Danvers: Charles H., b. 30 Nov., 1853. Mabel Annah, b. 1 Dec., 1860. Irving Kingman, b. 22 Jan., 1867.

ANNIS.

Joseph E.,

m. 22 Aug., 1862, Co. B, 40th Inf.; dis. 25 Feb., 1863, disability.

b. So. Reading, 1 June, 1830; died Danvers, 14 Aug., 1879; m. Lynn, 13 Dec., 1847, Harriet Margaret Wilkins of Wenham. Ch.: Catharine O., b. 24 Jan., 1849. Ada, b. 3 April, 1858. Fred L., b. 24 Mar., 1859. Herbert L., b. 16 Jan., 1861. Eleline Ida, b. 30 Apr., 1863. Geo., b. 14 Aug., 1866.

ANSONBERGER.

Charles,

m. 5 July, 1861, Co. I, 1st H. A.; dis. 21 Jan., 1862, deserted.

b. Germany; æt. 25 at enl. Ch.: Charles, b. 21 Sept., 1857. Henry Alex, b. 5 Mar., 1861.

AVERY.

Daniel P.,

m. 20 Nov., 1862, 2 Batt'y L. Art'y, reenl. 26 Dec., 1863; deserted Jan., 1864, while on veteran furlough.

Æt. 21 at enl., resided in Boston.

BAILEY.

Edwin,

m. 1 May, 1861, Co. A, 5th Inf.; dis. 31 July, 1861, ex. term; m. 1 Oct., 1862, Co.

(Bailey Continued.)

K. 8th Inf., 1st Lt.: dis. 7 Aug., 1863, ex. term.

b. Parsonville, Me., 1836, son of John and Salome Bailey; m. Mary Ellen Black of Danvers, 17 Dec., 1874.

Thomas H.,
m. 19 Aug., 1864, Co. A, 4th H. A.; dis. 17 June, 1865, ex. term., as sergt.

Æt. 25 at enl.

Wallace,
m. 23 Aug., 1864, Co. A, 4th H. A.; dis. 17 June, 1865, ex. term.

Æt. 20 at enl.

BARNARD.
John W.,
m. 16 Sept., 1862, Co. C, 5th Inf.; dis. 2 July, 1863, ex. term. Credited to South Danvers.

b. 22 Jan., 1840, So. Danvers; d. Danvers, 24 Jan., 1895; son of Willis and Susan (Souschurch) Barnard of So. Danvers; m. 10 Mar., 1884, Alice E., dau. of John A. and Sarah (Sylvester) Learoyd, of Danvers. Music teacher, resident of Danvers since 1867. Past Commander Post 90.

BARNES.
Joseph E.,
m. 2 Jan., 1864, 4th Batt'y L. A.; dis. 14 Oct., 1865, ex. term. Credited to Templeton.

Æt. 23 at enl.; killed by elevator accident in Boston abt. 1888; leaving wid. and 4 sons.

BARNETT.
Thomas,
m. 1 Oct., 1862, Co. K, 8th Inf., serg.; dis. 8 Aug., 1863, ex. term.

b. Scotland, 1825; d. Haverhill, 22 Feb., 1885; son of James and Margaret Barnett; m. Catharine J. Hughes; m. 2 1, 17 Mar., 1871, Mary J. Port. Ch.: Clara P., b. 26 July, 1872 Inf., b. 20 Dec., 1873.

BATCHELDER.
George D.,
m. 5 July, 1861, Co I. 1st H. A.; dis. 4 Feb., 1865, exchanged prisoner of war. Taken prisoner in or prior to May, 1864.

Æt. 19 at enlistment. He was claimed by Wenham, where his mother had a residence.

BATTYE.
James,
m. 12 Aug., 1861, Co. B. 17th Inf.; dis. 3 Aug., 1864, ex. term.

b. England, 1818; d. Danvers, 14 Aug., 1864; son of James Battye; m. Sarah ——; Ch.: Barber, b. 8 Dec., 1844. Agly V., b. Jan., 1851. Rhoda J., b 31 July, 1854. Geo. Washington, b 31 Jan., 1854. Louis Kossuth, b. abt. 1858 Ella, m. —— Thomas of Peabody.

BEARD.
George,
m. 16 Aug., 1861, 2nd Co. S. S.; dis. 2 Oct., 1862, disability.

Æt. 35 enl., unm. Lives at Quincy.

BECKFORD.
Edwin,
m. 22 Aug., 1862, Co. B, 40th Inf.; dis. 23 Nov., 1863, died Beaufort, S. C.

b. Salem, 1843; son of William and Lucinda (Small) Beckford.

Horace,
m. 22 Aug., 1862, Co. B, 40th Inf.; dis. 16 June, 1865, ex. term.

b. Salem, 1842, bro. of Edwin; m. 1866, Lydia F. Hale of Beverly. Ch.: Horace Lincoln, b. 1 Mar.,1869. Lives in Lynn.

William F.,
m. 1 May, 1861, Co. H, 5th Inf.; dis. 31 July, 1861, ex. term; m. 28 July, 1862,

(Beckford Continued.)

Co. D, 1st H. A. corp.; dis. 8 July, 1864, disability.

b. Salem, 1839, bro. of Edwin; m. 7 May, 1865, Mary E. Haskell of Salem. Ch.: Frank Edwin, b. 4 Nov., 1865. Fred H., b. 11 Aug., 1867. Nellie May, b. 27 May, 1870. Ernest Elmu, b. 29 Jan., 1872.

BEDELL.
Charles D.,
m. 19 July, 1864, Co. D, 35th Inf.; transferred, 19 July, 1864, to 29 Inf.; dis. 29 July, 1865, as absent sick.

Æt. 21 at enl. Of Troy, N. Y., cred. to Danvers.

BEMIS.
John W.,
m. 6 Aug., 1862, Co. D, 17th Inf.; dis. 28 Jan., 1863, disability. Credited to Haverhill.

b. Worcester; m. Emeline Perkins, of Alton Bay, N. H. Ch.: Geo. W., b. 18 Sept., 1858. Fred Irving, b. 25 May, 1860.

BENJAMIN.
Charles W.,
m. 22 Aug., 1862, Co. B, 40th Inf.; tran. to Veteran Reserve corps, March 15, 1864; dis. from Co. D, 11th V. R. C., July 7, 1865.

b. Salem, 24 Jan., 1834, son of Charles and Hannah (Call) Benjamin.

BENSON.
Samuel D.,
m. 22 July, 1861, Co. C, 17th Inf.; dis. 11 Sept., 1861, disability; m. 29 July, 1863, Co. B, 2d H. Art'y; dis. 14 Oct., 1864, disability.

b. Hooksett, N. H., 1839, son of Joseph C. and J (Davis) Benson; m. 19 Apr., 1869, Caroline D. Wilson of Danvers, dau. of Chas. W. and A. P. Wilson.

BERRY.
Daniel,
m. 2 Jan., 1862, Co. H, 1st H. A.; dis. 20 Jan., 1862, disability.

Æt. 21 at enl., married.

Eugene,
m. 24 Aug., 1864, Co. B, 4th H. A.; dis. 17 June, 1865, ex. term. Credited to Chesterfield.

Æt. 19 at enl.

BIGELOW.
George W.,
m. 21 June, 1861, Co. F, 10th Inf., 2nd Lt.; 1st Lt., 16 June, 1862; Capt., 3 Nov., 1862; dis. 1 July, 1864, ex. term. Commissioned brevet Major, 13 Mar., 1865. Credited to Springfield.

Æt. 32 at enl., unmarried.

BLAKE.
Edward,
m. 4 Sept., 1861, Co. A, 23rd Inf.; dis. 13 Oct., 1864, ex. term. Confined in hospitals at Newberne, Apr., '62; Carolina City, May, '63; Cold Harbor, June, '64; Petersburg, Aug., 1864.

b. Danversport, 15 Jan., 1841, son of Henry Jackson and Dorcas (Mitchell) Blake of Danversport; m. 25 July, 1875, Myra C. Jordan. Ch.: Henry Jackson, b. 13 Dec., 1875. Wm. Edw., b. 11 Feb., 1878. Chas. Wilson, b. 9 July, 1879; since dec'd. Now resides at Danversport.

Joseph,
m. 25 Oct., 1861, Co. A, 23rd Inf.; corp. 17 Aug., 1863; dis. 13 Oct., 1864, ex. term.

b. Danvers, 8 Mar., 1839, son of Henry and Dorcas (Mitchell) Blake. Lives in Peabody. Past Com., Post 90.

TOWN OF DANVERS.

(Blake Continued.)
William O.,
m. 4 Oct., 1863, Co. D, 3d H.
A.; trans. to Co. M, 17 June,
1865; deserted 27 July, 1865.

Æt. 26 at enl.

BODWELL.
Albion W.,
m. 15 July, 1864, Co. I, 6th
Inf.; dis. 27 Oct., 1864, ex.
term.

b. Acton, 1847, son of John and L.
J. (Goodwin) Bodwell; m. Mary M.
Hurd, dau. of Andrew and Prudence Hurd, b. Sanford, Me.

Isaac,
m. 22 July, 1861, Co. C, 17th
Inf.; corp.; dis. 3 Aug., 1864,
ex. term; reen. 6 Sept., 1864;
Co. F, 2nd H. Art'y; died
(suddenly during night), 12
Dec., 1864, at Kingston, N.
C. Credited to Ashby on
2nd enl.

b. Methuen, Mass., 28 Oct., 1822,
son of Isaac and Sally (Fuller) Bodwell.

BONDS.
Luke,
m. 15 Feb., 1864, 42nd U. S.
C. Troops; enl. at Nashville,
Tenn.; credited to Danvers.

Æt. 22 at enl., resided in Gunnett
Co., Ga.

BRADBURY.
Jacob,
m. 1 Oct., 1861, Co. G, 23
Inf.; dis. 14 Mar., 1862, disability; m. 1 Oct., 1862, Co.
K, 8th Inf.; dis. 7 Aug., 1863,
ex. term; m. 9 Feb., 1864,
Co. D, 59 Inf.; tran. 1 June,
1865 to 57th Inf.; credited to
Essex; d s. 25 June, 1865,
disability. Wounded 22 June,
1864.

(Bradbury Continued.)
b. Buxton, Me., 6 Aug., 1817; m.,
Salem, 15 Nov., 1849, Seneth White,
who was b. in Scotland. Ch.: Geo.
b. 16 Nov., 1850.
Gave age as 41 at each enlistment.
Stated by Selectmen, in 1884, to
have been a resident of Danvers for
many years. Credited to Essex,
but later to Danvers from Naval
Surplus.

BRADY.
William,
m. 1 Oct., 1862, Co. K, 8th
Inf.; dis. 7 Aug., 1863, ex.
term; m. 20 Oct., 1863, Co.
G, 3rd H. A.; dis. 6 Feb.,
1865, disability.

b. Ireland, 1830, son of Patrick and
Dolly Brady; m. Catharine Gray.
Ch.: Patrick Henry, b. 22 Apr.,
1859, Mary Ann, b. 18 Oct., 1861.

BRENNAN.
Patrick,
m. 27 Aug., 1862, Co. B, 40th
Inf., corp.; dis. 16 June,
1865, ex. term.
Wounded at Oulustee, Fla.

Æt. 22 at enl.

BRIGGS.
Henry T.,
m. 1 May, 1861, Co. A, 5th
Inf.; taken prisoner 21 July,
1861; exchanged 1862; m. 20
Nov., 1863, Co. H, 3rd H. A.;
dis. 18 Sept., 1865,' ex. term.

b. So. Scituate, 26 Oct., 1840; son
of Charles and Rhoda (Reed)
Briggs; m. 27 Nov., 1862, Eudora
Decosta, b Charlestown. Ch.:
Henry A., b. 14 May, 1864, Inf., b.
18 Dec., 1868.
Lives at Danvers Centre.

BROWN.
Charles E.,
m. 5 July, 1861, Co. I, 1st
H. A.; trans. 85th Co., 2nd
Batt., V. R. C., 1 Mar., 1864;

(Brown Continued.)

dis. 9 May, 1864, for disability.

b. Bethel, Me., 15 Apr., 1824; son of Benj. and May Brown.

Charles F.,

m. 22 July, 1861, Co. C, 17th Inf., corp.; serg.. Co. E, 6 Aug., 1862; dis. 3 Aug., 1864, ex. term.

Æt. 27 at enl., married. Lives Standish, Me.

Charles R.,

m. 21 Nov., 1863, Co. D, 1st H. A.; corp., 1 Jan., 1865; dis. 16 Aug., 1865. Confined in hospital at Petersburg, City Point and Washington, July 14, Sept., 1864. Wounded in groin by spent ball, during the charge at Petersburg.

b. Weymouth, N. S., 1842; son of John and Mary E. (Wyman of Yarmouth) Brown; m. 17 Mar., 1869, Alzina H. Trafton of Shapleigh, Me.; m. 2nd., Mary A. Merrill. Ch.: Elena Wyman, b. 29 Feb., 1872. Alicia Belle, b. 18 Apr., 1875.
Lives at South Lancaster.

Gustavus,

m. 5 July, 1861, Co. I, 1st H. A.; dis. 8 July, 1864. Wounded Battle of the Wilderness, Va.

b. Winthrop, Me., 1838; son of Wm. (jr.) and Melinda (Hopkins) Brown; m. 14 Sept., 1860, Matilda E. Frost, b. Bridgton, Me.

James,

m. 11 June, 1861, Co. D, 9th Inf.; deserted 13 Dec., 1862, at Fredericksburg, Va. Credited to South Danvers.

John T.,

m. 7 Aug., 1863, Co. K, 20th Inf.; dis. 8 Dec., 1863, disa-

(Brown Continued.)

bility. Enlisted, 23 Aug., 1864. V. R. C.; dis. 15 Aug., 1865. Credited to Danvers. Substitute.

Æt. 33 at enl., married; of Boston.

Sylvester,

m. 19 Aug., 1862, Co. F, 35th Inf.; dis. 13 Jan., 1863, disability. Credited to Middleton.

Æt. 23 at enl.

William,

m. 19 July, 1864, Co. G, 2nd H. A.; dis. 3 Sept., 1865.

Of Hampton Falls, N. H. Æt. 18 at enl.

BRUMMITT.

George,

m. (enl. at Templeton), 4 Jan., 1864, 4th Light Batt'y; dis. 7 Jan., 1864. Credited to Templeton.

b. 31 Jan., 1837, at Hartford, Conn.; son of Abel and Abigail (Terry) Brummitt of Danvers; m. Elizb. Griffin of Danvers. Ch.: Frederick Abel, b. 14 May.—— John David, b. 26 Mar. Susan Jane, b. 26 Jan., ——.

Lives in Tapleyville.

Joseph,

m. 6 Aug., 1862, Co. C, 33rd Inf.; dis. 11 June, 1865, ex. term. Wounded 29 Oct., 1863.

"Of Framingham;" b. New Haven, Conn., 19 July, 1840; bro. of George; m. —— 1861, Addie F. Porter. Resides at Wolfboro, N. H.

BUCKLEY.

Bartholomew S.,

m. 5 July, 1861, Co. G, 1st H. A.; dis. 16 Mar., 1865, ex. term. Credited to Salem.

b. Ireland; m. Ellen Rearaden, b. Ireland. Ch.: Honora Elizb., b. 12 June, 1866. Mary Ellen, b. 14 Aug., 1868.

(Buckley Continued.)

Daniel,
m. 11 June, 1861, Co. E, 9th Inf.; dis. 21 June, 1864. ex. term. Wounded at Gains Mill, 7 June, 1862.
Æt. 18 at enl.

BURCHSTEAD.

Charles A.,
m. 22 July, 1861, Co. C. 17th Inf.; dis. 3 Aug., 1864, ex. term.
b. Beverly, 1839; son of H. and Lydia (Hart) Burchstead; m. 3 July, 1861, Mary E. Hartman. b. Norwich, Conn.
Lives at Danversport.

Joseph N.,
m. 22 July, 1861, Co. C. 17th Inf.; dis. 5 Sept., 1862, disability; reenl. 24 Oct., 1862, Co. I, 47th Inf.; dis. 1 Sept., 1863, ex. term.
b. Beverly, 11 July, 1833; son of Hewitt and Lydia Burchstead of Danversport; m. 18 May, 1850, Phebe G., dau. of Wm. and Phebe Shepard. Ch.: Phebe Ann, b. 19 Feb., 1851. Wm. N., b. 12 Aug., 1853. Ella Frances, b. 16 July, 1855. Lydia M., b. 23 June, 1857. Joseph Albert, b. 8 Aug., 1859. Clara N., b. 7 Mar., 1862. Mary Alice, b. 7 Jan., 1865. Lives at Danversport.

BURKE.

Ulick,
m. 11 June, 1861, Co. F, 9th Inf.; dis. 30 Oct., 1862, disability. Credited to South Danvers.
Æt. 24 at enl.

BURNHAM.

Ansel,
m. 19 Mar., 1862, 1st Co. SS, died 12 Sept., 1862; but according to Roll of Honor, vol. 2, p. 15, 22 Nov., at Washington.
"Of Andover." b. Essex, 12 Sept., 1823; son of Zebulon and Judith Burnham; m. 24 Nov., 1844, Elizb. W., dau. of Isaac W. and Charlotte R. Roberts.

BURROWS.

James H.,
m. 22 July, 1861, Co. C, 17th Inf.; dis. 16 Dec., 1861, died at Drumington, Va.
Æt. 25 at enl.; married. Son of James Burrows who died at Wrentham.

William,
m. 1 May, 1861, Co. A, 5th Inf.; dis. 31 July, 1861, ex. term.
Brother of James.

BURTON.

Jacob,
m. 1 May, 1861, Co. A, 5th Inf.; dis. 31 July, 1861, ex. term.
b. ———, 1836, Washington, Vt.; son of Stephen and Judith (Clark) Burton; m. 21 July, 1858, Ellen L., dau. of Morris Webber. b. Hamilton. Ch.: Alice, b. 17 Dec., 1865.

BUSH.

Richard,
m. 11 June, 1861, Co. E, 9th Inf.; dis. 21 June, 1864, ex. term. Credited to South Danvers.
b. Ireland. Æt. 32 at enl.; m. Mary. Ch.: Ellen, b. 4 Nov., 1853.

BUSHBY.

Joseph,
m. 16 Sept., 1862, Co. C, 5th Inf.; dis. 2 July, 1863, ex. term. Of South Danvers.
Member of Post 90. Lives Danversport.

CAIRD.

Alexander,
m. 1 July, 1862, Co. B, 7th Inf.; dis. 31 Dec., 1862, ex. term. See also Naval Service.
b. Danvers, 21 Sept., 1843; son of William and Jeannette (Wright) Caird. Lives in Chicago.

(*Caird Continued.*)
Francis S.,
m. 12 Oct., 1861, Co. F, 23d Inf.; wounded 8 Feb., 1862, at Roanoke Island; dis. 5 Sept., 1862, disability.

b. Lowell, 27 Sept., 1837, son of Wm. and Jeannette (Wright) Caird; m. 17 Dec., 1864, Margaret A. Hyde, of Ossipee, N. H. Ch.: Emme E. Jessie May, b. 22 May, 1876. Francis H. Lives Tapleyville.

CALDWELL.
Thomas,
m. 24 Sept., 1861, Co. F, 22d Inf.; dis. 20 Aug., 1862, disability; m. 30 July, 1864, V. R. C.; dis. 17 Nov., 1865, ex. term.

b. Ulster Co., Ireland. Died Thompsonville, Conn. Æt. 34 at enl., and married.

CALLAHAN.
Edward,
m. 5 July, 1861, Co. I, 1st H. A., corp.; dis. 5 July, 1864, ex. term.

Wounded. Æt. 21 at enl.

CANN.
Lewis,
m. 22 July, 1861, Co. C, 17th Inf.; 1st sergt.; promoted 2d Lt., 26 Apr., 1863; promoted 1st Lt., 4 Aug., 1864; promoted Capt., 21 Nov., 1864; dis. 11 July, 1865, ex. term.

b. Yarmouth, N. S., 1837; son of Sam'l and Mary Cann; m. 3 June, 1858, Eliza A. Webb, of Danvers. Ch.: Lewis Austin, b. 29 Nov., 1858. Herbert L., b. 15 Mar., 1861. Wm. Webb, b. 11 July, 1872. A son, b. 1 Sept., 1875. Lives in Lynn.

CARNEY.
Thomas,
m. 1 Oct., 1862, Co. K, 8th Inf.; dis. 7 Aug., 1863, ex. term; m. 2 Apr., 1864, Co. I,

(*Carney Continued.*)
59th Inf.; trans. 1 June, 1865, to 57th Inf.; dis. 30 July, 1865.

Lives in Danvers. Born 1822.

CARR.
Patrick,
m. 4 Aug., 1861, Co. B. 17th Inf.; dis. 23 June, 1863, disability.

b. Ireland, 1828; m. Mary ———; Ch.: Mary Ann, b. 15 May, 1851. Ellen, b. 26 Dec., 1852. John, 14 Feb., 1854. James, b. 29 July, 1855. Sarah Jane, b. 18 Oct., 1857. Agnes, b. 24 April, 1862. Lives in Lowell.

CARTER.
Andrew O.,
m. 16 Aug., 1861, Co. I, 1st H. A., sergt; dis. 28 Jan., 1863; promoted 2d Lt., 29 Jan., 1863; dis. 8 Oct., 1864, from Co. H.

b. Wayland; æt. 22 at enl.; son of Albert F. and Cynthia (Hammond) Carter; m. 24 Mar., 1861, Adelaide, dau. of Curtis C. and Matilda (Howard) Carter. Ch.: Andrew O., b. 8 Apr., 1861. Resides in Lynn.

CASHMAN.
Dennis,
m. 4 Jan., 1864, Co. B. 17th Inf.; dis. 11 July, 1865, ex. term, from Co. C. Credited to South Danvers.

Æt. 18 enl. Lives in Danvers.

CASKIN.
Daniel A.,
m. 15 July, 1864, Co. I, 6th Inf.; dis. 27 Oct., 1864, ex. term.

Died Peabody, 25 Mar., 1884, leaving family; m. ——— Noonan.

CHADWICK.

William H.,

m. 22 Aug., 1863, Co. II, 3d H. A., corp.; dis. 18 Sept., 1865, ex. term as corp.

b. Cambridgeport, 12 Mar., 1843; son of John (b. Methuen) and Martha (Childs, b. Charlestown) Chadwick: died unm. in Danvers, 18 Dec., 1872.

CHALK.

Henry T.,

m. 5 July, 1861, Co. I, 1st H. A., corp.; dis. 10 Dec., 1863, to reenlist; final dis. 5 June, 1865, disability.

Æt. 23 at enl. Lives in Salem.

CHANNELL.

William H.,

m. 22 Aug., 1862, Co. B, 40th Inf.; killed at Cold Harbor, Va., 1 June, 1864.

b. Wenham, 22 Oct., 1833; son of Wm. Channell; m.———. Also appears on rolls as Wm. H. Chandler.

CHAPLIN.

George H.,

m. 5 July, 1861. Co. D, 1st H. A.; dis. 8 July, 1864, ex. term.

b. Danvers, 14 Feb., 1840; son of Benj. G. and Susan (Webb) Chaplin; m. 13 Nov., 1865, Betsey C. Moore. Ch.: Mary Ann, b. 5 May, 1866.

Nathaniel W.,

m. 28 Sept., 1861, Co. A, 23d Inf.; dis. 28 Sept., 1864, ex. term.

b. Danvers, 1 Feb., 1838; d. there, 8 July, 1874; son of Benj. Gage (b. Rowley, 27 Sept., 1808) and Susan (Webb, b. Danvers, 24 June, 1812) Chaplin; m. Mary A. Edwards. Ch.: Carrie Adella, b. 3 Aug., 1860.

William A.,

m. 28 Sept., 1861, Co. A, 23d

(Chaplin Continued.)

Inf.; dis. 13 Oct., 1864, ex. term.

b. Danvers, 14 Nov., 1844; son of Benj. G. and Susan (Webb) Chaplin; m. 15 June, 1870, Nellie E. Taylor, b. Lyman, Me.

CHASE.

Charles W.,

m. 1 May, 1861, Co. H, 5th Inf.; dis. 31 July, 1861. ex. term.

CHOATE.

George D.,

m. 28 Sept., 1861, Co. C, 23d Inf., sergt.; dis. 18 Feb., 1864 ; transferred to V. R. C. Mar., 1864; dis. 3 Oct., 1864 as of Co. F, 19th V. R. C.

CLARK.

Edward A.,

m. 1 May, 1861, Co. H, 5th Inf.; dis. 31 July, 1861, ex. term; m. 14 Dec., 1861, Co. H, 29th Inf.; dis. 7 May, 1864, disability.

Æt. 33 at enl., unm.

George G.,

m. 5 July, 1861, Co. I, 1st H. A.; dis. 14 Dec., 1863, to reenlist. Discharged to date 5 Aug., 1865; charge of desertion removed, letter War Dept. of 20 Nov., 1893.

Æt. 28 at enl., married; of Topsfield. He was claimed by Topsfield, with consent of Danvers, but credited to Danvers.

CLOUGH.

Daniel Prescott, jr.,

m. 2 Sept., 1861, Co. A, 22d Inf.; (Washington Light Guards), dis. 14 Feb., 1863, disability; m. 22 Dec., 1863, Co. K, 2d H. A., sergt.; dis. 3 Sept., 1865, ex. term.

(Clough Continued.)

b. Danvers, 31 May, 1844, son of Daniel Prescott and Lucy Bray (Rust) Clough; m. 21 Dec., 1865, Margaret, dau. of Nath'l and M'g't McCreary, of England.

Orion Waterman,

m. 1 Oct., 1862, Co. K, 8th Inf.; dis. 7 Aug., 1863, ex. term. m. 22 Dec., 1863, Co. K, 2d H. A., corp.; dis. 3 Sept., 1865, ex. term.

b. Danvers, 31 Oct., 1846; son of Daniel Prescott and Lucy Bray (Rust) Clough; m. 6 Feb., 1886, at Somerville, Alice Eugenia, dau. of Geo. and Keziah Dunn, of Cornwallis, N. S. Photographer; lives Somerville. Ch.: Lucy Elizh., b. 26 Aug., 1887. Chas. Waterman, b. 22 July, 1889; died same day.

COCHRAN.

Burton,

m. 19 Aug., 1862, Co. F, 35th Inf.; dis. 12 Nov., 1862, disability.

Credited to Malden. Æt. 26 at enl.

James,

m. 22 July, 1861, Co. C, 17th Inf.; corp. 18 June, 1862; dis. 3 Aug., 1864, ex. term.

Æt. 23 at enl. Removed to New Orleans.

COFFIN.

Enoch,

m. 13 June, 1861, Co. H, 11th Inf.; reenl. 29 Dec., 1863; transferred to Navy, q. v.; dis. 7 July, 1865. Enlisted from Danvers, but claimed by and credited to Middleton, where his wife resided. Died at Danversport.

John H.,

m. 5 July, 1861; æt. 24 and married. "Of Danvers," no further record.

(Coffin Continued.)

Reuben H.,

m. 27 Jan., 1862, Co. C, 17th Inf.; dis. 22 Jan., 1865, ex. term.

b. Maine, æt. 29 at enl.; m. Hannah Burchsted, b. Beverly. Ch.: Lulu Gertrude, b. 24 Dec., 1866. Lives in Ipswich.

Simeon,

m. 22 July, 1861, Co. C, 17th Inf.; dis. 25 Dec., 1861, died at Baltimore, Md.

b. Gloucester, 1839; son of Simeon and Mary A.; married prior to enl.

COLBY.

Francis B.,

m. 1 Aug., 1862, Co. I, 1st H. A.; reenl., 29 Dec., 1863, Co. I, 1st H. A.; dis. 15 Oct., 1864; died at Andersonville, Ga.

Æt. 19 at enl.; "of Salisbury"; credited to Danvers.

COLCORD.

William G.,

m. 19 Aug., 1862, Co. F, 35th Inf.; dis. 6 May, 1863; trans. to V. R. C.; dis. Co. A, 3 V. R. C., 6 July, 1865.

b. Danvers, 24 July, 1842; son of Eben Payson (b. Turner, Me., 1813,) and Sarah (Towne, b. Danvers, 1 April, 1810) Colcord.

COLEMAN.

David,

m. 12 Aug., 1861, Co. B, 17th Inf.; dis. 3 Aug., 1864, died Danvers, 27 July, 1882 (? 7 Apr., 1877).

b. Ireland, 1815, (æt. "44" at enl.)

COLLINS.

Frederick,

m. 23 Aug., 1864, Co. M, 3d H. A.; dis. 17 June, 1865; corp. Cred. to North Chelsea.

Æt. 19 at enl.; m.; lives in Danvers.

(*Collins Continued.*)
Henry 2d,
m. 1 Oct., 1862, Co. K, 8th Inf.; dis. 7 Aug., 1863, ex. term.

b. Ireland, 1835; son of Christopher and Ellen (Cleary) Collins; m. 16 Apr., 1873, Sarah Kenney. Ch.: Edward W., b. 24 July, 1876. Lives in Danvers.

James M.,
m. 22 Dec., 1863, Co. K, 2d H. A.; dis. 3 Sept., 1865, ex. term.

Æt. 23 at enl.; m. Esther, dau. of Thomas Hynds. Ch.: Geo. Ola. Lives at Hartford, Conn.

Patrick,
m. 1 Oct., 1862, Co. K, 8th Inf.; dis. 7 Aug., 1863, ex. term; m. 15 July, 1864, Co. I, 6th Inf.: dis. 27 Oct., 1864, ex. term.

b. Ireland, 1843; son of Henry and Margaret Collins; died, Danvers, 22 July, 1880.

Richard,
m. 22 Aug., 1864, 29 Unatt. Co., H. A.; dis. 16 June, 1865. Credited to Andover. Resident of Danvers.

Æt. 35 and m., at enl.

Thomas,
m. 1 Oct., 1862, Co. K, 8th Inf.; dis. 29 May, 1863, disability.

b. Ireland, 1836; son of Christopher and Ellen (Cleary) Collins. Deceased.

William,
m. 1 Oct., 1862, Co. K, 8th Inf.; dis. 7 Aug., 1863, ex. term; m. 15 July, 1864, Co. I, 6th Inf.; dis. 27 Oct., 1864, ex. term.

b. Ireland, 1846, bro. of Thomas; m. 17 Oct., 1860, Hannah Conner of Danvers. Lives in Danvers.

CONGDON.
Nicholas,
m. 22 July, 1861, Co. G, 17th Inf.; dis. 18 Dec., 1861, disability.

Æt. 25 at enl.; married Anne Barbour. Lives Elmyra. N. Y.

CONNELL.
William (O.),
m. 11 June, 1861, Co. I, 9th Inf.; dis. 16 July, 1862, disability. Credited to South Danvers.

Æt. 26 at enl.

CONNERS.
John,
m. 11 Aug., 1862, at New Orleans (place also of enlistment); Co. I, 26th Inf.; dis. 7 Nov., 1864, ex. term.

b. Munster Co., Ireland, 1835; d. in Soldiers Home, Togus, Me. Ch.: Johanna; Mary Ellen.

COOK.
Andrew,
m. 22 July, 1861, Co. C, 17th Inf.; 1st serg.: promoted 2d Lt., 13 Aug., 1862; resigned 26 Apr., 1863.

b. Antrim Co., Ireland, 1831; shoemaker; son of Hugh and Henrietta Cook; m. 17 Nov., 1855, Jennette Lang, of Danvers. Ch.: Henrietta, b. 7 Sept., 1856. Jennetta F., b. 9 June, 1872. Lives Thompsonville, Conn.

David,
m. 22 July, 1861, at Lynnfield, Co. C, 17th Inf.: corp.; dis. 3 Apr., 1863, disability.

Shoemaker. Lives in Tapleyville, b. Antrim Co., Ireland; æt. 35 at enl. (b. 1827 personal record, 1818 town records); m. Mary Mitchinson, b. North of England, 18 May, 1818. Ch.: Danvers, *Mary Ann, b. 7 Apr., 1841. Alfred, b. 13 Sept., 1851. David, b. 9 Sept., 1855. Clara, b. 25 Dec., 1857. *Mary Fuller, b. 28 Aug., 1861. Ellen Susanna, b. 10

(*Cook Continued.*)
Jan., 1864. Chas. Henry. b. 16 May, 1866. Alice Maria, b. 14 Mar., 1869.
*Deceased.

Jeremiah,
m. 8 Oct., 1861, Co. F. 23d Inf.; dis. 25 Sept., 1862, disability; m. 12 Sept., 1864, V. R. C., credited to Salem; dis. 17 Nov., 1865.

Æt. 35 at enl.; b. Newburyport; m. Eveline E. L. Smith. Ch.: James O. H., b. 15 Mar., 1862.

COOLEY.
Joseph H.,
m. 22 July, 1861, Co. G, 17th Inf.; dis. 5 Dec., 1863, to re-enlist, dis. (from Co. B,) 11 July, 1865, ex. term.

Æt. 18 at enl. Lives in Natick.

COOPER.
Thomas Y.,
m. 15 Feb., 1864, 42d U. S. Col. Troops, enl. at Nashville, Tenn.; credited to Danvers.

Æt. 18 at enl.; resided Ginnett Co., Ga.

COTHRAN.
Elbridge,
m. 22 Aug., 1864, Co. A, 4th H. A.; dis. 17 June, 1865, ex. term.

CRAWFORD.
James,
m. 29 Dec., 1863, Co. K, 1st Cav.; corp. Co. A, dis. 29 June, 1865, ex. term, sick in hospital. Credited to Salem. Received gun shot wound in leg in Wilderness.

b. Scotland, 1844, son of James and Jennie Crawford.
Lives on Lawrence St., Lowell.

William R.,
m. 22 July, 1861, Co. C, 17th Inf.; dis. 9 Dec., 1863, to re-

(*Crawford Continued.*)
enl. same Reg. and Co.; deserted 15 Nov., 1864, from Co. B, while on veteran furlough, in N. Y.

Æt. 19 at enl.; b. Lowell. Res. Danvers. Also appears as Wm. R. Coffin.

CRESSY.
Albert T.,
m. 28 July, 1862, Co. A, 23d Inf.; dis. 2 Dec., 1863, to re-enlist; dis. 25 June, 1865.

b. Danvers, 22 Dec., 1844; died Revena, O., 14 Apr., 1866; son of Enoch and Sally (Whittier) Cressy.

Eben F.,
m. 26 May, 1862, Salem Cadets; dis. 11 Oct., 1862, ex. term; m. 22 Aug., 1864, Co. A, 4th H. A.; dis. 17 June, 1865, ex. term.

b. Danvers, 1 Aug., 1842; son of Enoch T. and Sally (Whittier) Cressy; m. 7 Jan., 1866, Lizzie A. Whittier, of Newton, N. H. Ch.: Herbert J., b. 2 Mar., 1868, Mabel T., b. 25 July, 1874. Lulu W., b. 4 Apr., 1878.
Died in Danvers, 1894.

CROFT.
William H.,
m. 22 July, 1861, Co. C, 17th Inf.; killed 27 Apr., 1864, Washington, N. C.

Æt. 17 at enl.

CROSBY.
Lyman D.,
m. 1 May, 1861, Co. A, 5th Inf.; dis. 31 July, 1861, ex. term.

b. Nova Scotia; m. Lizzie Harris. Ch.: Mary Alice, b. 13 Feb., 1864. Lives in Tapleyville.

CROWELL.
George M.,
m. 1 May, 1861, Co. C, 5th Inf.; dis. 31 July, 1861, ex.

(Crowell Continued.)
term: m. 1 July, 1862, Co. B, 7th Inf. serg.; dis. 31 Dec., 1862. ex. term: m. 15 July, 1864, Co. I, 6th Inf.. 2d Lt.; com. 2d Lt., 15 July, 1864, dis. 27 Oct., 1864, ex. term.

b. Nova Scotia, 21 Aug., 1829; d.———; m. 12 July, 1852, Sarah Elizb. Dow, b. Charlestown, 10 Mar., 1834. Ch.: Sarah Elizb., b. 4 Jan., 1853, at Danvers. M. 2d, Jennette Smith. Mrs. Crowell lives in Mulberry St., Lynn.

CROWLEY.
Florence H.,
m. 26 May, 1862, Salem Cadets; dis. 11 Oct., 1862. ex. term; m. 23 Aug., 1864, Co. A, 4th H. A.; dis. 17 June, 1865. ex. term.

b. Danvers, 23 Nov., 1843; died Danvers, 5 Sept., 1874; son of Daniel and Ann (Crowley) Crowley. Currier in Danvers and Peabody.

Timothy D.,
m. 23 Aug., 1864, Co. A. 4th H. A.; dis. 17 June, 1865. ex. term. Enl. U. S. A., 15 Sept., 1869; dis. 15 Sept., 1874, as sergt., in Co. I, 13th U. S. Inf.

b. Danvers, 26 Apr., 1849; son of Daniel and Ann (Crowley) Crowley; m. Annie M., dau. of Thos. G. and Ann Howell. Ch.: Alice J., b. 20 Mar., 1878, d. in inf. Stationed in the West from 1869 to 1874. Past Commander, Post 90. Lives in Danvers.

CUNNINGHAM.
David H.,
m. 3 Sept., 1861, Co. E. 24th Inf.; dis. 3 Jan., 1864, to reenlist; dis. 20 Jan., 1866.

Æt. 18 at enl. Lives in Middleborough.

John L.,
m. 16 Aug., 1861, Co. C, 17th

(Cunningham Continued.)
Inf.; dis. 4 Jan., 1864, to reenlist; dis. 11 July, 1865, Co. B.

Æt. 31 at enl.; married. Lives in South Salem.

William,
m. 5 July, 1861, Co. I, 1st H. A.; dis. 8 July, 1864, ex. term, prisoner of war.

Æt. 19 at enl.

CURTIS.
Oscar F.,
m. 5 July, 1861, Co. I, 1st H. A.; died 19 May, 1864, at Washington, of wounds.

Æt. 22 at enl.; b. Boxford.

CUTHBERTSON.
Hugh,
m. 4 Nov., 1861, Co. B, 23d Inf.; dis. 26 Oct., 1862, disability. Wounded in the head, 14 Mar., 1862, at Newberne. Credited to Lynnfield.

b. Scotland, 1815; d. Danvers, 8 Aug., 1863; son of John and Ellen Cuthbertson.

DALE.
William C.,
m. 5 July, 1861, Co. I, 1st H. A.; dis. 8 July, 1864, ex. term, prisoner of war.

b. New York, 1838; d. 29 Oct., 1867; m. 17 Sept., 1857. Emily E. Rollins (b. Salem). Ch.: Mary E., b. 10 July, 1860.

DARLING.
Edward,
m. 1 Oct., 1862, Co. K, 8th Inf.; deserted 28 Dec., 1862. Newberne, N. C.

Ezekiel B.,
m. 18 Aug., 1862, Co. A, 39th Inf.; dis. 2 June, 1865, ex. term; credited to South Danvers. Wounded 6 Feb., 1865.

Æt. 29 at enl.

DAVIS.

William F.,
m. 5 July, 1861, Co. I, 1st H. A.; dis. 6 Dec., 1863, to re-enlist, m. 6 Dec., 1863, same Co., corp.; dis. 31 July, 1865, ex. term.

Æt. 23 at enl.

DAY.

George H., junior,
m. 22 Aug., 1862, Co. B, 40th Inf.; dis. 13 Jan., 1865, disability. Absent in hospital in Mass. since 1 June, 1864.

Æt. 18 at enl.; lives in Danvers.

Lewis W.,
m. 19 Aug., 1862, Co. F, 35th Inf.; dis. 16 Feb., 1863, disability; m. 22 Aug., 1864, Co. A, 4th H. A.; dis. 17 June, 1865, ex. term.

b. Shapleigh, Me., 1832; son of Samuel and Lydia Day; m. 22 July, 1854, Louisa Plaisted, of Wenham. Ch.: Lewis P., died 30 Aug., 1878. Lives in Danvers.

Stephen S.,
m. 22 Aug., 1862, Co. B, 40th Inf.; dis. 4 Sept., 1862, at Boxford, Mass., m. 22 Aug., 1864, Co. A, 4th H. A.; dis. 26 May, 1865, for disability; transferred to V. R. C. 2d Co. 2d Bat.

b. Wells, Me., 1826; son of Robert and Mary Day; m. Mary Susan Adams. Ch.: Grace E., b. 1855. John A., b. 1857. Hattie Maria, b. 12 July, 1860. Clarence E., b. 1866.

DELAND.

Moses,
m. 22 Aug., 1861, 2d Co. S. S.; killed at Spottsylvania, 30 May, 1864.

Æt. 22 at enl.; unm. His family were of Peabody.

DeMERRITT.

George S.,
m. 24 Dec., 1863, Co. K, 2d H. A.; dis. 3 Sept., 1865.

Æt. 31 at enlistment. "Of South Danvers." Credited to Danvers.

DEWAN.

John G.,
m. 26 May, 1862, Salem Cadets; dis. 11 Oct., 1862, ex. term.

DICKEY.

James W.,
m. 22 July, 1861, Co. C, 17th Inf.; dis. 16 Jan., 1863, disability; m. 27 Feb., 1864, 14th Batt'y Lt. Art'y; dis. 15 June, 1865, credited to Roxbury.

Æt. 19 at enl.; lives in Roxbury.

William G.,
m. 22 Aug., 1864, Co. A, 4th H. A.; dis. 17 June, 1865, ex. term.

b. Brighton, 7 July, 1825; m. Martha S. Chaplain, of Danvers, (b. 1 Nov., 1826) 3 May, 1845, d. 1894. Ch.: Martha C., b. 10 July, 1846. Susan B., b. 5 Apr., 1849. William Geo., b. 22 Mar., 1851. Lives in Danversport.

DOCKHAM.

George Frank,
m. 26 May, 1862, Salem Cadets; dis. 11 Oct., 1862, ex. term.

Æt. 18 at enl. Son of Henry G.

Henry G.,
m. 19 Aug., 1862, Co. F, 35th Inf.; dis. 27 June, 1863, disability.

b. Lynn, æt. 43 at enl.; died, Salem, 1889; m. 11 Mar., 1841, Irene H. Rhodes. Ch.: Wm. H., Geo. F., John G. Laura E., b. 8 Dec., 1850. Chas. Leonard, b. 18 Apr., 1858.

John G.,
m. 26 May, 1862, Salem Ca-

TOWN OF DANVERS. 15

(Dockham Continued.)
dets; dis. 11 Oct., 1862, ex. term.

b. Salem, 1847; son of Henry G. and Irene H. (Rhodes); m 1867, Abbie M. Brown, dau. of Winthrop and Abby Brown of Lynn.

William H.,
m. 5 July, 1861, Co. D, 1st H. A.; dis. 8 July, 1864, ex. term.

Æt. 21 at enl. Died in Salem. Son of Henry G.

DODGE.
Alonzo P.,
m. 28 Sept., 1861, Co. G, 23d Inf. sergt.; dis. 2 Dec., 1863, to reenlist; 2d Lt., 1 June, 1865; dis. 25 June, 1865, ex. term.

b. Topsfield. 2 Jan., 1838; son of Benjamin C. (b. Beverly, 9 Jan., 1817) and Almira (Bickford, b. Topsfield, 25 Mar., 1815) Dodge. Lives in Marlboro.

Charles W.,
m. 19 Aug., 1862, Co. F, 35th Inf.; dis. 18 Sept., 1862, accidently wounded, died of wounds.

b. Beverly, 1835; son of Charles and Mary C. Dodge; m.

Francis S.,
m. 9 Oct., 1861, Co. F, 23d Inf. corp.; 9 Oct., 1861, transferred to 1st U.S. colored Cav., 20 Dec., 1863, as 1st Lt.: Capt., 6 July, 1865; dis. 12 Feb., 1866; 1st Lt., 9th Cav. U. S. A. 28 July, 1866; Capt., 31 July, 1867; Major and Paymaster, 13 Jan., 1880. Now stationed at Walla Walla, Washington.

b. Danvers, 11 Sept., 1842; son of Francis (b. Salem, 25 Jan., 1817) and Rebecca Appleton (Brown, b. 23 Jan., 1821); m. 3 Dec., 1878, Mary Hunt Weston of Danvers. She b. 8 Oct., 1847.

(Dodge Continued.)
Judson Ward,
m. 1 Oct., 1862, Co. K, 8th Inf.: dis. 7 Aug., 1863, ex. term; m. 26 Aug., 1864, Co. M, 3d H. A.; credited to Boxford on second enl.: dis. 17 June, 1865.

b. Wenham, 21 July, 1833; son of Adoniram J., and Julia A. (Perley) Dodge; m. 8 Oct., 1866, Mrs. Elizb. G. Perley née Hood, b. Ipswich, 16 June, 1838. Ch.: Elmer Addison, b. 24 Mar., 1868. Lives in Danvers.

Thomas S.,
m. 22 Aug., 1864, Co. A, 4th H. A.: dis. 17 June, 1865, ex. term.

b. Danvers, 26 Jan., 1845; son of Wm. and Mary (Shed) Dodge. Lives in Danvers.

Warren P.,
m. 1 July, 1861, Co. B. 7th Inf.: dis. 31 Dec., 1861, ex. term; m. 15 July, 1864, Co. I, 6th Inf.; dis. 27 Oct., 1864, ex. term.

b. Danvers, 2 Feb., 1839; son of Ezra Dodge (who was b. New Boston, N. H., 9 Sept., 1812) and Martha Bradstreet (b. Danvers. 11 Apr., 1816); m. 29 June, 1862, Julia M. Carroll. Ch.: Henry Porter, b. 30 Nov., 1863. Mary Abby, b. 26 Nov., 1865.

DOLE.
George H.,
m. 22 July, 1861, Co. C, 17th Inf.: dis. 1 Dec., 1863, to reenlist: dis. 11 July, 1865, ex. term. from Co. B.

Æt. 28 at enl. Lives in Lowell.

William C.,
m. Co. I, 1st H. A.: captured at Petersburg, Va., confined at Richmond. 25 June, 1864; sent to Lynchburg, Va., 29 June, 1864. No further information.

DONARTH.
Ernest,
m. 23 July, 1864, Co. F, 35th Inf.: trans. to Co. F, 24th Inf.; died at Salisbury, N. C., a prisoner of war, 12 Dec., 1864. Credited to Boston.

Æt. 24 at enl.; b. Germany; substitute for Jos. W. Colburn, of Boston.

DOWDELL.
Charles,
m. 11 June, 1861, Co. F, 9th Inf. corp.; dis. 21 June, 1864, ex. term. Credited to Salem.

b. Ireland, 1841; son of James and Ann Dowdell; m. 14 May, 1865, Bridget Loftus. Ch.: James Henry, b. 22 Feb., 1865. John, b. 14 Apr., 1867. Chas. Dennis, b. 16 July, 1869. Wm. Francis, b. 3 May, 1871. Joseph Russell, b. 29 Sept., 1873.

John,
m. 13 Dec., 1861. Co. E, 28th Inf.; dis. 1 Jan., 1864, to re-enlist: m. 2 Jan., 1864, Co. E. 28th Inf.; dis. 30 June, 1865, ex. term, from Co. B.

b. Ireland, 1844; son of James and Ann Dowdell: m. 12 Nov., 1868, Catherine Loftus.

DOWNS.
Thomas J.,
m. 25 May, 1861, Co. F, 2d Inf.: dis. 4 Oct., 1861, for disability. Of Ipswich, enlisted 14 Jan., 1864, 2d B. L. A. as of Boston, rejected 17 Jan., 1864; enl. 18 Jan., 1864, m. 1 Mar., 1864, Co. E, 58th Inf.; wounded 3 June, 1864; trans. V. R. C., 10 June, 1865. Credited to Dartmouth. Claimed by Danvers, as of "Co. F," 10 Aug., 1864 as a resident of Danvers. His first two enlistments æt. 22 and 23, shoemaker, of Ipswich; third enl., "married" æt. 23, resident of Grover.

DRESSER.
Charles F.,
m. 5 July, 1861, Co. I, 1st H A.; reenl. 7 Dec., 1863, ditto, died of disease at City Point Hospital. Va., 15 Nov., 1864.

Æt. 23 at enl : of Salem.

DRIVER.
George Hibbert Smith,
m. 7 Oct., 1861, Co. F, 23d Inf.; dis. 28 Sept., 1862, disability.

born Salem, 4 Feb., 1842; son of Stephen and Susanna (Payson) Driver; m. 19 Nov., 1868, Lucretia G., dau. of Michael and Ellen M. (Rae) Larkin, of Boston, b. 23 Dec., 1842. Ch.: Lucretia L., b. Lynn, 14 Sept., 1870. Israel G., b. Boston, 25 Nov., 1872. Geo. Benj., b. 16 Mar., 1874, d. y. Harold B., b. Lynn, 3 Oct., 1877. Geo. H., b. Lynn, 6 May, 1879.

DRYESDALE.
James,
m. 5 July, 1861, Co. I, 1st H. A.: dis. 8 July, 1864. ex. term, absent sick.

Æt. 35 at enl.; born in Scotland. Died leaving a dau. Mary, and other children.

DUNLEY.
Patrick,
m. 8 Aug., 1862, Co. K, 33d Inf.: dis. 8 Aug., 1862, transferred to 35th Inf. Not found on rolls of 35th reg.

Æt. 18 at enl.

DURGIN.
George F.,
m. 5 Mar., 1864, Co. C, 2d Cav.: dis. 20 July, 1865; Credited to Weymouth; residence on rolls given as West Epping, N. H.

Æt. 18 at enl.; given by selectmen of Danvers in their list, 1864.

TOWN OF DANVERS.

(Durgin Continued.)

Samuel W.,
m. 22 July, 1861, Co. C, 17th Inf.; dis. 3 Aug., 1864, ex. term.

b. Epping, N. H., 1839; son of Geo. and Susan (West) Durgin; m. 25 Aug., 1860, Lucy A. Fish. Ch.: Geo. West, b. 8 Feb., 1867, Alice May, b. 5 May, 1868, James Edwin, b. 13 Feb., 1873.
Lives in Danvers.

DWINELL.

George H.,
m. 22 Aug., 1862, Co. B, 40th Inf.; dis. 14 Sept., 1863; died Folly Is., S. C.

b. Danvers, 20 Oct., 1836; son of Hezekiah (b. Danvers, 30 Oct., 1804) and Sophronia (Bomer, b. Beverly, 23 Dec., 1804) Dwinnell; married.

EARLE.

George W.,
m. 5 July, 1861, Co. I, 1st H. A.; dis. 13 Sept., 1864, died Andersonville, Ga.

Æt. 23 at enl. and married.

EATON.

Alpheus,
m. 1 May, 1861, Co. H, 5th Inf.; dis. 31 July, 1861, ex. term.

EDWARDS.

John L.,
m. 17 Sept., 1861, 4th L. B.; dis. 3 Jan., 1864, to reenlist; m. 4 Jan., 1864, 4th L. B.; dis. 14 Oct., 1865. ex. term.

b. Salem, 1839; son of Lowell and Elizabeth (Cross) Edwards; m. 23 May, 1863, Bertha L. Cobb (born in Wellfleet).

ELLIOTT.

George A.,
m. 29 July, 1863, Co. B, 2d H. A., sergt.; dis. 2 July, 1865, died Newberne, N. C., of fever.

(Elliott Continued.)
b. Gloucester, 1838; son of Richard (b. Danvers) and Sophronia (Hill, b. Salem) Elliott.

ELWELL.

George A.,
m. 11 Aug., 1862, Co. I, 12th Inf.; dis. 30 Aug., 1862, missing in battle.

b. Detroit, Mich., 1834; m. Angeline G. E. Smith. Ch.: Florence A., b. 29 July, 1862. George A.

ENGLISH.

Henry F.,
m. 1 Oct., 1862, Co. K, 8th Inf.; dis. 7 Aug., 1863, ex. term.

EVANS.

Isaac O.,
m. 5 July, 1861, Co. I, 1st H. A.; reenlisted 7 Dec., 1863, final dis. 15 Dec., 1864, disability.

b. Beverly, 18 May, 1843; son of Isaac W. (b. Lyman, Me., 18 Oct., 1811) and Elizb. (Stone, b. Danvers, 17 May, 1818); m. 26 Mar., 1874, Mary Kelley, of North Reading.
Lives in Danvers.

John T.,
m. 19 Aug., 1862, Co. F, 35th Inf.; dis. 9 June, 1865, ex. term, credited to Lyman, Me.

Æt. 19 at enl.

William S.,
m. 18 Aug., 1862, Co. A, 39th Inf.; taken prisoner 19 Aug., 1864, died in rebel prison, 1864. Æt. 21 at enl.

EVELETH.

John F.,
m. 19 Aug., 1862, Co. F, 35th Inf.; dis. 13 June, 1865, ex. term; taken prisoner, by Stuart's Cav., 2 May, 1864, at Elysford, Rappidan River, Va., confined at Andersonville

(*Eveleth Continued.*)

from May, 1864, to March 26, 1865, when he was paroled and taken to Union Lines at Vicksburg. In hospital, Jefferson Barr., St. Louis, Mo., Apr. 25, to May 1, 1865; confined in Confed. Prison Hosp., at Andersonville, Ga., winter of 1864.

b. Danvers, 20 July, 1843; son of Francis (b. Danvers, 5 Apr., 1816) and Lucy Johnson (Stoker, of Beverly. b. 15 Feb., 1821) Eveleth. Resides Danversport.

FARMER.

Anderson,
m. 6 Dec., 1864, 5th Ill. Cav.; enl. at Vicksburg, Miss., credited to Danvers.

Æt. 24, residence Capiote, Miss.

FAY.

William T.,
m. 1 Oct., 1862, Co. K, 8th Inf.; dis. 1 June, 1863, disability.

b. Nova Scotia, m. Lydia Jane —— Ch.: Angeline Florence. b. 8 Apr., 1860. Emma Harriett, b. 10 May, 1863. Willie Lebette, b. 19 Aug., 1865.

FIELD.

Charles H.,
m. 8 Oct., 1861, Co. F, 23d Inf.; dis. 8 July, 1862, disability; enl. V. R. C., Co. I, 13th Reg., 12 Sept., 1864; dis. 17 Nov., 1865, cred. to Salem.

b. Boston, 4 Oct., 1814; son of Charles (b. Malden) and Harriet (Von Hegan, b. N. Y.) Field. Ch.: Sarah Jane, b. Dover, N. H., 6 July, 1847. Antinette, b. Danvers, 18 Feb., 1852. Chas. Henry, b. 2 Aug., 1854.
Shoemaker. Lives in Danvers.

George W.,
m. 19 July, 1864, Co. D, 35th Inf.; never reported; de-

(*Field Continued.*)

serted from 35th Inf., 18 Aug., 1864, " of Philadelphia," credited to Danvers.

Æt. 21 at enl.

FINNEKAN.

James,
m. 20 Nov., 1863, Co. H, 2d H. A.; deserted 1 Apr., 1865.

Æt. 35 at enl.

FINNERTY.

James,
m. 15 Feb., 1862, Co. D, 17th Inf.; dis. 3 Aug., 1864, disability.

Æt. 23 at enl. Died in Tenn.

FISH.

Henry,
m. 22 Aug., 1862, Co. B, 40th Inf.; dis. 15 Mar., 1865; trans. to V. R. C., dis. Co. I, 12th V. R. C., 28 June, 1865.

b. Danvers, 2 Sept., 1846; son of Levi and Betsey (Putnam) Fish.

James L.,
m. 1 Oct., 1862, Co. K, 8th Inf.; dis. 11 Aug., 1863, ex. term.

b. Danvers, 13 Nov., 1845; died in Danvers, in 1892; son of Levi (b. Danvers, 5 Aug., 1811) and Nancy W. (Wilkins, b. Middleton, 6 Apr., 1821) Fish; m. Josie M. Tuttle, of Salem. Ch.: Nellie E., b. Philadelphia. Carrie M., b. Delemco, N. Y.

Nehemiah Putnam,
m. 5 July, 1861, Co. I, 1st H. A.; dis. 8 July, 1864, ex. term, prisoner of war.

b. Middleton, 4 Feb., 1842; died Danvers, 9 Aug., 1884, unm.; bro. of James L. In Washington General Hospital. Confined in Libby Prison; paroled.

FITZPATRICK.

John,
m. 13 Dec., 1861, Co. D, 28th Inf.; died of wounds received in action, 15 Sept., 1862, a sergt.

Æt. 32 at enl.

John,
m. 11 June, 1861, Co. B, 9th Inf.; transferred to Co. A; deserted at Washington, D. C. 12 Sept., 1862.

Æt. 26 at enlistment, married.

FLEET.

George E.,
m. 5 July, 1861, Co. I, 1st H. A.; cred. to Salem; reenl. 7 Dec., 1863, Co. I, 1st H. A.; dis. 22 June, 1864; killed at Petersburg, Va.

Æt. 30 at enl.

FLYNN.

William,
m. Co. G, 59th N. Y. Inf.; dis. 30 June, 1862, for disability; enl. 1863, Co. C, 10th Batt. V. R. C., credited to Worcester: dis. 31 Mar., 1865, for disability.

Æt. 43 at enl. in V. R. C.

FORBUSH.

George W.,
m. 16 July, 1864, Co. D, 6th Inf.; dis. 27 Oct., 1864, ex. term.

b. Carlisle, 17 Nov., 1844; son of George and Harriet A. (Richardson) Forbush; m. Fannie M. Clark. Machinist. Danversport.

FOSTER.

Warren B.,
m. 22 Dec., 1863, 2d H. A.; dis. 3 Sept., 1865, ex. term.

Æt. 18 at enl.; m. Miss Legro. Lives at Danvers Centre.

FOWLE.

William,
m. 1 Oct., 1862, Co. K, 8th Inf.; dis. 7 Aug., 1863, ex. term.

b. Danvers, 10 Aug., 1821; son of Samuel (b. W. Cambridge, 29 Sept., 1793) and Rebecca (Perry, b. Danvers, 27 Dec., 1795) Fowle; m. Esther W. Phillips, b. Salem, 1826. Lives in Danvers.

FOWLER.

Addison W.,
m. 24 May, 1862, Salem Cadets; dis. 11 Oct., 1862, ex. term; m. 5 Oct., 1863, Co. E, 2d H. A., sergt.; dis. 3 Sept., 1865, ex. term.

b. Danvers, 26 May, 1841; son of Henry (b. Danvers, 15 Sept., 1809) and Sally H. (Putnam, b. 11 Feb., 1816); m. Mary E. Lowe, b. Beverly. Ch.: Jessie Florence, b. 15 Nov., 1863.

Albert A.,
m. 22 Dec., 1863, Co. K, 2d H. A.; dis. 3 Sept., 1865, ex. term. "Sick in N. Y. since April."

b. Danvers, 4 June, 1841; died in Alabama, 6 Mar., 1882; son of Augustus (b. Danvers, 11 Nov., 1812) and Emily (b. Danvers, 31 Dec., 1814) Fowler.

Henry P.,
m. 5 July, 1861, Co. D, 1st H. A., serg.; prom. 2d Lt., 5 Sept., 1863; dis. 7 Oct., 1864, ex. term.

b. Danvers, 24 Feb., 1839; son of Henry (b. Danvers, 15 Sept., 1809) and Sally H. (Putnam, b. Danvers, 11 Sept., 1816) Fowler.

Samuel Page, jr.,
m. 1 Oct., 1862, Co. K, 8th Inf., sergt.; dis. 7 Aug., 1863, ex. term.

b. Danvers, 6 Dec., 1838; son of Samuel Page (b. 22 Apr., 1800) and Harriet (Putnam, b. 11 May, 1806) Fowler. Lives in Danvers.

FOX.

Lawrence,
m. 22 July, 1861, Co. B, 17th Inf.; dis. 3 Aug., 1864, ex. term; m. 15 Aug., 1864, Co. C, 17th Inf.; cred. to Salem; dis. 11 July, 1865, ex term. Wounded in the knee, Wisesfork, N. C., 1865, confined in regimental hospital, in 1862, at Foster.

b. Rosscommon Co., Ireland, 1821; son of Michael and Hannah (Burns) Fox; m. 1846, in Ireland, Bridget McDermot; m. 2d in Ireland, 1852, Bridget Welch. Ch.: Sarah J., b. 18 Oct., 1847. Michael, b. 26 Sept., 1849. Mary, b. 28 Oct., 1854. Annie E., b. 15 Nov., 1856. Lawrence, b. 15 Nov., 1858. Patrick, b. 17 Mar., 1861. John, b. 12 June, 1867. Wm.; Mgt.; Mgt. M.; Wm. J.

Resides Tapleyville. Shoemaker.

FRYE.

Hiram S.,
m. 20 July, 1864, Co. I, 7th V. R. C.; dis. 14 Oct., 1865, for disability.

Æt. 33. Borne on War Dep't rolls as Foy.

FULLER.

Benjamin M.,
m. 28 Sept., 1861, Co. A, 23d Inf.; dis. 2 Dec., 1863, to reenlist; prisoner of war in Libby prison, 16 May, 1864, died there 7 June, 1864.

b. Isle of Tristan d'Acunha, 10 Sept., 1844; brother of Richard W. Fuller.

Cyrus,
m. 1 Oct., 1862, Co. K, 8th Inf.; dis. 7 Aug., 1863, ex. term.

Son of Daniel Fuller; died in N. H.

Daniel,
m. 28 Sept., 1861, Co. B, 23d Inf., corp.; dis. 27 Sept., 1864, ex. term.

(Fuller Continued.)

b. Salem, 1838; died Danvers 2 Apr., 1888; son of Nehemiah P. and Mary A. (Perkins) Fuller; m. 21 June, 1870. Mrs. Carrie K. Arie (née Thompson).

David A.,
m. 25 May, 1861, Co. C, 2d Inf.; dis. 12 July, 1862, disability; m. 18 Feb., 1864, Co. I, 4th Cav.; dis. 14 Nov. 1865. Credited on second enl. to Easton, but claimed by Danvers.

b. Middleton, æt. 28 at enl.; son of N. P. and Mary A. Fuller, m. Annie M. Carroll. Ch.: Mary Jane, b. 19 Jan., 1863. Annie. Lives in Danvers.

Edwin A.,
m. 5 July, 1861, Co. I, 1st H. A.; dis. 8 July, 1864, ex. term, absent wounded.

b. Newton, m. Harriet K———. Ch.: Charles Putnam, b. 2 Nov., 1853.

George H.,
m. 1 May, 1861, Co. A, 5th Inf.; dis. 31 July, 1861 ex. term; m. 29 July, 1863, Co. B, 2d H. A.; dis. 3 Sept., 1865, ex. term.

b. 1837, d. in So. America; son of Nehemiah P. and Mary A. (Perkins) Fuller.

Moses F.,
m. 4 Mar., 1864, Co. G, 59th Inf.; trans. 1 June, 1865, to 57th; dis. 30 July, 1865, from Co. G. Credited to Sherborn.

Claimed 10 Aug., 1864, as a resident of Danvers, at date of enrollment, and that he and family were always residents of Danvers.

Nehemiah P. junior,
m. 21 Aug., 1861, Co. C, 17th Inf., captain; transferred 30 July, 1863 to Co. B, 2d H. A., capt.; prom. major, 2 Oct.,

(Fuller Continued.)
1864; dis. 3 Sept., 1865, ex. term.

b. Middleton, 17 May, 1830; died Danvers, 3 Feb., 1884; son of N. P. and Mary A. (Perkins) Fuller; m. Maria L. Fuller, of Danvers, 7 Aug., 1863. Ch.: Isabella Glass, b. 22 July, 1866. Lucy Putnam.

Richard W.,
m. 12 Aug , 1861, Co. C, 17th Inf.; dis. 7 Dec., 1863, to re-enlist; dis. 11 July, 1865, from Co. B, as sergt.

b. Isle of Tristan d'Acunha, 10 Oct., 1841; son of Joseph J. (b. Nottingham West, 5 June, 1811) and Mary A. (Glass, b. 22 Apr., 1817) Fuller, m. 4 Sept., 1887, Laura A. Marston. Ch.: Waldron M., b. 18 Mar., 1879.

Solomon,
m. 1 Oct., 1862, Co. K, 8th Inf.; dis. 7 Aug., 1863, ex. term.

b. Middleton, 4 Nov., 1835; son of Joseph and Clarissa (Wilkins) Fuller; m. 5 Aug., 1860, Sarah E. Fletcher, b. Randolph. Ch.: Ella Elizb., b. 16 Sept., 1861. Lorin S., b. 14 Feb., 1863. Arthur Endicott, b. 10 Apr., 1870.
Farmer, Danvers.

FRANCIS.
William,
m. 16 May, 1864, 13th unatt. Inf.; dis. 15 Aug., 1864, ex. term.

b. Danvers, 1 May, 1807; son of William (b. Beverly, 2 Oct., 1777) and Leafy (Brown, b. Hamilton, 29 Dec., 1784) Francis; m. 1852, Betsey R. Warren, of Lynn. Ch.: Arthur W., b. 12 Feb., 1856. Edwin.

GEORGE.
Horace,
m. 26 Jan., 1864, 6th Lt. B't'y; corp. 20 June, 1865; trans. 5 Jan., 1865, 15th L. B.; dis. 7 Aug., 1865, cred. to Falmouth.

Æt. 25 at enl. Lives in Kansas. Brother of John S.

(George Continued.)
John S.,
m. 24 Aug., 1864, Co. A, 4th H. A.; dis. 17 June, 1865, ex. term, sergt.

b. Sandwich, N. H., 1840; son of John and Mary A. (Quimby) George; m. 2 Aug., 1860, Mary A. Fogg (b. Sandwich, 1842).

Thomas B.,
m. 24 Aug., 1864, Co. A, 4th H. A.; dis. 17 June, 1865, ex. term.

b. Sandwich, N. H., 1837; son of John and Mary A. (Kent) George; m. Emily C. Wadleigh (b. Sandwich, N. H.).

GETCHELL.
Edwin J.,
m. 5 July, 1861, Co. I, 1st H. A.; killed 15 July, 1862; killed near Ft. Barnard, near Alexandria, Va., by being run over on railroad.

b. Sanford, Me., 1839; son of Isaiah and Dorothy Getchell.

Ephraim,
m. 5 Aug., 1862, Co. G, 17th Inf.; dis. 18 Jan., 1863, died at Newberne, N. C.

b. Wakefield, Me., 19 Dec., 1826; son of Josiah and Dorothy Getchell; m. Isabella P. Goodale (b. Danvers). Ch.: Hetta P., b. 1 Oct., 1851. Louisa Bell, b. 24 Oct., 1853. Warren L. b. 18 Jan., 1856.

GIDDINGS.
Charles W.,
m. 1 Oct., 1862, Co. K, 8th Inf.; dis. 15 Nov., 1862, disability.

GILES.
Charles H.,
m. 1 May, 1861, Co. A, 5th Inf.; dis. 31 July, 1861, ex. term; m. 15 July, 1864, Co. I, 6th Inf.; dis. 27 Oct., 1864, ex. term.

(Giles Continued.)
b. Boston, 22 Dec., 1843; son of Charles Sias (b. Brookfield, 17 Nov., 1809) and Sarah (Ricker, b. Shapleigh, Me., 16 Sept., 1816) Giles; m. 24 May, 1862, Ellen J. Cambell, (b. Scotland). Ch.: Allen W., b. 11 Apr., 1863. Clara, b. 8 Sept., 1866. Fred'k W., b. 12 Apr., 1868. Chas. E., b. 31 Oct., 1869. Lives in Tapleyville.

James A.,
m. 2 Dec., 1864, 11 Lt. Art'y dis. 15 June, 1865, credited to Provincetown.

Æt. 18 at enl.

GILMAN.
Charles A.,
m. 1 Oct., 1862, Co. K, 8th Inf.; dis. 14 Nov., 1862, minor.

John. T. (?F),
m. 1 May, 1861, Co. A, 5th Inf.; dis. 31 July, 1861, ex. term.

GLIDDEN.
Mark,
m. 1 Oct., 1862, Co. K, 8th Inf.; dis. 7 Aug., 1863, ex. term.

b. Barre, Vt., 1817; m. 7 July, 1846, Harriet Holden. Ch.: Elmer, b. 10 Sept., 1849. Harriet Holden, b. 29 Feb., 1852. He m. 2d, Mary A. Batchelder. Ch.: Marion, b. 28 Mar., 1855. Miller H., b. 2 May, 1856. Irving Joseph, b. 18 Apr., 1860. Lives in Salem.

GLOVER.
Samuel,
m. 1 Oct., 1862, Co. K, 8th Inf.; dis. 7 Aug., 1863, ex. term.

b. Marblehead, 1809; d. 11 Oct., 1864, in Danvers; son of Samuel and Elizh. Glover.

GOLDTHWAIT.
Charles M.
m. 22 July, 1861, Co. D, 17th

(Goldthwait Continued.)
Inf.; dis. 31 May, 1862, disability.

b. Danvers, 10 Aug., 1839; son of William jr. (b. 29 July, 1800) and Sally (Andrews, b. 19 Dec., 1799) Goldthwait.

George D.,
m. 22 Aug., 1863, Co. D, 2d H. A.; dis. 26 May, 1865, ex. term.

GOODALE.
Lewis E.,
m. 25 May, 1861, Co. C, 2d Inf.; dis. 9 Mar., 1863, disability: m. 14 Apr., 1864, U. S. Sig. Corps: dis. 29 Aug., 1865.

b. Danvers, 21 Feb., 1844; son of Ebenezer (b. Danvers, 15 Dec., 1811) and Emily Hannah Purdy (Sullivan, b. 19 June, 1817, at Yarmouth, N. S.); m. 1868, Sarah J. Finley, of Peabody.

GOODWIN.
Andrew J.,
m. 22 Dec., 1863, Co. K, 2d H. A.; dis. 3 Sept., 1865, ex. term.

Æt. 21 at enl.

Charles M.,
m. 18 Aug., 1862, Co. A, 39th Inf.; dis. 15 May, 1865, ex. term. Credited to Boxford. Wounded 6 May, 1864.

b. Shapleigh, Me., 1838; son of Moses and Armini (Jellison) Goodwin; m. 1861, Elizabeth M. Fremir. Lives in Danvers.

John,
m. 5 July, 1861, Co. I, 1st H. A.; dis. 6 Dec., 1863, to reenlist; killed Petersburg, Va., 20 June, 1864.

b. Shapleigh, Me., 1825; son of Moses and Mary Goodwin; m. Abby Rogers. Ch.: Mary Jane, b. 15 Oct., 1852, d. y. Mary, b. 15 Oct., 1853. Charles, b. 6 Sept., 1854. Ella E. b. 1 July, 1862.

(Goodwin Continued.)

Warren F.,
m. 5 July, 1861, Co. I, 1st H. A.; dis. 6 Dec., 1863, to re-enlist; final dis. 16 Aug., 1865.

b. Danvers, 20 Dec., 1842; son of Ivory (b. Sanford, Me., 30 Jan., 1814) and Mary (Coffin, b. Sanford, 19 Apr., 1820) Goodwin.

William W.,
m. 1 Oct., 1862, Co. K, 8th Inf.; dis. 7 Aug., 1863, ex. term.

GOOTHER.

Charles,
m. 1 Oct., 1862, Co. K, 8th Inf.; dis. 7 Aug., 1863, ex. term.

GOSS.

George H.,
m. 22 July, 1861, Co. C, 17th Inf.; dis. 3 Aug., 1864, ex. term; reenl. 8 Mar., 1865, Co. B, 17th Inf.; dis. 11 July, 1865.

b. Danvers, 5 Feb., 1843; son of Joshua and Rachel Fuller Goss; m. 14 Mar., 1865, Hattie J. Clark (b. Charlestown).
Lives in Charlestown.

Joshua,
m. 22 July, 1861, Co. C, 17th Inf.; dis. 4 Dec., 1862, disability; m. 31 Aug., 1863, Co. H, 3d H. A.; dis. 18 Sept., 1865, ex. term.

b. Marblehead, 6 Mar., 1817; son of Wm. and Abigail (Hammond) Goss; m. 1st, Rachel Fuller (b. Danvers, 15 July, 1820); m. 2d, 7 Oct., 1867, Catharine G. Clark. Father of Geo. H.
Lives in Charlestown.

Richard,
m. 26 Sept., 1861, 2d Co. S. S., dis. 22 Sept., 1862, disability.

b. Mendon, 17 Apr., 1821; son of Wm. and Abigail Goss, m. 20 Oct., 1850, Hannah Jane Tedford. Ch.:

(Goss Continued.)
Walter Solon, b. 6 May, 1853. Orrison, b. 7 June, 1854, Geo. B., b. 12 Nov., 1855. Arthur L., b. 4 Oct., 1857. Mary Alice, b. 17 Nov., 1859. Benj. Lewis, 10 Jan., 1861. Milford Tedford, b. 29 Aug., 1863.
Lives in Beverly.

GOUDEY.

Charles W. C.,
m. 21 Nov., 1863, Co. D. 1st H. A.; died 24 May, 1864, of wounds at Washington, D. C.

b. Yarmouth, N. S.

GOULD.

Cleaveland,
m. 1 Oct., 1862, Co. K, 8th Inf.; dis. 26 Apr., 1863, disability.

Daniel Herbert,
m. 1 Oct., 1862, Co. K, 8th Inf.; dis. 7 Aug., 1863, ex. term; m. 26 Oct., 1863, Co. A, 1st Cav.; died 20 Nov., 1864, Salisbury, N. C.; credited to Boston, 2d enlistment.

b. Topsfield, 5 Oct., 1845; son of Daniel, (b. Topsfield, 12 June, 1820) and Mary Ann (Sears, b. Danvers) Gould.

William W.,
m. 22 July, 1861, Co. C, 17th Inf.; corp. 18 Aug., '63; dis. 3 Aug., 1864, ex. term; credited to Boxford.

Æt. 25 at enl.; b. Danvers, son of Mrs. Peter Roberts, of Danvers.
Lives Pittsfield, N. H.

GOURLEY.

Edward F.,
m. 23 Aug., 1864, Co. A, 4th H. A.; dis. 17 June, 1865, ex. term.

GRAY.

Alonzo,
m. 26 May, 1862, Salem Cadets; dis. 24 July, 1862, died Fort Warren, Mass.

(*Gray Continued.*)
b. Danvers, 4 Sept., 1837; son of Josiah (b. Beverly, 2 Aug., 1800) and Eunice (Fuller, b. Danvers, 4 Feb., 1802) Gray.

Samuel Fairfield.
m. 26 May, 1862, Salem Cadets; dis. 11 Oct., 1862. ex. term.

b. Danvers, 9 Mar., 1835; son of Josiah and Eunice (Fuller) Gray; m. Abigail Whitehouse Foster, of Beverly. Ch.: Arthur F., b. 9 Jan., 1855. Francis A., b. 9 Aug., 1859. Rosa F., b. 10 May, 1862. Mabel, b. 28 Mar., 1865. Marion, b. 7 Feb., 1867. Annie H., b. 31 Mar., 1873. Brickmaker, Danversport.

GREEN.
James A.,
m. 19 July, 1862, Co. F, 35th Inf.; dis. 9 June, 1865. ex. term as corp.

Æt. 21 at enl.

Thomas E.,
m. 19 July, 1862, Co. F, 35th Inf.; dis. 1 Nov., 1863, disability.

b. Lower Canada, 1839; son of Wm. and Jane (Gaffney) Green; m. 25 Dec., 1860, Henrietta W. Porter, of Danvers. Ch.: Alice E., b. 6 Aug., 1831. Marietta, b. 28 June, 1875. Eliza, b. 20 June, 1877. Frank Cameron, b. 29 May, 1879.

GRIFFIN.
Eben J.,
m. 22 Dec., 1863, Co. K, 2d H. A.; dis. 3 Sept., 1865, ex. term.

b. Danvers, 11 Oct., 1846; son of Joseph (b. Danvers, 22 Mar., 1812) and Eliza Ann (Jackson, b. Charlestown, 17 Sept., 1818) Griffin; m. 17 Nov., 1869, Sarah M., dau. of John C. Putnam. Ch.: Ernest Jackson, b. 5 Aug., 1876. Sarah Elizabeth, b. 18 Mar., 1879.
Lives in Danvers.

John D.,
m. 14 Sept., 1861, Co. B, 30th Inf.; dis. 17 Oct., 1864, ex.

(*Griffin Continued.*)
term. Credited to Lowell.

Æt. 18 at enl., b. Danvers; son of David.

GROUT.
Samuel S. (W.),
m. 20 Jan., 1862, Co. I, 1st H. A.; captured at Petersburg, Va., 22 June, 1864; confined at Richmond, 25 June, 1864. Sent to Lynchburg, Va., 29 June, 1864. No further record.

b. Danvers, 20 Nov., 1844; son of John (b. Kirby, Vt., 17 July, 1807) and Sally P. (Smith, b. 9 June, 1807) Grout.

GROVER.
Benjamin F.,
m. 23 Aug., 1864, Co. A, 4th H. A.; dis. 17 June, 1865, ex. term.

GUILFORD.
David Augustus,
m. 1 May, 1861, Co. H, 5th Inf.; dis. 31 July, 1861, ex. term; m. 28 Oct., 1861, Co. C, 24th Inf., corp.; 6 Mar., 1864, transferred to V. R. C.; final dis. 12 Nov., 1864, from 2d Batt. V. R. C.

b. Danvers, 27 Mar., 1827; son of David M. and Harriet (Grover) Guilford; m. 28 June, 1849, Frances E. Lilley, (b. Boston). Ch.: Sarah E. C., b. 31 Oct., 1851. Clara, b. 17 Oct., 1853. Annie L., b. 22 Feb., 1867. David F., b. 12 Jan., 1869. Geo. Francis, b. 18 July, 1877. Horace M., b. 5 Dec., 1857.
Helped guard Mason and Slidell at Ft. Warren, Boston, 27 Dec., 1861; was detached in command of 20 privates to man the guns on the Vidette, in the Burnside Coast Expedition. After the battle of Newberne was engaged in detached service in making reconnoissances. Among the engagements in which he participated was 1st Battle Bull Run. Wounded at Roanoke, by a piece of shell in right shoulder.

TOWN OF DANVERS.   25

(Guilford Continued.)
Was in Mason Hospital, Boston, July and Aug., 1863, and Regimental Hospital, St. Augustine, Fla. Dec., 1863, was hospital steward on the Cosmopolitan, in 1864.
Resides in Danvers. Boxmaker.

Elbridge Henry,
m. 1 May, 1861, Co. H, 5th Inf., corporal; dis. 31 July, 1861; m. 7 Oct., 1861, Co. C, 24th Inf., sergt.; dis. 8 Oct., 1864, ex. term. Confined in hospital at Beaufort, S. C., and at Beaufort, N. C.
b. Danvers, 26 Jan., 1843; son of David M. (b. Danvers, 26 Sept., 1799) and Harriet (Grover, b. Salem, 16 Dec., 1804) Guilford; m. 17 Mar., 1866, Mary F. Hay. Ch.: Alice E., b. 12 Oct., 1868. Florence F., b. 13 July, 1871. Elbridge Henry, b. 17 June, 1875. Harriet F., b. 19 Sept., 1877. Wm. H., b. 25 Oct., 1881. Ruth C., b. 2 Sept., 1884. Bernard G., b. 10 Apr., 1890.
Resides Beaver Brook, Danvers.

Elbridge W.,
m. 5 July, 1861, Co. A, 1st H. A.: 1st Sergt.; prom. 2d Lt., 18 Jan., 1862; 1st Lt., 9 Feb., 1862; dis. 11 July, 1864, dismissed.
b. Danvers, 20 May, 1829; son of Elbridge Gerry (b. Danvers, 2 Nov., 1802) and Susanna Haywood (Whipple, b. 11 Jan., 1807) Guilford; m. Mary E. Fletcher. Ch.: Frank Oscar, b. 15 June, 1854. Lander E., b. 19 Aug., 1866.

Jacob O.,
m. 18 Aug., 1862, Co. A, 39th Inf.; dis. 29 Dec., 1863, disability; credited to Middleton.
Æt. 21 at enl.; d. s. p., in Lynn; Son of Levi Guilford.

William Francis,
m. 1 May, 1861, Co. H, 5th Inf.; dis. 1 Aug., 1861, ex. term. Credited to South Danvers.
b. Danvers, 5 Jan., 1840; son of David M. and Harriet (Grover) Guilford; d. Danvers, 5 Sept., 1861, of typhoid fever contracted at Washington. He was an engineer.

GUPPY.

Charles A.,
m. 24 Aug., 1864, Co. A, 4th H. A.; dis. 17 (22) June, 1865, ex. term.
b. Lowell, 22 Sept., 1834; son of Samuel (of Rochester, N. H.) and Philena (Andrews of Essex) Guppy; m. Almira A. Smith, of Newfield, Me. Ch.: Luther A., b. 18 Feb., 1856. Annie W., b. 29 Nov., 1862. Herbert A., b. 24 May, 1873.
Of Danvers. Shoemaker.

Orlando C.,
m. 5 July, 1861, Co. I, 1st H. A.; dis. 8 July, 1864, ex. term.
Æt. 26, married; bro. of Charles A.

HADLEY.

Horace L.,
m. 13 June, 1861, Co. H, 11th Inf.; m. 5 Jan., 1864, Co. H, 11th Inf.; corp.; dis. 25 May, 1865, disability. Credited to Danvers.
"Of North Andover"; b. Sandwich, N. H., 1837; son of Winthrop and Sybil Hadley; m. 11 Sept., 1868, S. Lizzie, dau. Daniel Emerson of Danvers.
He was claimed by Middleton. Lives at Washington Court House, Ohio.

HAGGERTY.

Robert B.,
m. 22 July, 1861, Co. C, 17th Inf.; deserted 20 Aug., 1861.
Aged 22 at enl.; enl. at Lynnfield.

HALL.

Everson,
m. 7 Nov., 1863, Co. D, 1st H. A.; dis. 19 May, 1864; killed at Battle of North Anna, Va.
Æt. 30 at enl.; of Danversport, shoemaker.

Stephen A.,
m. 22 Aug., 1862, Co. E, 38th Inf.; dis. 18 Dec., 1863, disa-

(Hall Continued.)
bility; credited to So. Danvers.

b. Lynn, 1844; son of Stephen W. and Louisa R. (Williams) Hall; m. 13 May, 1872, Mary E. Colburn, of Salem.

HAM.
Charles H.,
m. 19 July, 1862, Co. F, 35th Inf.: corp.: dis. 9 June, 1864, ex. term. Wounded.

b. Georgia, 20 Mar., 1838; son of Daniel and Sarah (Watson) Ham; m. 13 Mar., 1867, Elizb. A. Craft of Danvers. Ch.: Albert Henry, b. 10 Oct., 1867; Wm. Henry, b. 5 Apr., 1872; Herbert C., b. 4 Nov., 1875; a dau., b. 16 Dec. 1870. Lives in Danvers.

Daniel A.,
m. 19 Aug., 1862, Co. F, 35th Inf.; corp.: dis. 15 Oct., 1862, disability. Credited to E. Weldon, N. H.
Æt. 22 at enlistment.

James H. (M.),
m. 5 July, 1861, Co. I, 1st H. A.; dis. 9 Sept., 1864; died Andersonville, Ga.
Æt. 21 at enlistment.

HANSON.
Charles W.,
m. 18 Aug. 1862, 1st sgt., Co. A, 39th Inf.; serg.-major; 6 Dec., 1862; prom. 2d Lt. 25 Jan., 1863; 1st. Lt. 8 Nov., 1863; Capt. 8 Sept., 1864; dis. 22 Apr., 1865, for disability. Credited to South Danvers. Æt. 26 at enl.

George W.,
m. 19 Aug., 1862, Co. F, 35th Inf.; dis. 9 June, 1865, ex. term; (trans. V. R. C. corp. 18 Dec., 1863, but sent back to regiment). Æt. 19 at enl.

Jonathan B.,
m. 5 July, 1861, Co. I, 1st H. A., 1st sergt.; prom. 2d Lt.

(Hanson Continued.)
22 Sept., 1861; prom. 1st Lt., 18 Jan., 1862: capt. 22 May, 1864, of Co. E.: dis. 12 Mar., 1865; 2d Lt. 39th U. S. Inf., 7 March, 1867; 1st Lt. 1 Jan., 1869; assigned to 10th U. S. Inf., Jan. 1, 1871. Died 2 Nov., 1876, at Washington, D. C.

b. Danvers, 16 May, 1831; son of Isaac Remerick (b. Wakefield, N.H.) and Elizb. (Batchelder) Hanson; married Phebe, dau. of John Grout.

HARRIGAN.
Bartholomew,
m. 13 Dec., 1861, Co. C, 28th Inf.; dis. 14 Mar., 1863, disability; m. 22 Aug., 1864, Co. G, 4th H. A.; dis. 17 June, 1865, ex. term.

b. Ireland, 1828; m. Ann Farrell. Ch.: Francis, b. Danvers, 6 Apr., 1853. Mary Ann, b. Danvers, 5 Nov., 1860. David J., b. Lowell.

HARRIS.
John,
m. 14 Oct., 1864, 3d U. S. Col. Art'y: enl. at Vicksburg, Miss.; credited to Danvers.
Æt. 19 at enl.; resided Rankin Co., Miss.

John C.,
m. 22 Dec., 1863, Co. K, 2d H. A.; dis. 3 Sept., 1865, ex. term.

b. Wilmot, N. S., 1840: son of Thomas and Mary (Bonley) Harris: m. 11 Nov., 1866, Belle M. Fraim (b. Brookfield).

HART.
Rufus,
m. 22 July, 1861, Co. C, 17th Inf.; dis. 18 Sept., 1863, disability.

b. Danvers, 15 June, 1835; son of Martin (b. Lynnfield, 31 Mar., 1794) and Elizb. (Swinton, b. 19 Aug., 1791) Hart: m., 1866, Emma Speed: m. 2d, 1872, Sarah B. Thorme. Ch.: Emma Florence, b. 21 Apr., 1874. Lives in Danvers.

HARTMAN.

Charles,
m. 22 July. 1861. Co. C, 17th Inf.; musician; trans. to Co. B; dis. 4 Jan., 1864, to reenlist; final dis. from Co. H, 11 July, 1865, ex. term.

b. 1844 at Saxonville, Mass.; son of Thomas and Charlotte P. (Taylor) Hartman; m. 4 Apr., 1867, at Sanford, Me. Elizb. J. Welch. Ch.: Chas. E.; Ernest A.; Herbert Henry and Hervey L., twins, b. 8 Feb., 1873. Ethel; Maud. Resides in Danvers.

Thomas,
m. 22 July, 1861, Co. B, 17th Inf.; dis. 13 Aug., 1862, disability; died 5 July, 1862.

b. Scotland, 1805 (age at enlistment "58"); son of Thomas Hartman; m. Charlotte P. Taylor (b. Conn.). Ch.: Albert, b. 27 Sept., 1851. Geo., b. 16 Mar., 1854. Louise, b. 21 Dec., 1856. Caroline, b. 21 Nov., 1859. Served in the English Army for 21 years; was a sergeant.

Thomas, junior,
m. 22 July, 1861, Co. C, 17th Inf.; dis. 24 Apr., 1863, disability; m. 15 July, 1864, Co. I, 6th Inf.; dis. 27 Oct., 1864, ex. term.

Æt. 29 at enl.; son of Thomas, q. v. Lives in Danvers.

HAWKES.

Timothy,
m. 22 July, 1861, Co. C, 17th Inf.; dis. 12 Sept., 1862, disability.

b. Salem, 16 May, 1816; d. in Danvers; son of Timothy Hawkes; m. 12 July, 1836, Mary Ann Smith (b. Boston, 3 Mar., 1816). Ch.: Timothy, q. v.; John; Philip; Robert; Thorndike; Thorndike; George; Elizb.; Abbie; Walter.

Timothy, junior,
m. 22 July, 1861, Co. C, 17th Inf., corp.; trans. to Co. B; dis. 5 Jan., 1864 to reenlist, 6 Jan., 1864 same Co., serg.:

(Hawkes Continued.)
taken prisoner; prom. 2d Lt., 24 Mar., 1865; prom. 1st Lt., 1 June, 1865.; dis. 11 July, 1865, ex. term, from Co. D.

b. Danvers. 24 May, 1836; died Danvers, 19 Jan., 1884: son of Timothy Hawkes; m. 28 July, 1860, Eliza Jane Leach.

HAYWARD.

Charles,
m. 22 Aug., 1864, Co. A, 4th H. A.: dis. 17 June, 1865, ex. term. Credited to Marblehead.

HENDERSON.

Albert (H.),
m. 5 July, 1861, Co. I, 1st H. A., corp.: dis. 5 July, 1864, ex. term.

b. Danvers, 7 Apr., 1838; died Danvers, 1 Apr., 1877; son of Benjamin, (b. Salem, 8 Aug., 1798) and Elenor (Rowell, b. Boston) Henderson.

HENNESSY.

John V. (B.),
m. 5 July, 1861, Co. I, 1st H. A.: dis. 5 July, 1864. ex. term. Æt. 22 at enl.

HILL.

James,
m. 1 May, 1861, Co. A, 5th Inf.; dis. 31 July, 1861, ex. term: m. 6 Aug., 1862, Co. C, 33d Inf., sergt.; 1st sergt. 15 Aug., 1862; prom. 2d Lt. 7 June, 1863; killed at Lookout Mountain, 29 Oct., 1863.

b. Kidderminster. Eng.. 1841: son of James and Sarah Hill.

HILLER (Hilliar).

Charles,
m. 5 July, 1861, Co. I, 1st H. A.; dis. 5 July, 1864.

b. Boston, 1840; son of Haskett and Harriet Hiller; m. 21 June, 1868, Etta Bedler, b. Springvale, Me., 1847.

HINDS.
Ambrose,
m. 19 Aug., 1862, Co. F, 35th Inf.; killed at Antietam, Md., 17 Sept., 1862.

Æt. 25 at enlistment, widower.

HINES.
John M.,
m. 1 May, 1861, Co. H, 5th Inf.; dis. 31 July, 1861, ex. term; m. 17 Feb. 1862, Co. D. 1st H. A.; dis. 20 Feb., 1865.

b. Danvers, 5 Mar., 1840; son of John (b. 7 Nov., 1803) and Louisa (Potter, b. Manchester, 7 Oct., 1807) Hines.

HOBBS.
John,
m. 5 July, 1861, Co. I, 1st H. A.; dis. 10 Dec., 1863, to reenlist; final dis. 16 Aug., 1865.

b. Danvers, 1 Jan., 1841; son of Abraham Richardson (b. Topsfield, 13 Nov., 1806) and Mercia (Brown, b. Tewksbury, 8 June, 1808); m. Annie Gentley (b. Salem). Ch.: Annie Antoinette, b. 9 Jan., 1868

HOLT.
James A.,
m. 9 Dec., 1861, Co. C, 17th Inf.; dis. 12 Sept., 1862, disability.

b. Danvers, 24 July, 1829; son of James (b. Danvers, 25 Feb., 1797) and Mary (Smith, b. Danvers, 9 Oct., 1796) Holt.

HOOD.
Joseph E.,
m. 19 Aug., 1862, Co. F, 35th Inf.; dis. 10 Apr., 1865, sergt.; wounded (leg lost) 30 July, 1864, at Petersburg, Va.

b. Danvers, 26 Mar., 1841; son of John (b. Wenham, 8 Mar., 1806) and Rebecca (Standley, b. Beverly, 6 Jan., 1808) Hood; m. 13 Nov., 1866. Mattie E. Gilpatrick (b. Shapleigh, Me., 1843). Ch.: Ralph Otho, b. 5 July, 1870, Chas. E., b. 22 Jan., 1873, Lee Roy Standley, and Mabel Electa, twins, b. 26 June, 1877.

(*Hood Continued.*)
Richard,
m. 17 Oct., 1861, Co. G, 23d Inf.; dis. 21 Oct., 1862, disability.

b. Topsfield, 9 Dec., 1802; died 20 Apr., 1881; son of John and Ruth Hood; m. 22 Sept., 1825, Asenath Smith (b. Hanover?, N. H., 21 Sept., 1798). Ch.: Richard Brainard, b. 31 Jan., 1826. Ruth, b. 30 Jan., 1827, above at Topsfield. Frances Melvena, b. 4 Jan., 1829. Wm. I., b. Danvers, 4 May, 1830. Adoniram Judson, b. 7 Apr., 1832. Elsa Asenath, b. 10 Jan., 1834. Alonzo LeRoy, b. 7 Aug., 1836. May Asenath, b. 25 Apr., 1838. M. 2d, 27 Jan., 1861, Harriet Parker of Groton. Ch.: Wallace Parker, b. 3 Dec., 1863.

Wendell P.,
m. Co. A, 10th R. I.; dis. 1 Sept., 1862, ex. term; m. 7 Nov., 1862, Co. F, 48th Inf.; acting Hospital steward at Port Hudson, and at Arsenal Hosp., at Baton Rouge, La.; dis. 3 Sept., 1863, ex. term.

b. Danvers, 25 Feb., 1839; son of John (b. Wenham, 8 May, 1806) and Rebecca (Standley, b. Beverly, 6 Jan., 1808) Hood; m. 27 Mar., 1866, Maria Phelps Putnam. Ch.: Robert Putnam, b. 17 Feb., 1868. Wm. Phelps, b. 2 Apr., 1870, d. 4 Aug., 1870. Susie Mabel, b. 10 May, 1876. At time of first enl. was a student at Brown U., Providence. He was a volunteer nurse on one of the ships in Banks Expedition to the Gulf Dept. Spotted fever was prevalent. Now a resident of Melrose.

HOPKINS.
James,
m. 6 Aug., 1862, Co. C, 33rd Inf.: wounded in action; dis. 10 Aug., 1864, trans. to V. R. C., dis. 89th Co. 2d Batt'l, 28 July, 1865.

b. St. Johns, N. B., 1841, son of John and Catharine; m. 1862, Ann Marion Murphy. Ch.: James P. Lives in Danvers.

TOWN OF DANVERS.

(Hopkins Continued.)

John, junior,
m. 15 Aug., 1862, Co. H, 20th Inf.; dis. 15 Dec., 1862, disability.

Æt. 21 at enlistment; son of John and Catharine (Lunney) Hopkins. Now at Togus, Me.

HORNE.

Abial A.,
m. 1 Oct., 1862, Co. K, 8th Inf., corp.; dis. 16 Mar., 1863.

b. New Hampshire; died in Conn. on way home, 31 Mar., 1863.

HOWARD.

John H.,
m. 1 May, 1861, Co. A, 5th Inf.; dis. 31 July, 1861, ex. term; m. 1 July, 1862, Co. B, 7th Inf., corp.; dis. 31 Dec., 1862, ex. term.

b. Jackson, Me., 1842; son of Levi H. and Bethia A. (Page) Howard; m. Saluce D. Goodwin, 21 Apr., 1862. Ch.: Geo. Henry, b. 16 Nov., 1863. Susan Bertha, b. 30 May, 1865. Cordelia Burleigh, b. 25 Apr., 1868. Abbie G., b. 23 Jan., 1871. Lorenzo G., b. 14 July, 1874.
Lives in West Peabody.

Levi H.,
m. 5 July, 1861, Co. I, 1st H. A.; died 27 Aug., 1863, at paroled prisoners camp, Annapolis, Md.

b. Me., aged 42 at enlistment; m. Bethiah A. Page. Ch.: John H., b. Jackson, Me., 1842. Wm. A., b. do. 1849. Ezra M., b. do. 1857. Mary E. and Edward Fletcher, twins, b. Danvers, 27 Apr., 1860.

HOWE.

Elias W.,
m. 13 Aug., 1864, Co. E, 1st Batt'y H. Art'y; dis. 28 June, 1865, as Q. M. sergt.; credited to Hopkinton.

Æt. 22 at enl.; deceased.

HUFF.

Orisk K.,
m. 15 July, 1864, Co. I, 6th Inf.; dis. 27 Oct., 1864, ex. term.

Lives in Maine.

HUNT.

Ebenezer,
m. 29 July, 1864, 8th Inf., M. V. M., Asst. Surg.; dis. 10 Nov., 1864, ex. term.

b. Nashua, N. H., 13 Apr., 1799; died Danvers, 27 Oct., 1874; m. 18 June, 1828, Sarah F. Cheever, of Danvers. Ch.: Catharine Elizb., b. 16 Mar., 1829, M. 2d. Elizb. Smith Cheever, of Danvers. Ch.: Sarah Cheever, b. 20 July, 1834. Mary Addine, b. 23 Dec., 1835. Wm. Augustus, b. 30 Sept., 1837. Moses Nowell, b. 11 Dec., 1839. John Melton, b. 7 Feb., 1842. M. 3d, Mrs. Mary P. Putnam. Ch.: Sarah Elizb., b. 22 June, 1849.

HURD.

Charles,
m. 5 July, 1861, Co. I, 1st H. A.; dis. 10 Dec., 1863, to reenlist; m. 11 Dec., 1863, same Co.; dis. 16 Aug., 1865, ex. term. Aged 22 at enlistment.

HUSE.

David S.,
m. 2 Sept., 1861, 1st Co. S. S.; dis. 11 Jan., 1862, disability.

Æt. 18 at enl.

HUTCHINSON.

James M.,
m. 11 Aug., 1862, Co. I, 32d Inf.; dis. 4 Jan., 1864, to reenlist, same Reg. and Co.; final dis. 29 June, 1865, ex. term. Credited to Charlestown.

Æt. 21 at enl.

HYDE.

Daniel A.,
m. 22 July, 1861, Co. C, 17th Inf.; dis. 10 May, 1863, disability.

(*Hyde Continued.*)

b. Tamworth, N. H., 1823: Uncle of Henry G. Hyde.
Lives in Danvers Centre.

Henry Gould,

m. 22 July, 1861, Co. C, 17th Inf., sergt.; dis. 29 Feb., 1864, to reenlist same day and Co., as 1st sergt.; prom. 2d Lt., 4 July, 1864; prom. 1st Lt., 1 Sept., 1864; dis. 11 July, 1865, ex. term.

b. Danvers, 19 Feb., 1842: son of Elisha G. (b. Ossipee, N. H., 4 July, 1803) and Eliza J. (Cass, b. Meredith, N. H., 20 June, 1808) Hyde; m. 1 Feb., 1866, L. Marion (dau. of Wm. and Lydia Endicott) Endicott. Ch.: Marion E., b. 23 Mar., 1875. Mary Endicott, b. 7 Jan., 1877. Henry Cass, b. 10 Nov., 1879.
Lives in Boston.

HYND.

Thomas,

m. 22 July, 1861, Co. C, 17th Inf.; dis. 3 Aug., 1864, ex. term.

b. Dunfermlines, Fiffeshire, Scotland, 18 Oct., 1820; "aged 34 at enlistment"; son of John and Maria (Williamson) Hynd; m. 4 July, 1847, Susan Best (b. London, Eng., 25 Mar., 1829, dau. of Geo. and Jane [Colbett] Best). Ch.: John, b. Conn., 1848. Esther, b. Danvers, 14 Apr., 1850. Jennie E., b. Conn., 1854. Irene B., b. (1 July, 1866.
Lives in Tapleyville.

INGALLS.

Charles Nathan,

m. 3 Sept., 1861, 1st Co. S. S.. serg.; dis. 5 Dec., 1862, disability.

b. North Andover, 9 July, 1820; died Hawley, Minn., 9 Aug., 1886; son of Francis and Elizb. B. (Foster) Ingalls; m. 16 Dec., 1845, Hannah Jaquith Abbott of Andover, who d. 29 Dec., 1898. Ch.: Sarah E., b. 8 Nov., 1846, Chas. F., b. 28 Jan., 1849. Geo. Wm., b. 26 Mar., 1851. Francis, b. 8 June, 1853. Albert A., b. 18 Apr., 1856. M. 2d, 26 Oct., 1871, Mary Jane Morse, of

(*Ingalls Continued.*)

Portland, Me. Ch.:. Chas. H., b. 22 Apr., 1873.
Settled in Danvers in 1851, architect and builder.

INGRAM.

George,

m. 5 July, 1861, Co. I, 1st H. A.; taken prisoner; dis. Feb., 1865, ex. term.

b. England, 1838; died Danvers, 18 Feb., 1878; son of Geo. and Elizb. (Suthaland) Ingram; married Miss Sheldon.

INMAN.

James,

m. 22 July, 1861, Co. C, 17th Inf., sergt.; prom. 2d Lt., 26 Apr., 1863; dis. 3 Aug., 1864.

b. England, 1838; son of Thos. and Susannah (Brooks) Inman; m. 9 Dec., 1858, Sophia E. Clement (dau. of Mrs. Sophia Putnam). Ch.: Arthur Nelson, b. 6 Aug., 1860.
Lives in Denver, Col.

Joseph,

m. 9 July, 1863, Co. F, 3d H. A.; dis. 18 Sept., 1865, ex. term.

b. England, 1840; son of Thos. and Susannah (Brooks) Inman; m. 20 Oct., 1860, Angie E. Smart, dau. of J. T. G. and Prudence (Tuttle) Smart. Ch.: Fred'k P., b. 4 May, 1861. James and Joseph, twins, b. 12 May, 1868.
Lives in Denver, Col.

William S.,

m. 15 July, 1864, Co. I, 6th Inf.; dis. 27 Oct., 1864, ex. term.

b. Simsbury, Conn., 1848; died Boston, 8 July, 1885; son of Thomas and Susannah (Brooks) Inman; m. 21 Apr., 1873, Marcia D. Brown, dau. of Chas. W. and Lydia (Hood) Brown. Ch.: Chas. T., b. 24 June, 1874. Hattie Goodhue, b. 27 Nov., 1877.

JEFFS.

Tristram C.,

m. 28 Sept., 1861, Co. G, 23d

TOWN OF DANVERS.

(Jeff's Continued.)

Inf., corp.: dis. 14 Oct., 1864: died in Florence Prison, S. C.

b. Lynn, 1828; m. Caroline F. Grant, of Beverly. Ch.: Martha Helen, b. 23 July, 1861.

JELISON.
George W.,

m. 22 Dec., 1863, Co. K. 2d H. A.; dis. 3 Sept., 1865, ex. term.

b. Shapleigh, Me., 2 Aug., 1846; son of Enoch E. and Mercy (Webber) of Sanford, Me.) Jebison; m. 23 Aug., 1868, Hattie A. Wiggin, dau. of Joseph F. and Mary Ashby Wiggin. Ch.: Joseph Walter, b. 14 Feb., 1869, Geo. Melvin, b. 13 Apr., 1872. M. 2d, 20 Sept., 1885, Hannah D. Clark of Augusta, Me. Lives in Danversport.

JENNESS.
Lorenzo W.,

m. 10 Oct., 1861, Co. F, 23d Inf.; dis. 13 Oct., 1864, ex. term. (? Credited to Mhd.)

b. Plymouth, N. H., 1835; son of Benjamin (of Lynn) and Maria (Pinkham of Boothbay, Me.) Jenness; m. Eliza Hawkes of M'h'd. Ch.: Blanch, b. Lynn, Howard, b. Lynn. M. 2d, 23 Oct., 1889, Ellen, dau. of G. W. and H. J. (Hines) Remick. Resides in Danvers.

JESSUP.
Robert W.,

m. 22 Oct., 1861, Co. A, 17th Inf.; dis. 14 Oct., 1864, ex. term.

b. England, 25 Oct., 1823; aged "35" at enlistment; died 21 July, 1887; m. 15 June, 1845, Louisa Langdon Rhodes, (b. Waterborough, Me., 14 Aug., 1823) of Danvers. Ch.: Wm. Walter, b. 15 Apr., 1846, Lydia Emeline, b. 17 Dec., 1849, Robert E., b. 15 Mar., 1859.

William W.,

m. 22 Aug., 1862, Co. B, 40th Inf.; dis. 21 Sept., 1863; died Folly Is., S. C.

b. Danvers, 15 Apr., 1846, son of Robert W. and Louisa L. (Rhodes) Jessup.

JOHNSON.
Franklin,

m. 22 Dec., 1863, Co. K. 2d H. A.; dis. 3 Sept., 1863, ex. term from Co. H. Æt. 18 at enl.

George,

m. 24 Oct., 1861, Co. I. 1st Inf.: recn. 4 Jan., 1864; trans. to 11th Inf., 21 May, 1864: dis. from Co. A, 11th Inf., 14 July, 1865.

b. Boston, 1822; son of———and Rachel (Baxter) Johnson, of Gloucester; m. Georgiana F. Williams of Salem. Ch.: Geo. Henry, b. 1860, Mary Alice, b. Oct., 1878. Resides at Danversport, Mass.

JONES.
George H.,

m. 5 July, 1861, Co. I, 1st H. A.; dis. 14 Dec., 1863, to reenlist; final dis. 16 Aug., 1865.

b. Alton Bay, N. H., 1 Aug., 1842; died Danvers, 1892; son of Wm. and Elizb. L. (Perkins) Jones; m. 14 Feb., 1864, Mrs. Roxana (Lowe) Welch, dau. of Ivory W. and Louisa C. Lowe. Ch.: Lewis Edw., b. 26 July, 1866, Minerva, b. 21 Feb., 1871, Elmer Francis, b. 28 Sept., 1874.

JOYCE.
Michael,

m. 13 Oct., 1862, Co. E, 48th Inf.: deserted 25 Dec., 1862.

KEEFE.
John,

m. 14 Sept., 1861, Co. B, 24th Inf.; dis. 14 Sept., 1864, ex. term: m. 9 Feb., 1865, V. R. C.; dis. 3 Jan., 1866, ex. term; credited to Salem.

b. Ireland, 1827; son of John and Annora O'Keefe; m. 1853, Catharine Manah, dau. of Mathew and Bridget Flannegan, b. Ireland. Ch.: Carry May, b. 3 May, 1870, Amanda. Lives in Danvers Centre.

KELLEY.

Andrew,
m. 19 Aug., 1861, Co. C, 17th Inf.; dis. 12 Sept., 1862, disability.

b. Pelham, N. H., 30 Apr., 1821; m. Elizb. Holden (b. 30 Aug., 1821, in Paisley, Scotland). Ch.: Andrew, b. 15 Feb., 1844. Mary Ellen, b. 31 Mar., 1846. Lydia, b. 29 Dec., 1848. A son, b. 10 Dec., 1854. Rebecca Holden, b. 23 Mar., 1859.
Lives in Milbury.

Archie P. B.,
m. 28 July, 1863, Co. A, 2d H. A., musician; dis. 3 Sept., 1865, ex. term.

b. 12 Dec., 1846; son of James (q. v.) and Bathsheba; m. 10 Aug., 1875, Susan Scampton. Ch.: Grace S., b. 24 Feb., 1876. Robert Stanley, b. 24 Aug., 1877.
Lives in Lynn.

Charles F.,
m. 5 July, 1861, Co. I, 1st H. A., serg't; dis. 28 Dec., 1863, to reenlist; final dis. 18 July, 1865, for disability.

b. Danvers, 12 Mar., 1839; died Salem, Apr., 1887; son of John B. (b. Alton, N. H., 1 Sept, 1812) and Hannah N. (Goodale, b. Danvers, 24 Feb., 1815) Kelley; m. 22 June, 1831, Nancy E. Munsey, dau. of C. C. and Matilda (Howard) Munsey.

Francis G.,
m. 22 July, 1861, Co. G, 17th Inf., sergt.; dis. 22 June, 1863, disability; credited to Lynn. Wounded 17 Dec., 1862.

b. Danvers, 7 Oct., 1838; son of James, q. v. and Bathsheba Kelley.

James,
m. 2 Aug., 1862, Co. A, 23d Inf.; dis. 30 May, 1863, disability. Wounded 14 Oct., 1862.

b. Deering, N. H., 14 Dec., 1808; m. 8 Dec., 1829, Bethsheba Needham

(Kelley Continued.)
(b. Salem, 3 Feb., 1809). Ch.: James W., q. v.; Thomas B., q. v. Francis G., q. v. Archie P. B., q. v.

James H.,
m. 29 July, 1863, Co. B, 2d H. A.; dis. 3 Sept., 1865, ex. term.

b. Danvers, 20 Oct., 1843; brother of Chas. F. Kelley; m. 20 Aug., 1864, Louisa A., dau. of Benj. and Fanny Young, b. Danvers, 7 Apr., 1840. Ch.: James Augustus, b. 26 Dec., 1864. Nellie L., b. 21 Jan., 1867. Fred Alden, b. 7 Dec., 1870. Ernest W., b. 9 Apr., 1873. Wm. Young, b. 27 Apr., 1875.
Lives in Haverhill.

James W.,
m. 28 Sept., 1861, Co. A, 23d Inf.; wounded 14 Mar., 1862; dis. 2 Jan., 1864, to reenlist; killed at Drury's Bluff, Va., 16 May, 1864. Credited to South Danvers.

b. Danvers, 4 Oct., 1834; son of James, q. v. and Bethsheba Kelley; m. 24 May, 1858, Ellen Poor, dau. of Joseph and Eliza M. Poor, of South Danvers.

John,
m. 19 Aug., 1864, Co. A, 4th H. A.; dis. 17 June, 1865, ex. term.

b. Manchester, Eng., 1840; died Danvers, 19 July, 1882; son of James and Bridget (who were b. in Ireland) Kelley.

Thomas B.,
m. 28 Sept., 1861, Co. A, 23d Inf.; dis. 13 Oct., 1864, ex. term.

b. Danvers, 7 Aug., 1842; son of James (above) and Bathsheba Kelley.

KELLY.

Edward,
m. 1 May, 1861, Co. H, 5th Inf.; dis. 31 July, 1861, ex. term.

(Kelly Continued.)

b. Ireland, 1835; m. Mary Calbart. Ch.: Edw., b. 8 Aug., 1860. Mary Ellen, b. 2 Jan., 1862. John, b. 12 May, 1863. M'g't Lizzie, b. 14 Sept., 1865. Mary Ann, b. 23 May, 1868. Katie Ellen, b. 19 June, 1870.

John,
m. 22 July, 1861, Co. C, 17th Inf.; dis. 3 Aug., 1864, ex. term.

b. 1825, Ailsford, N. S.; d. Danvers, 25 Mar., 1878; son of James and Eliza Kelley; m. 27 June, 1852, Lucy G. Hill, b. Kittery, Me., dau. of Wm. and Jane Neil.

KENNEDY.
Elbridge,
m. 22 Aug., 1864, Co. A, 4th H. A.; dis. 17 June, 1865, ex. term.

b. Danvers, 28 May, 1847; died Danvers, 12 May, 1885; son of James (b. Washington, N. H., 13 Dec., 1818) and Elizb. Hatch (Coffin, b. Sanford, Me., 21 May, 1823) Kennedy; m. Harriet E. Martin. Ch.: Harry Clinton, b. 12 Feb., 1874. Grace May, b. 30 June, 1877. Ernest, b. 14 Jan., 1879.

Jackson,
m. 22 July, 1861, Co. C, 17th Inf.; dis. 3 Aug., 1864, ex. term.

b. 29 May, 1829, at Somerville, Me.; son of Samuel and Harriet Kennedy; m. Mary E.——— Ch.: Emeline. Elbridge. Other children. Lives in West Peabody.

KENNEY.
Arthur C.,
m. 26 May, 1862, Salem Cadets; dis. 11 Oct., 1862, ex. term.

b. 18 July, 1839; d.—; son of Wm. J. C. (b. Middleton, 1 Dec., 1809) and Elizb. (Whittier, b. Danvers, 4 Oct., 1811) Kenney; m. 7 Feb., 1866, Nellie L. Bartlett, b. Portland, Me., dau. of Isaac and Mary (Ward) Bartlett

(Kenney Continued.)

George W.,
m. 21 Aug., 1861, Co. G, 17th Inf., capt.; wounded 17 Dec., 1862; dis. 3 Aug., 1864, ex. term; m. 30 Aug., 1864, 29th unatt. Co., H. A., capt.; dis. 16 June, 1865, ex. term.

b. Danvers, 12 Apr., 1830; died 9 Mar., 1891; son of Wm. J. C. Kenney, bro. to Arthur C.; m. 6 Apr., 1858, Gertrude Stickney (b. N. H.). Ch.: Willis Herbert, b. 8 Aug., 1858. Gertrude S., b. 4 Mar., 1868.

KENISTON.
Hiram B.,
m. 27 Sept., 1861, 2d Co. S. S.; dis. 30 Jan., 1863, disability.

b. Alton, N. H., 13 Sept., 1827; m. Lucinda Meader. Ch.: Malissa Helen, b. 11 Feb., 1853. Sarah E., b. 17 Dec., 1863. Henry M., b. 17 June, 1857. Lives in Danvers.

KENT.
Moses A.,
m. 28 Sept., 1861, Co. A, 23d Inf.; died Newberne, N. C., 7 Oct., 1862.

b Danvers, 31 Jan., 1841; son of Moses (b. Newbury, 27 Oct., 1779) and Hannah (Green, b. 23 Jan., 1801) Kent.

KIMBALL.
Albert,
m. 13 Feb., 1864, Co. A, 23d Inf.; dis. 25 June, 1865, ex. term.

b. Danvers, 20 Nov., 1845; son of Jeremiah (b. 25 Mar., 1808) and Mary D. (Kenney, b. 24 Mar., 1814) Kimball.

Ezra D.,
m. 22 July, 1861, Co. C, 17th Inf.; dis. 2 Apr., 1862, disability; m. 20 Nov., 1863, Co. H, 3d H. A.; dis. 18 Sept., 1865, ex. term.

(*Kimball Continued.*)

b. Danvers, 21 Feb., 1838; died California about 1875; son of Dean (b. Meridith, N. H., 25 Dec. 1796) and Polly (Batchelder, b. Danvers, 9 Sept., 1810) Kimball; m. 1 Jan., 1864, Mrs. Mary A. Gould, dau. of Chas. G. and Amanda G. (Sanborn) Decoston.

Horace,
m. 3 Sept., 1861, 1st Co. S. S.; dis. 16 Mar., 1864, trans. to 24th Reg., V. R. C.; dis. 5 Sept., 1864.

b. Danvers, 1826; son of Caleb and Mary (Ponsland) Kimball, of Beverly; m. 16 Sept., 1849, Elizb. dau. of Josiah and Eunice Gray. Ch.: H. Freeman, b. 19 Mar., 1854. Alice G., b. 4 Apr., 1856. Mary P., b. 17 June, 1858. Frank B., b. 11 June, 1860. Lizzie C., b. 15 Oct., 1861. Alonzo G., b. 18 Aug., 1870. Caleb W., b. 14 Feb., 1872.

KIRBY.
Jeremiah,
m. 15 July, 1864, Co. I, 6th Inf.; dis. 27 Oct., 1864, ex. term.

b. Ireland, 1845; son of Michael and Ellen (Downing) Kelley; m. 15 Jan., 1870, Mary, dau. of Dennis and Kate (Splane) Fogarty. Ch.: John, b. 6 Nov., 1870. Kate Ellen, b. 25 June, 1872. Mary Ann, b. 24 Dec., 1873. Annie L., b. 23 Sept., 1878. Lives in Danvers.

Michael,
m. 22 July, 1861, Co. C, 17th Inf.; dis. 2 Apr., 1862, disability.

b. 1842, (æt. "21" at enlist.) Ireland; d. abt. 1892; son of Michael and Ellen (Downing) Kirby; m. 13 May, 1870, Mary, dau. of Daniel and Marg't (O'Neal) Murphy.

KITTREDGE.
Frank S.,
m. 5 July, 1861, Co. I, 1st H. A., corp.; dis. 6 Dec., 1863, to reenlist; dis. 16 Aug., 1865.

Æt. 20 at enlistment.

KNIGHTS.
Samuel Leaverett,
m. 19 Aug., 1862, Co. F, 35th Inf.; dis. 1 July, 1865, disability.

b. Danvers, 7 Dec., 1835; son of Allen (b. Middleton, 13 Apr., 1811) and Maria Theresa (Clark, b. Topsfield, 4 Sept., 1813) Knights; m. 4 Oct., 1866, Marg't E., dau. of Wm. and Hannah (Benson) Skinner, b. Lynnfield. Ch.: Sarah E., b. 16 Sept., 1867. Geo. Allen, b. 8 Apr., 1869.
Moved to Davenport, Iowa.

KROUSE.
Herman,
m. 5 Mar., 1862, Co. K, 4th Cav., bugler; reenl. 21 Apr., 1864; dis. 14 Nov., 1865, ex. term.

Æt. 19 at enl., "of Boston." Lives in Peabody; has a son Albert L.

LANDERS.
Richard,
m. 15 July, 1864, Co. E, 33d Inf.; dis. 8 June, 1865, ex. term. Prisoner from 12 Feb., to 28 Apr., 1865.

Of Bangor, Me., credited to Danvers. Æt. 22 at enl.

LANE.
Solomon (Salmon) B.,
m. 11 Oct., 1862, Co. C, 42d Inf.; dis. 20 Aug., 1863, ex. term; m. 9 Nov., 1863, Co. H, 3d H. A.; dis. 18 Sept., 1865, ex. term.

LANG.
David P.,
m. 22 July, 1861, Co. C, 17th Inf.; dis. 3 Aug., 1864, ex. term.

b. Lowell, 1838; son of Archibald and Jane (Pulson) Lang; m. 14 Apr., 1868, Mary L., dau. of Joseph and Lucy (Welch) Dwinnell of Danvers. Ch.: Ralph Ernest, b. 11 Oct., 1877. A dau.
Lives Danversport.

LARRIBEE.
Benjamin F.,
m. 16 Sept., 1863, Co. F, 3d H. A., corp.: dis. 8 May, 1865, disability.

b. Peabody. 1836; died Danvers. 25 Sept., 1881.

LEAVITT.
Joseph,
m. 22 Nov., 1861, Co. H, 17th Inf.; dis. 24 Apr., 1863, disability; m. 2 Jan., 1864, Co. F, 2d H. A.; died Newberne, N. C., 14 Nov., 1864, of yellow fever.

b. Shapleigh, Me., 28 Jan., 1815; æt. 43 at enl.; m. 1 Sept., 1841, Hannah Hall (b. Nottingham, N. H., d. Danvers, 28 Feb., 1842). M. 2d, 22 Dec., 1844, Ruth Maria Hatch (b. Andover, 31 Jan., 1821). Ch.: Caroline Augusta, b. 11 Dec., 1845. Laura Frances, b. 24 Oct., 1847. Mary Isabella, b. 14 Sept., 1849. Austin. b. 25 Jan., 1852. Emily Maria, b. 9 Aug., 1853. Geo. P., b. 11 Apr., 1856. Eliza M., b. 1 Aug., 1858. Inez Josephine, b. 3 May, 1862.

LEE.
James,
m. 22 July, 1861, Co. C, 17th Inf.; dis. 3 Aug., 1864, ex. term.

b. Ireland, aged 22 at enl.; d. at Bridgewater about 1890.

LEFFLAU.
Samuel A.,
m. 5 July, 1861, Co. I, 1st H. A.; dis. 6 Dec., 1863, to reenlist; killed Petersburg, Va., 16 June, 1864. Credited to Rockport on first enl.; to Danvers on second enl.

Aged 22 at enl.; b. in Salem.

LEIGHTON.
Reuben,
m. 4 Mar., 1864, Co. G, 5th Cav.; dis. 31 Oct., 1865, ex. term.

Æt. 18 at enl.

LEGRO.
Charles P.,
m. 19 Aug., 1862, Co. F, 35th Inf.: dis. 6 May, 1863; trans. V. R. C.; dis. Co. H, 7th V. R. C., 29 June, 1865.

b. Danvers, 1836; son of Edmund R. and Maria (Putnam) Legro; m. 1858, Adaline A. Solaris, dau. of Francis and Nancy Solaris. Lives in Danvers.

LEWIS.
Samuel W.,
m. 7 Oct., 1861, 3d Cav., "Reids Rangers"; corp., 20 May, 1862; sergt. 1 Sept., 1862; 1st sergt., 1 Jan., 1863; prom. 2d Lt., 22 Aug., 1863; dis. 26 Nov., 1864.

b. Newburyport. 1837; son of Andrew and Lucy M. (Jewell) Lewis; m. 26 Jan., 1865, Mrs. Lydia A. Ross, dau. of Joseph and Mehitable (Hawks)———.
Lives in Newburyport.

LOWE.
Darling,
m. 19 Aug., 1861, Co. C, 17th Inf.; dis. 5 Sept., 1862, disability.

b. Shapleigh, Me., 2 Aug., 1813; d. in Lynn about 1880. Ch.: Alonzo, James W., two daus., one of whom m. O. D. Ham.

George S. (E.),
m. 5 July, 1861, Co. I, 1st H. A.: dis. 14 Dec., 1863, to reenlist; dis. 16 Aug., 1865.

b. Maine, 1842; son of Ivory and Louisa (Pinkham) Lowe. Wounded. Lives at Danvers Centre.

James Wesley,
m. 1 May, 1861, Co. H, 5th Inf.; dis. 31 July, 1861, ex. term.

b. Danvers, 26 Mar., 1842; son of Darling (b. Shapleigh, Me., 2 Aug., 1813) and Phebe (Rhodes, b. Waterborough, Me., 9 Apr., 1812) Lowe. m. 25 Jan., 1865, Adrienne M. W. Canney (b. Norton). Lives in Lynn.

LOWELL.
James E.,
m. 22 July, 1861, Co. C, 17th Inf.: died 10 Feb., 1862, at Baltimore, Md.

b. 1838 in Maine; d. of diphtheria, at Baltimore.

LUFKIN.
William H.,
m. 1 May, 1861, Co. A, 5th Inf.: dis. 31 July, 1861, ex. term.: m. 28 Sept., 1861, Co. G, 23d Inf.; trans. 8 Feb., 1864, to V. R. C.; credited to Beverly.

Lives in Danvers.

LYONS.
Charles H.,
m. 26 Oct., 1863, Co. E, 1st Cav.; killed at Ashland, Va., 11 May, 1864. Credited to Boston.

Aged 21 at enl.; son of Levi R. and Mary Lyons.

MACK.
James,
m. 5 July, 1861, Co. I, 1st H. A., sergt.; dis. 7 Dec., 1863, to reenlist; prom. 1st Lt., 31 July, 1865; dis. 16 Aug., 1865, ex. term.

Æt. 29 at enl., b. Charlottetown, P. E. I.; son of John and Jane Mack; m. 1850, Eliz. E. dau. of Abraham and Edar Smith, b. Wenham. Ch.: a son, b. 13 Oct., 1859. William, b. 13 Sept., 1866.
Lives in Elmira, N. Y.

MADDEN.
James,
m. 19 Sept., 1864, 29th unatt. H. A.; dis. 16 June, 1865. Credited to Ashland. Æt. 18 at enl.

MALLEY.
Melville,
m. 22 July, 1861, Co. C, 17th Inf.: dis. 3 Aug., 1864, ex.

(Malley Continued.)
term.; reenl. 20 Sept., 1864, Co. D, 17th Inf.; credited to Quincy; dis. 30 June, 1865, from Co. H; sergt. 4 Mar., 1865.

Aged "19" at enl.; deceased.

MALONEY.
Thomas,
m. 5 July, 1861, Co. I, 1st H. A.; dis. 6 Dec., 1863, to reenl.; dis. 3 Feb., 1865. Æt. 20 at enl.

MANGOLD.
Daniel,
m. 22 Dec., 1863, Co. K, 2d H. A.; dis. 3 Sept., 1865, ex. term. Credited to Rockport; disputed credit; allowed to Danvers, from naval surplus. "For ten years previous to enl., a resident of Danvers."

Æt. 38 at enl.; b. in Germany. Had a son Daniel. Deceased.

MARGERSON.
James Parker,
m. 1 Oct., 1862, Co. K, 8th Inf.: dis. 7 Aug., 1863, ex. term.

b. Nova Scotia; m. Martha A. White. Ch.: Martha E., b. 27 Apr., 1855. Lizzie, b. 13 Jan., 1857. Carrie Estella, b. 4 June, 1858.

MARR.
Frederick,
m. 16 Sept., 1863, Co. F, 3d H. A.; trans. to Co. M; deserted 20 June, 1865. Æt. 20 at enl.

MARSHALL.
Edward (Edwin) H.,
m. 29 July, 1863, Co. B, 2d H.A.; dis. 3 Sept., 1865, as corp.

Æt. 25 at enl.

(Marshall Continued.)
George H.,
m. 3 Sept., 1862, Co. K, 40th Inf. ; deserted 9 July, 1863, from Gen. Hospital ; credited to Beverly. Not on War Dept. records.

Æt. 18 at enl.

John D.,
m. 5 June, 1862, Co. G, 23d Inf. ; dis. 4 June, 1865, ex. term. Credited to Beverly. Trans. to V. R. C. Æt. 16 at enl.

MARTIN.
John M.,
m. 1 Oct., 1862, Co. K, 8th Inf. ; dis. 7 Aug., 1863, ex. term.

b. N. H.; m. Sarah Gilman. Ch.: Ida May, b. 28 May, 1862.

Joseph G.,
m. 22 July, 1861, Co. C, 17th Inf. ; sergt., Co. B ; trans. to Co. G ; dis. 29 Feb., 1864 to reenlist ; m. 1 Mar., 1864, 1st sergt. ; prom. 2d Lt., 16 June, 1865 ; dis. 11 July, 1865, ex. term.

b. Scotland, 1826; d. Danvers, 26 Feb., 1895; m. Agnes Arbucklie. Ch.: Mary L., b. Lawrence, 1855. Agnes Arbucklie, b. 7 June, 1858. Lived in Danvers Centre.

MASURY.
Charles Henry,
m. 5 July, 1861, Co. D, 1st H. A., sergt. ; dis. 25 Feb., 1863 ; prom. 2d Lt., 8 Mar., 1863 ; dis. 8 July, 1864, ex. term. from Co. M ; Batt'l Adj.— Post ordnance officer, wounded at Petersburg in head, 16 June, 1864 ; confined in hospital at Petersburg and at Campbell Hospital, Washington.

(Masury Continued.)
b. Wenham, 11 Feb., 1842; son of Thomas and Lucy (Andrews) Masury; m. 1 Mar., 1877, Eveline A. dau. of Alfred and Nancy (Putnam) Fellows. Ch.: Alfred Fellows, b. 2 Sept., 1882.
Lives in Danvers.

MAUD.
Henry,
m. 31 Aug., 1863, Co. B, 2d H. A. ; dis. 3 Sept, 1865, from Co. B.

b. England, 1826; d. Philadelphia; son of David Maud; m. Jane. Ch.: Thomas, b. 10 Nov., 1857. Martha, b. 12 July, 1862.

MAYHEW.
Edward P.,
m. 8 Oct., 1863, Co. F, 2d H. A. ; dis. 23 June, 1865.

b. Danvers, 6 Apr., 1849, (æt. "18" at enl.); son of George (b. Danvers, 31 Mar., 1824) and Harriet Augusta (Morris, b. Harvard, 25 Dec., 1825) Mayhew.

McAULIFF.
John,
m. 1 Oct., 1862, Co. K, 8th Inf. ; dis. 7 Aug., 1863, ex. term.

b. Ireland, 1833; d. Danvers, 12 Feb., 1871; son of John and Mary McAuliff; m. 19 Jan., 1857, Ellen Moriarty, (b. Ireland). Ch.: Ellen, b. 16 Jan., 1860. John, b. 20 Nov., 1861. Timothy, b. 20 Jan., 1866. Catherine, b. 6 Jan., 1868. Margaret, b. 2 May, 1870.

Michael,
m. 12 Aug., 1862, Co. D, 11th Inf. ; dis. 23 Apr., 1863 ; died Washington, D. C.

b. Ireland, 1840; son of John and Mary McAuliff.

McCARTHY.
James,
m. 22 July, 1861, Co. B, 17th Inf.; dis. 2 Dec., 1861, disability.

(*McCarthy Continued.*)
Aged 47 at enl.; died Danvers; left a dau. Anne and sons James and John.

McCOY.
John,
m. 2 Jan., 1864, Co. E, 2d H. A.; dis. 15 July, 1865. Cred. to So. Danvers.

Æt. 39 at enl.; married.

McCREARY.
John,
m. 22 July, 1861, Co. C, 17th Inf.; dis. 3 Aug., 1864, ex. term; m. 24 Jan., 1865, V. R. C.; dis. 15 Dec., 1865.

b. Ulster Co., Ireland, 1825; d. in Lynn; son of Patrick McCreary; m. 1854, Mrs. Sarah Bird (b. England). Ch.: Elisha, b. 6 Mar., 1859.

McDEVITT.
Dominick,
m. 15 Feb., 1862, Co. D, 17th Inf.; dis. 14 Feb., 1865, ex. term.

b. Ireland, aged 30 at enl. Lives in Weymouth.

McGILL.
Charles (B.) L.,
m. 21 Nov., 1863, Co. D, 1st H. A.; dis. 16 Aug., 1865, disability, from Co. I.

b. Yarmouth, N. S., 1844; son of Wm. J. and Lucinda (Pickering) McGill; m. 10 May, 1866, Maria, dau. of Alvin Ellenwood.

McINERY.
John,
m. 24 Jan., 1865, 3d Reg., V. R. C., Co. F.; dis. 15 Dec., 1865. On rolls as John Mc-Cresey. Æt. 44 at enl.

McKEIGUE.
Thomas,
m. 20 Nov., 1863, Co. H, 3d H. A.; dis. 18 Sept., 1865, ex. term.

(*McKeigue Continued.*)
b. Ireland, 1844; died Danvers, 8 Oct., 1877; son of Edw. and Elizb. (Acton) McKeigue; m. Ann Kelly; Ch.: Maude A., b. 4 Feb., 1876.

McKENNEY.
Joseph,
m. 18 July, 1864, Co. F, 33d Inf.; said to never have joined his regiment.

Of N. Y. City; cred. to Danvers; æt. 23 at enl.

McKENNY.
Robert,
m. 20 Dec., 1861, Co. H, 20th Inf.; m. 30 Mar., 1864, Co. H, 20th Inf.; dis. 27 July, 1865, ex. term.

b. Nova Scotia, 1830; m. Mary.

McLAUGHLIN.
James,
m. 11 June, 1861, Co. F, 9th Inf., corp.; dis. 21 June, 1864, ex. term. Wounded in thigh at Hanover Court Ho., 27 May, 1862.

b. Ireland; æt. 23 at enl.; m. Mary Maddin. Ch.: Catharine Elizb., b. 2 Feb., 1867.

MEADER.
Charles E.,
m. 3 Sept., 1862, Co. K, 40th Inf.; dis. 6 Nov., 1863; died Folly Is., S. C., 5 Nov., 1863. Æt. 18 at enl.

MEEHAN.
Matthew (Nathaniel),
m. 22 July, 1861, Co. G, 17th Inf.; dis. 3 Aug., 1864, ex. term; credited to Salem. Æt. 17 at enl.

MERRILL.
John,
m. 5 July, 1861, Co. I, 1st H. A.; died 2 Nov., 1862, of disease at Ft. Tillinghast, Va.

b. Salem, 1834, d. 25 Nov., 1862; son of Joseph (b. Amesbury) and Phebe (Felton, b. Danvers) Merrill.

MESSER.
Frank B.,
m. 15 July, 1864, Co. I, 6th Inf.; dis. 27 Oct., 1864, ex. term.

b. Danvers, Jan., 1846; son of Albert and Sophronia Messer.

METZGER.
Christopher,
m. 19 Aug., 1862, Co. F, 35th Inf.; dis. 8 Apr., 1865, wounded; gunshot wound in right arm received at Weldon R. R., Va., 19 Aug., 1864.

b. Oberolm, Hessen Darmstatt, Germany, 17 Apr., 1843; brother of John, q. v.: m. Mary Jane Herrick; m. 2d, Edwina Frances Butler. Ch.: Butler, b. 27 Mar., 1874. Mary J. H., b. 26 Aug., 1876. Laura, b. 30 Apr., 1882. Chas. H., b. 24 Dec., 1884. Albert, b. 3 Mar., 1887. John, b. 19 Jan., 1890.
Now a resident of Lynn.

John,
m. 5 July, 1861, Co. I, 1st H. A.; dis. 4 Nov., 1862, disability.

b. Oberolm, Hessen Darmstatt, Germany, 1 Mar., 1834; son of Henry P. and Eliza (Rosenzweig) Metzger, of Danvers; m. 12 Jan., 1856, Barbara Schloager of Danvers. Ch.: Elizb., b. 26 Feb., 1858. John, b. 1 Jan., 1861. Fred'k, b. 31 July, 1865. Catharine, b. 2 July, 1867. Annie, b. 1 Apr., 1869. John, b. 24 Nov., 1870.
Resides in Danvers.

William,
m. 23 July, 1864, Co. C, 5th Inf.; dis. 16 Nov., 1864, ex. term; reenl. 5th Cav.

b. Roxbury, 1847, d. Galloupes Island, Boston Harbor, 10 Mar., 1865; son of Fred'k and Catharine (Peters) Metzger.

MILLER.
Arthur J.,
m. 6 Sept., 1861, Co. D, 22d Inf.; dis. 17 Oct., 1864, ex. term; credited to Salem.

Æt. 19 at enl.; m. dau. of Lorenzo Rogers. Lives in Danvers.

MILES.
Benjamin D.,
m. 5 July, 1861, Co. I, 1st H. A.; reenlisted 8 Dec., 1863, corp.; dis. 16 Aug., 1865. On first enlistment, credited to Wenham; on second enl., to Danvers, but disputed and allowed to Wenham.

b. Maine; æt. 27 at enl. "of Wenham"; d. at Lynn; m. Hannah H. Medom. Ch.: Hannah D., b. 8 May, 1869.

MITCHELL.
Edward,
m. 16 Sept., 1863, Co. F, 3d H. A., 1st sergt.; dis. 27 Sept., 1865, prom. 2d Lt., 27 Sept., 1865.

Æt. 26 at enl.; married.

MOIR.
Alexander,
m. 22 July, 1861, Co. C, 17th Inf.; dis. 24 Apr., 1863, disability.

b. Scotland; æt. 43 at enl.; m. Jennie———; Ch.: Elizb. M'g't. Jennie. Mary.
Lives in Danvers.

MOORE.
George E.,
m. 22 July, 1861, Co. C, 17th Inf.; dis. 3 Aug., 1864, ex. term; reenl. 9 Feb., 1865, Co. D, 17th Inf.; cred. to Shutesbury; prom. principal musician; dis. 11 July, 1865.

b. Candia, N. H., 1837; d. Danvers; son of Herbert and Sally Moore; m. 1857, Dorothy N., dau. of Samuel and Sarah Philbrick, of Danvers. Ch.: Edw. E., b. 1859; d. abt. 1889.

John K.,
m. 22 July, 1861, Co. C, 17th Inf.; dis. 15 June, 1862, disability.

b. Pembroke, N. H., 1820; son of Herbert and Sally S. Moore; m. 26

(*Moore Continued.*)

Nov., 1851, Maria J., dau. of Nathan and Lydia Shaw (b. Yarmouth, N. S.). Lives in Haverhill.

Lewis D.,
m. 22 July, 1861, Co. C, 17th Inf.; dis. 12 Mar., 1862.

Aged 18 at enl.; brother of John K. Moore, q. v.

MOORES.
John B.,
m. 22 July, 1861, Co. C, 17th Inf.; dis. 4 Jan., 1864, to re-enlist; dis. 11 July, 1865; corp., Co. B, 1 Mar., 1865; sergt., 4 Mar., 1865 from Co. G.

b. England, 1835; son of Henry Moores; m. 5 Apr., 1855, Jane Mitchenson (b. in England, dau. of Richard). Ch.: John Henry, b. 22 May, 1864. Samuel Mitchenson, b. 6 May, 1866. Three daus. Lives Danvers Centre.

MORE.
John,
m. 22 July, 1861, Co. C, 17th Inf.; dis. 4 Jan. 1864, to re-enlist; dis. 11 July, 1865, from Co. B.

b. Ireland, 1840; died Peabody, 29 Dec., 1875; son of Michael and Peggy (Call) More; m. 6 Sept., 1856, Matilda J., dau. of Wm H. and Hannah Lus om. She m. 2d ———Tufts. Left two daus.

MORAN.
James,
m. 7 Jan., 1862, Co. B, 11th Inf.; dis. 29 Aug., 1862, killed at 2d Bull Run, Va. Credited to Salem.

b. Ireland, æt. 34 at enl.; m. Ellen Cochran. Ch.: Michael, b. 22 July, 1859. Ellen, b. 14 Jan., 1861. James, b. 9 June, 1862.

MORRILL.
Edwin F.,
m. 10 May, 1863, Co. F, 3d H. A.; dis. 18 Sept., 1865, ex. term. Æt. 18 at enl.

MORRISON.
Archibald,
m. 22 July, 1861, Co. C, 17th Inf.; dis. 3 Aug., 1864, ex. term.

Aged 26 at enl.; b. Scotland. Lives in Providence; married.

MOSER.
Charles T.,
m. 22 Dec., 1863, Co. K, 2d H. A.: dis. 3 Sept., 1865, ex. term.

b Nova Scotia, 1845; son of Wm. and Eliza A. Moser; m. Sarah J. Jowder. Ch.: Ethel Maria, b. 24 July, 1883. Lives in Danvers.

John H.,
m. 1 May, 1861, Co. A, 5th Inf.: dis. 31 July, 1861, ex. term; m. 28 Sept., 1861, Co. D, 22d Inf., corp.: dis. 4 Mar., 1863, disability; wounded in right leg and back, 13 Dec., 1862 at Fredericksburg, and left arm, 1 July, 1862 at Melvin Hills, Va. In hospital at Washington. 16 Dec., 1862; trans. to Portsmouth Grove, R. I.

b. Dover, N. H., 11 Mar., 1843; son of Wm. H. and Eliza Ann (Brown) Moser; m. 30 Nov., 1864, Emma J., dau. of J. C. and Emma Shaw, b. Moultonborough, N. H., 1848. Ch.: Joseph Wm., b. 19 Sept., 1865. Hattie Stimpson, b. 12 Mar., 1868. Arthur W., b. 12 Sept., 1873. One of the first to enlist in Danvers (16 Apr., 1861). Lives in Danvers.

William H.,
m. 5 July, 1861, Co. I, 1st H. A.; dis. 8 July, 1864; m. 22 Aug., 1864, Co. M, 3d H. A.; dis. 19 June, 1865, ex. term.

b. Nova Scotia, 1846; died Danvers, 7 July, 1881; m. Eliza A. Brown. Ch.: John H., b. Dover, N. H., 1842. Maria A., b. Wenham, 1846. Ann G., b. Danvers, 1853.

MOULTON.

George H.,
m. 22 July, 1861, Co. C, 17th Inf.; dis. 3 Aug., 1864. ex. term.

b. Wells, Me., aged 28 at enl.; m. Marg't H. Connor (b. Glasgow, Scotland). Ch.: Henry C., b. Salem, 13 Jan., 1861. Lives in Haverhill.

MULLEN.

Andrew,
m. 1 May, 1862, Co. C. 17th Inf.: dis. 1 Jan., 1864, to re-enlist; dis. 11 July, 1865, from Co. B.

Æt. 24 at enl. "of Boston"; enlisted at Newberne; died in Wakefield.

MUNDIE.

John,
m. 22 July, 1861, Co. C. 17th Inf.; dis. 3 Aug., 1864. ex. term.

b. England, 27 Jan., 1834: son of George and Mary Ann Mundie; d. Lawrence.

MUNSEY.

Joseph C.,
m. 1 May, 1861, Co. A, 5th Inf.; dis. 31 July, 1861, ex. term.

MURPHY.

Edward,
m. 11 Mar., 1862, Co. L, 1st H. A.; trans. to Co. A, 31 July, 1865; dis. 17 Mar., 1864, to reenlist; dis. 16 Aug., 1865.

b. Scotland, 1840; d. Charlestown; brother of Owen Murphy, q. v.; m. Catharine Claney. Ch.: James Patrick, b. 29 Nov., 1876. James, b. 7 Nov., 1877.

Hugh,
m. 15 July, 1864, Co. I, 6th Inf.; dis. 27 Oct. 1864, ex. term; m. 3 Mar., 1865, Co. H, 17th Inf.; dis. 11 July, 1865; credited to Salem.

(Murphy Continued.)
Æt. 21 at enl.; b. in Danvers; son of Henry and Sarah (McLaughlin) Murphy.
Lives in Haverhill.

Jeremiah,
m. 30 Dec., 1861, Co. A, 28th Inf.; dis. 16 Oct., 1864; died Salisbury, N. C. Wounded at Chantilly, 1 Sept., 1862. Æt. 26 at enl.

Owen,
m. 22 July, 1861, Co. C, 17th Inf.; dis. 3 Aug., 1864; re-enl. 20 Sept., 1864. Co. C. 17th Inf.; cred. to Hingham; (sergt. of Co. H. 4 Mar., 1865; trans. to Co. B); dis. 30 June, 1865, from Co. H.

b. Aberdeen, Scotland, 1836; died Danvers, 8 Apr., 1881; son of Patrick (b. Ireland) and Julia (Riley) Murphy.

William Joseph,
m. 22 July, 1861, Co. C, 17th Inf.; dis. 3 Aug., 1864, ex. term.

b. Andover, 1833; son of Henry Murphy; half-brother of Hugh Murphy, q. v.; m. 1854, Mary, dau. of Wm. Glinon, b. Ireland. Ch.: Phebe Ann, b. 12 Apr., 1857. Mary, b. 18 Jan., 1859. Sarah Winnford, b. 6 June, 1861. Chas. Edmund, b. 19 Sept., 1865. Marg't Eliza, b. 19 Apr., 1867. Catharine Matilda, b. 13 Mar., 1869. Nellie J., b. 3 Nov., 1871. Frances Agnes, b. 2 June, 1877.
Lives in Danvers.

MURRAY.

George W.,
m. 28 July, 1862, Co. I, 1st H. A.; dis. 8 July, 1864, ex. term; credited to Salem. Æt. 22 at enl.

James,
m. 28 July, 1862, Co. D, 1st H. A., corp.; dis. 8 July, 1864; sick in hospital since 17 May, 1864.

(Murray Continued.)
b. Scotland, 1838; son of David and Elizabeth Murray; m. Sarah E., dau. of Allen and Sally Jacobs. Ch.: James Warren, b. 23 Sept., 1861. Susan Frances, b. 25 Sept., 1865. Lives in Lynn.

Martin,
m. 22 July, 1861, Co. C, 17th Inf.; dis. 3 Aug., 1864, ex. term.

b. Roscommon Co., Ireland, 1 Nov., 1840; son of Martin and M'g't Murray; m. 23 May, 1880, Frances L.— Lives in Beverly.

Patrick (enl. as John Stonehall),
m. 25 May, 1861, Co. C, 2d Inf.; dis. 9 Aug., 1862, killed at Cedar Mountain, Va.

Brother of Martin Murray; b. 1842, Ireland. Enlisted as John Stonehall.

Simon R.,
m. 5 July, 1861, Co. I, 1st H. A.; dis. 8 July, 1864, ex. term; absent, wounded. Æt. 25 at enl.

MUSGRAVE.
Thomas A.,
m. 22 July, 1861, Co. C, 17th Inf.; dis. 9 Aug., 1861; died 9 Aug., 1861, at Lynnfield. Credited to Lynnfield.

b. North Sidney, 1842; son of Chas. and Ann Leslie (Dundee) Musgrave. First man in regiment to die.

NALOR.
Mark,
m. 22 Aug., 1863, Co. D, 2d H. A.; dis. 3 Dec., 1864, died Florence, S. C. Credited to Springfield.

Resided in Thompsonville, Conn.; æt. 40 at enl.

NASH.
Prince W.,
m. 16 Sept., 1863, Co. F, 3d H. A., sergt.; dis. 18 Sept., 1865, ex. term.

(Nash Continued.)
b. Weymouth, 12 Feb., 1845; son of Prince E., (b. Weymouth, 1 Feb., 1821) and Sarah (Field, b. 6 Sept., 1826) Nash.

NEWHALL.
Benjamin E.,
m. 1 Oct., 1862, Co. K, 8th Inf., 2d Lt.; dis. 7 Aug., 1863, ex. term.

b. Augusta, Me., 4 Sept., 1834; son of Benj. S. and Caroline M. (Gray) Newhall; m. 20 Sept., 1864, Mary A. Ropes, who d. 20 June, 1866; m. 2d, 11 June, 1868, Caroline A. Derby, dau. of Henry and Mary Derby. Ch.: Arthur Derby, b. 20 Feb., 1869. Alice Henderson, b. 6 Dec., 1869. Walter, b. 21 May, 1872. Benj. Simonds, b. 22 Oct., 1874. Frank Warren, b. 22 July, 1879. Lives in Danvers.

Charles,
m. 24 Aug., 1864, Co. A, 4th H. A.; dis. 17 June, 1865, ex. term.

b. Salem, 1838; bro. of Benj. E., q. v.; m. 3 Oct., 1861, Flora Kimball, dau. of Dean and Polly (Batchelder) Kimball. Ch.: Chas. K., b. 20 Jan., 1864. Lives in Danvers.

George A.,
m. 6 May, 1862, Co. F, 23d Inf.; dis. 5 May, 1865, ex. term.

Æt. 18 at enl.

NICHOLS.
Jefferson,
m. 27 May, 1862, Co. A, 23d Inf.; dis. 26 Mar., 1863, disability.

Æt. 46 at enl.

NORTH.
Abram,
m. 2 June, 1862, Co. K, 23d Inf.; dis. 17 Oct., 1862, disability; m. 31 Aug., 1863, Co. D, 2d H. A., sergt.; dis. 3 Sept., 1865, ex. term, from Co. B.

TOWN OF DANVERS.   43

(North Continued.)

b. England, 1824, (æt. "30" at enl.) d. Danvers, 17 Jan., 1890; m. Marg't Douglas. Ch.: Isabel C. Francis, b. 14 July, 1853. Marg't, b. 17 Aug., 1856. Wm. Sillars, b. 6 Jan., 1862. Edward, q. v. James D. Abram. Soldier in the English army.

Edward,

m. 21 Jan., 1862, Co. C, 17th Inf.; dis. 31 Jan., 1863, disability: m. 15 July, 1864, Co. I, 6th Inf.; dis. 27 Oct., 1864, ex. term.

Æt. 20 at enl.; son of Abram North. Resides in Lynn, 1894.

James D.,

m. 1 May, 1861, Co. A, 5th Inf.; dis. 31 July, 1861, ex. term.

b. Scotland, 26 May, 1840; son of Abram North, q. v. Resides in Lynn.

NOURSE.

Allen,

m. 23 July, 1861, Co. C, 17th Inf., sergt.; 6 Aug., '62, trans. to Co. E.; dis. 21 Oct., 1862, died 31 Oct., 1862, at Newberne, N. C.

b. Danvers, 12 Nov., 1839; bro. of Sam'l W. Nourse, q. v.

Samuel Walter,

m. 23 July, 1864, Co. C, 5th Inf.; dis. 16 Nov., 1864, ex. term.

b. 19 Aug., 1841; son of Sam'l Putnam (b. 14 Feb., 1806) and Mary Endicott (Proctor, b. 31 Mar., 1812) Nourse; m. 27 May, 1863, Mary E. B. Seidmore. Ch.: Allen Francis, b. 30 Jan., 1865. Ernest Proctor, b. 8 Sept., 1867. Walter Endicott, b. 13 July, 1870. Lives in Peabody.

NUGENT.

Thomas,

m. 4 Aug., 1863, Co. F, 3d H. A.; dis. 8 May, 1865, disability.

Æt. 37 at enl.

NUTTER.

Stephen L.,

m. 11 Aug., 1862, Co. B, 13th Inf.; dis. 1 Aug., 1864, ex. term.

b. Sandwich, N. H., 1840; son of Dan'l W. and Betsey C. (Cook) Nutter; m. 4 Oct., 1861, Elmira Jane, dau. of Wm. and Abigail (Griffin) Goodale. Ch.: Albert Lewis, b. 8 Dec., 1862.

OBER.

William,

m. 5 Aug., 1862, Co. G, 17th Inf.; dis. 3 Aug., 1864, ex. term.

b. Beverly, 1835; son of Wm. and Lucy Ober; m. 20 Jan., 1859, Susan R., dau. of Stephen and Salome Small, b. Lynnfield. Ch.: Arthur Wm., b. 5 June, 1860. Emma Susan, b. 31 Jan., 1864. Geo. Arthur, b. 24 July, 1867. Lives in Lynn.

O'BRIEN.

William, junior,

m. 4 Feb., 1864, Co. E, 59th Inf.; trans. 1 June, 1865, to 57th Inf.; dis. from 57th, 30 July, 1865, as corp. Credited to South Danvers.

"A minor, resident with his father for a long time in Danvers." Deceased.

OGDEN.

David H.,

m. 22 July, 1861, Co. C, 17th Inf.; corp. 2 July, 1863; dis. 3 Aug., 1864.

Æt. 23 at enl.; son of James and Elizb. (Buckley) Ogden; married 1859, Ann Finnerty, dau. of Patrick and Mary Finnerty. Living at Edena, Mo. Ch.: Mary Elizb., b. 7 June, 1865. Wm. Francis, b. 25 Feb., 1870.

William H.,

m. 22 July, 1861, Co. C, 17th Inf., corp.; reenl. 1 Jan., 1864; sergt., Co. B, 4 Mar., 1865; dis. 11 July, 1865, ex. term, from Co. G.

(*Ogden Continued.*)
b. Poughkeepsie, N. Y., 1838; (æt. "21" at enl.) d. about 1868, in Danvers; son of James and Elizb. Ogden; m. Clarissa E. Fuller, dau. of Daniel W. and Clarissa (Putnam) Fuller. Ch.: Ella, m. Allen Giles, Wm. II., died in Hudson, N. H.

O'GRADY.
Patrick R.,
m. 12 Aug., 1863, Co. E, 28th Inf.; dis. 18 May, 1864, killed at Spottsylvania, Va. Credit to Danvers.

Residence, Brookline, single.

O'NEIL.
William,
m. 1 Oct., 1862, Co. K, 8th Inf.; dis. 7 Aug., 1863, ex. term.

b. Ireland, 1824, died about 1889, in Danvers; son of Thos. and E. (Kennifle) O'Neil; m. Mary. Ch.: John, b. 1 Dec., 1853. Mary, b. Nov., 1855. Thos., b. 13 Dec., 1857. Wm., b. 13 Apr., 1859.

OSGOOD.
Edward T.,
m. 18 May, 1861, Co. I, 8th Inf.; dis. 1 Aug., 1861; m. 28 Sept., 1861; dis. 13 Oct., 1864, ex. term, Co. A, 23d Inf., sergt.: credited to Salem.

b. Boston. Ch.: Edw. Fisher, b. 19 Mar., 1866. Lucius Warren, b. 27 Jan., 1870. Wm. M., b. 22 Oct., 1871.

Thaddeus,
m. 15 July, 1864, Co. I, 6th Inf.; dis. 27 Oct., 1864, ex. term.

b. Danvers, 5 Sept., 1847, died Danvers; son of Thaddeus (b. Alfred, Me., 9 Nov., 1825) and Rebecca (Hood, b. Boston, 5 Aug., 1830) Osgood; m. 2 July, 1866, Anna M., dau. of Simeon and Charlotte Allen, b. Beverly.

PAGE.
James H.,
m. 26 Aug., 1864, Co. M, 3d

(*Page Continued.*)
H. A.: dis. 17 June, 1865, ex. term; credited to Boxford.

Æt. 34 at enl.

PARKER.
William H.,
m. 22 Aug., 1862, Co. B, 40th Inf.; dis. 1 Nov., 1863, died at Folly Is., S. C.

b. Salem, 1830; son of Eben and Jane Parker; married.

PARRY.
Albert,
m. 1 Oct., 1862, Co. K, 8th Inf.; dis. 7 Aug., 1863, ex. term; m. 22 Aug., 1864, Co. A, 4th H. A.; dis. 17 June, 1865, ex. term.

Æt. 36 at enl.; died Danvers, 19 Dec., 1883.

PATON.
Andrew,
m. 22 July, 1861, Co. B, 17th Inf.; dis. 3 Aug., 1864, ex. term.

b. Edinburg, Scotland, 1823; died Danvers, 1 Feb., 1879; son of Adam and Henrietta (Houston) Paton, of Scotland; m. Mary S. Tullock. Ch.: Andrew H., b. 15 July, 1849. Henrietta. Florence.

PATTERSON.
George,
m. 31 July, 1861, Co. I, 1st H. A.; m. 7 Dec., 1863, Co. I, 1st H. A.; dis. 28 Jan., 1864, trans. to Navy, q. v.: dis. 26 July, 1865.

Æt 19 at enl.; of Andover. Also on rolls as Peterson.

PEABODY.
Allen,
m. 22 Dec., 1863, Co. K, 2d H. A.: dis. 1 Aug., 1865, disability.

TOWN OF DANVERS. 45

(Peabody Continued.)

b. 15 July, 1816; son of Allen and Rebecca Peabody; married. Under date of 22 Jan., 1864, Selectmen of Danvers say he was a citizen of Wenham; but he was credited to Danvers nevertheless.

George W.,

m. 27 Nov., 1861, Reed's Rangers ; dis. 26 Apr., 1862 ; died on Mississippi River on ship North America, 23 Apr., 1862. Credited to Middleton.

b. Topsfield, 1838; son of Wm. (b. Me.) and Almira (b. Middleton) Peabody.

Joseph S.,

m. 22 Dec., 1863, Co. K, 2d H. A. ; dis. 3 Sept., 1865, ex. term, from Co. H.

Æt. 18 at enl.; of Wenham, credited to Danvers.

William A.,

m. 19 Aug., 1862, Co. F, 35th Inf. ; dis. 9 June, 1865, ex. term. Aged 21 at enl.

William Augustus,

m. 11 Aug., 1862, Co. B, 13th Inf. ; dis. 19 Feb., 1863 ; disability.

b. at Danvers, 4 June, 1834; son of Wm. (b. 29 June, 1806) and Hannah (Prince, b. 24 Sept., 1811) Peabody; m. 28 Apr., 1861, Adelaide, dau. of Jabez and Eliza D. (Green) Bigelow, b. Quincy. Lives in Danvers.

PEARSON.

Amos,

m. 1 Oct., 1862, Co. K, 8th Inf. ; dis. 7 Aug., 1863, ex. term ; m. 23 July, 1864, Co. C, 5th Inf. ; dis. 16 Nov., 1864, ex. term.

b. Alna, Me., 20 Feb., 1808; d. Danvers, 3 June, 1885; m. Martha Pinkham, Ch.: Wm. E., b. Boston, 1856.

Elbridge G.,

m. 5 July, 1861, Co. I, 1st H.

(Pearson Continued.)

A. ; musician ; dis. 8 July, 1864, ex. term.

Aged 28 at enl. ; married.

Sidney M.,

m. 5 July, 1861, Co. I, 1st H. A., corp. ; dis. 8 July, 1864, ex. term.

b. W. Newbury, 9 Feb., 1836; son of Wm. N. and Betsey Pearson; m. Aurela G. Ch.: Chas. A. b. 1853. Jessie F., b. 1855. Lives in Swampscott.

PEART.

Charles W.,

m. 1 Oct., 1862, Co. K, 8th Inf. ; dis. 7 Aug., 1863, ex. term.

b. Essex, 1840; d. Danvers, 11 Feb., 1873; son of Wm. B. (b. Manchester) and Mary J. (Burnham, b. Essex) Peart.

PERKINS.

Franklin,

m. 5 July, 1861, Co. I, 1st H. A. ; dis. 6 Dec., 1863, to reenlist ; died Andersonville, Ga., 3 Jan., 1865.

b. (æt. "27" at enl.) Meredith, N. H., 1836; m. Hannah Tarleton. Ch.: Hattie, b. 29 Nov., 1859. Albert Parker, b. 11 Jan., 1861. War Dept. Record of death 16 Sept., 1864, incorrect.

George W.,

m. 5 July, 1861, Co. I, 1st H. A. ; taken prisoner, 1862, at Fairfax Court House, Va., and sent in 10 days to Parole camp hospital, Annapolis, Md. : dis. 24 Mar., 1863, disability.

b. Westbrook, Me., 22 Dec., 1833; son of George and Martha (Smith) Perkins, of Charlestown; m. Sarah Jane Goodwin, (b. Amesbury). Ch.: Roselvena B, b. 16 Nov., 1857. George W., b. 25 Dec., 1860. Martha J. Now lives in Beverly.

(*Perkins* Continued.)
John H.,
m. 18 Aug., 1862, Co. A, 39th Inf.; dis. 9 June, 1865, ex. term. Had been taken prisoner of war.

b. Danvers, 30 Nov., 1838; d. there, 16 Oct., 1883; son of John (b. 28 Feb., 1803) and Martha (Fowler, b. Danvers, 20 Sept., 1808) Perkins; m. 8 Aug., 1862. Mary E., dau. of Isaac and Elizb. (Stone) Evans, b. Danvers. Ch.: Alice C., b. 19 Jan., 1863. Cora May, b. 2 Apr., 1868. Elvira G., b. 17 May, 1871. Mary Lizzie, b. 1 Sept., 1874.

PETTINGELL.
David,
m. 22 July, 1861, Co. C, 17th Inf.; dis. 3 Aug., 1864, ex. term.

b. Sandwich, N. H., 1830; killed at Boston, 1864; son of Sampson and Sally Brown Pettingell.

PHELPS.
Joel French,
m. 1 Oct., 1862, Co. K, 8th Inf.; dis. 7 Aug., 1863, ex. term.

b. 4 May, 1822, Northfield, N. H.; son of Elisha and Mary Phelps; m. 25 June, 1844, Mary E. Townsend, dau. of Samuel and Alice Townsend. Ch.: Ruth Ann, b. 12 July, 1846. Morris Franklin, b. 29 Nov., 1848; Jerome, b. 7 Aug., 1853. Homer B., b. 27 Aug., 1856. Lives in Danvers.

PHIPPEN.
Charles H.,
m. 1 May, 1861, Co. A, 5th Inf.; dis. 31 July, 1861. ex. term.

Lives in Salem.

PIERCE.
Shepard,
m. 22 Dec., 1863, Co. K, 2d H. A.; dis. 3 Sept., 1865, ex. term.

Æt. 18 at enl.; of So. Danvers, credited to Danvers.

PILLSBURY.
John F.,
m. 22 Dec., 1863, Co. K, 2d H. A.; dis. 3 Sept., 1865, ex. term, from Co. H.

b. Newbury, æt. 22 at enl.; son of Thomas Pillsbury.

PITMAN.
George,
m. 17 Aug., 1861, Co. B, 17th Inf.; dis. 15 Feb., 1864, to reenlist; dis. 11 July, 1865.

b. Barnstead, N. H., 21 June, 1814; d. Danvers, 1892; m. 6 Nov., 1836, Sarah Elliott Friend. Ch.: Sarah Trask, b. 13 Sept., 1839. Mary Ellen, b. 13 June, 1841. Geo., b. 27 Nov., 1844. q. v. Joseph, b. 27 May, 1848. Eva, b. 20 June, 1851.

George, junior,
m. 17 Aug., 1861, Co. B, 17th Inf.; dis. 25 Feb., 1864, to reenlist, same Co., corp.; taken prisoner 8 Mar., 1865; dis. 26 June, 1865, ex. term, from Co. C.

son of George Pitman, q. v.; drowned at sea.

Joseph F.,
m. 22 Aug., 1864, Co. A, 4th H. A.; dis. 17 June, 1865, ex. term.

b. Danvers, 28 May, 1848; son of Geo. and Sally (Friend) Pitman; m. 18 June, 1870, Emma F. Dockham, of Salem; m. 2d, 5 Sept., 1891, Susan Miller of Salem. Ch.: A. Laura, b. 8 Apr., 1871. E. Frank, b. 30 Jan., 1877.
Lives in Salem.

PLUMMER.
Oliver A.,
m. 5 July, 1861, Co. I, 1st H. A.; dis. 8 July, 1864, ex. term.

b. Sandwich, N. H., 5 Mar., 1834; son of Richard (b. Sandwich, 28 Dec., 1804) and Philena W. (Hutchins, b. 27 Sept., 1808, at Hadley, Me.) Plummer; m. 1854, Phebe W., dau. of Samuel Perkins, b. Wakefield, N. H.
Lives in Peabody.

TOWN OF DANVERS.

POPE.
Nathaniel A.,
m. 22 July, 1861, Co. C, 17th Inf., corp.: dis. 3 Aug., 1864, ex. term; m. 19 Oct., 1864; dis. 11 July, 1865 from Co. D.

b. Danvers, 24 Dec., 1837; son of Elijah jr. (b. Danvers, 13 July, 1809) and Eunice (Prince, b. Danvers, 19 May, 1811).
Lives in Danvers.

POOR.
Richard,
m. 22 July, 1861, Co. C, 17th Inf.; dis. 30 Oct., 1861, disability; m. 31 Jan., 1862, Co. C, 17th, Inf.; dis. 28 Feb., 1862, disability: m. 1 July, 1862, Co. B, 7th Inf.: dis. 31 Dec., 1862, ex. term; m. 15 July, 1864, Co. I, 6th Inf.: dis. 27 Oct., 1864.

b. P. E. I., 1842, d. Worcester, 1892; son of Mary Poor (b. Ireland, 1810). Left a fund for benefit of Post 90, amounting to about $2000.

PORTER.
Alfred,
m. 1 Oct., 1862, Co. K, 8th Inf., corp.: dis. 7 Aug., 1863, ex. term.

b. Danvers, 11 June, 1826, d. Danvers, 19 July, 1864; son of Warren (b. 30 Sept., 1789) and Ann (Welch, b. 22 Apr., 1800, Plaistow, N. H.) Porter.

George W.,
m. 26 June, 1861, Co. B, 12th Inf.: dis. 17 Sept., 1862, killed at Antietam, Md., credited to Great Falls, N. H.

b. Berwick, Me., 1832; son of James Porter; m. 17 Nov., 1855, Abby P. Ham (b. Shapleigh, Me.). Ch.: Caddie P., b. 17 Sept., 1857.

Samuel M.,
m. 22 Aug., 1862, Co. B, 40th Inf.; died 10 Sept., 1863, Folly Is., S. C.

(Porter Continued.)
b. N. S., 1822; son of Samuel and Mary Porter; m. Mary. Ch.: Arvilla, b. 15 Sept., 1847. Ann Augusta, b. 10 Sept., 1850. Mary Alice, b. 29 Aug., 1860.

POWELL.
Thomas,
m. 20 Feb., 1864, Co. C, 58th Inf.; dis. 24 May, 1865, paroled prisoner.

PRAY.
Samuel F.,
m. 6 Sept., 1861, Co. D, 22d Inf.; dis. 31 Mar., 1863, disability.

b. Salem, 21 July, 1839; bro. of R. B. Pray; m. 1861, Sarah J., dau. of Wm. and Lydia (Felton) Price. Ch.: Frances Estelle, b. 28 Aug., 1861.
Lives in Baltimore. Md.

PRESTON.
Daniel J.,
m. 19 Aug., 1862, Co. F, 35th Inf.; 1st Lt., 12 Aug., 1862; prom. Capt., 28 Sept., 1862: Major, 6 Dec., 1863, 36th U. S. C. T. Resigned as Major 36th U. S. Colored Troops, 29 Aug., 1864.

b. Danvers, 13 Feb., 1817, d. there 24 Dec., 1886; son of Daniel (b. 19 Jan., 1786) and Lucinda (Proctor, b. 30 Jan., 1795) Preston; m. 1843, Elizb. C. Hoyt, of Newburyport.

PRINCE.
James,
m. 28 Oct., 1861, Co. C, 17th Inf.; dis. 17 Nov, 1861.

b. England, æt. about 23.

PROCTOR.
John,
m 1 Oct., 1862, Co. K, 8th Inf.; dis. 7 Aug., 1863, ex. term.

b. Danvers, 4 Jan., 1828; son of Daniel and Mary (Perry) Proctor; m. 16 Oct., 1856, Martha W., dau. of Levi and Nancy Fish.

(Proctor Continued.)

Joseph M.,
m. 1 Oct., 1862, Co. K, 8th Inf.; dis. 7 Aug., 1863, ex. term.
Died in Salem.

PUTNAM.

Albert F.,
m. 1 Oct., 1862, Co. K, 8th Inf.; dis. 7 Aug., 1863, ex. term.

b. Danvers, 31 Jan., 1841; son of Edwin F. (b. 19 July, 1810) and Olivia (Woodbury, b. Beverly, 21 Mar., 1813) Putnam; m. 5 Nov., 1867, Irene E. Place, dau. of John and Julia M. Place, b. Frenchtown, Pa., 3 July, 1844. Ch.: Lena F., b. Windsor, Vt., 8 July, 1873.

Arthur A.,
m. 5 July, 1861, Co. I, 1st H. A., captain; dis. 14 Aug., 1861, resigned; m. 28 Oct., 1863, Co. I, 2d H. A., 1st Lt.: dis. 18 Sept., 1865, ex. term: Capt., 18 Sept., 1865.

b. Danvers, 18 Nov., 1829; son of Elias (b. 7 June, 1789) and Eunice (Ross, b. 3 May, 1798) Putnam; m. Helen Staples, of Blackstone. Ch.: Alden Lyon; Beatrice.
Author of an historical sketch entitled the "Putnam Guards," afterward Co. I, 1st H. A.

Augustus,
m. 25 Sept., 1861, Co. H, 1st Cav.; dis. 10 Jan., 1863, disability.

b. Danvers, 22 Apr., 1810; died Danvers, 6 Oct., 1892; son of Simeon (b. 22 Nov., 1776) and Deborah (Brown, b. 22 Oct., 1782) Putnam; m. 27 Jan., 1836, Abigail Ann Bomer. Ch.: Augustus B., b. 25 Apr., 1837. Abba Brown, b. 25 Apr., 1837. Chas. Henry, b. 24 Feb., 1840. John Brown, b. 22 Mar., 1842. Edw. Brown, b. 24 Jan., 1846. Jas. Oscar, b. 30 Apr., 1849. Harry Edw. Edwin R.

Charles Henry,
m. 22 July, 1861, Co. C, 17th Inf.; dis. 3 Aug., 1864, ex. term.

(Putnam Continued.)

b. Danvers, 24 Feb., 1840; d. Danvers about 1880; son of Augustus Putnam q. v.; m. 1870, Mrs. Elizb. (Huntress) Horne of Great Falls, N. H. Ch.: Harry E., b. 20 Sept., 1871.

Frederick M.,
m. 1 Oct., 1862, Co. K, 8th Inf.; dis. 7 Aug., 1863, ex. term.

b. Danvers, 21 Apr., 1841; son of James A. (b. 1 Dec., 1792) and Sarah (Marston, b. 3 June, 1795, at Methuen) Putnam; m. 20 Sept., 1865, Lydia C., dau. of Moses J. and Ruth Currier, b. Danvers, 17 Sept., 1846. Ch.: Ralph P., b. Lynn, 22 Feb., 1870. Alice.
Lives in Philadelphia.

George F.,
m. 22 July, 1861, Co. C, 17th Inf.; dis. 3 Aug., 1864, ex. term.

b. Danvers, 29 Aug., 1838; son of Orin (b. Danvers, 24 Sept., 1812) and Sally P. (Nourse, b. 3 Oct., 1813.); m. 28 July, 1864, Marianne Waldron, of Farmington, N. H. Ch.: Ralph W., b. 8 Aug., 1865. Herbert F., b. 24 Feb., 1870. Nellie F., b. 5 Apr., 1875; d. 1877. Willie O., b. 1 Mar., 1880.
Lives in Lynn.

Robert Winthrop,
m. 28 Aug., 1861, Co. F, 19th Inf.; wounded 30 June, 1862, at Malvern Hills, in the breast, and taken prisoner. Died 13 July, 1862, of wounds, in Libby Prison, Richmond, Va., the day after he was formally exchanged.

b. Danvers, 22 May, 1845; son of Wm. Richardson (b. 23 May, 1811) and Mary R. (Phelps, b. 17 Aug., 1810) Putnam.
In a letter dated 29 Apr., 1862, he writes "I left to help defend a Constitution that was second to none in the world, a Flag which every nation on earth respected. If I am to die, I shall be happy to die in the service of my country."

TOWN OF DANVERS. 49

(Putnam Continued.)

Wallace Ahira,
m. 21 June, 1861, Co. E, 10th Inf., 2d Lt.; com. 1st Lt., 28 July, 1862; dis. 24 Jan., 1863, resigned; m. 1 Aug., 1863, 56th Inf.; capt., 21 Nov., 1863; promoted major, 7 May, 1864. Died of wounds received 24 May, 1864, at the North Anna. 20 June, 1864, at Stoughton, Mass.

b. Danvers, 23 Feb., 1838; son of Ahira Herrick (b. 21 May, 1807) and Sarah (Bradstreet. b. 7 Mar., 1812) Putnam. The biographer of the 10th regiment said "many a tear was shed to the memory of the gallant Putnam." His name heads the lists of fallen heroes on the soldiers' monument in Danvers.

PUTNEY.
George H.,
m. 22 July, 1861, Co. C, 17th Inf., corp.; 1st sergt., 19 Mar., 1862; dis. 3 Aug., 1864, ex. term, from Co. E.

b. Bow, N. H., 1833; son of David and Mary Putney; m. 13 Dec., 1854, Ardelia S., dau. of Aaron and Ede Tapley. Ch.: Annie Cordelia, b. 29 Aug., 1861. Mary R., b. 2 May, 1865.
Died in Stoneham, 1891.

QUINT.
Lorenzo A.,
m. 3 Sept., 1862, Co. K, 40th Inf.; dis. 5 Dec., 1862, disability.

b. Sanford, Me., 1831; son of Edmund Stackpole Quint, jr.; m. 12 May, 1854, Abigail Allen, b. Danvers, 1835, dau. of Benj. Allen.

RACKLIFF.
Alonzo A.,
m. 22 Dec., 1863, Co. K, 2d H. A.; dis. 3 Sept., 1865, ex. term.

b. Danvers, 13 Aug., 1847; son of Geo. Knowles (b. Standish, Me., 20 Dec., 1819) and Mary Elizb. (Wait,

(Rackliff Continued.)
b. Danvers, 11 Apr., 1825) Rackliff: m. 1871, Minnie E. Perry, b. Nova Scotia.
Lives in Danvers.

RAYNER.
John G.,
m. 23 Aug., 1862, Co. A, 40th Inf.; dis. 16 Dec., 1865.

Æt. 41 and m.; "of Danvers."

REGAN.
Dennis W.,
m. 1 Oct., 1862, Co. K, 8th Inf.; dis. 7 Aug., 1863, ex. term.

b. Ireland, 1820; m. 5 June, 1852, Ellen Geary (b. Ireland, 15 Apr., 1820). Ch.: Maria Ann, b. 18 Mar., 1853. John, b. 1 Jan., 1860.
Lives in Danvers.

REYNOLDS.
Alexander,
m. 15 Feb., 1864, 42d U. S. C. troops, enl. at Nashville, Tenn.; credited to Danvers.

Æt. 21 at enl.; residence Gilman Co., Ga.

James,
m. 6 Aug., 1862, Co. C, 33d Inf.; dis. 27 Feb., 1865, disability. Wounded 14 May, 1864 at Resaca, Ga.

Æt. 18 at enl.; d. Danvers, 4 Nov., 1873; son of James and M'g't (Brady) Reynolds.

William,
m. 22 July, 1861, Co. C, 17th Inf.; dis. 6 Apr., 1863, disability: m. " æt 28 " 12 July, 1864, V. R. C.; dis. 13 Mar., 1865, disability.

b. Ireland, 1837; d. Danvers, 18 July, 1880; son of James and Margaret (Brady) Reynolds.

William,
m. 1 Oct., 1862, Co. K, 8th Inf.; dis. 7 Aug., 1863, ex. term.

(Reynolds Continued.)
b. Ireland, ("æt. 47" at enl.) 15 Mar., 1826; m. 26 Sept., 1850, Marg't Carley, b. Ireland, 31 Oct., 1828. Ch.: Mary Ann, b. 1 July, 1851. Elizb. Jane, b. 19 June, 1852. James, b. 1 Dec., 1867. James, b. 3 Dec., 1868. Lives in Danvers.

RICHARDSON.
Calvin F.,
m. 25 Aug., 1864, Co. M, 3d H. A.; dis. 17 June, 1865, ex. term, as corp.

b. Lynn, 24 Nov., 1843; son of William (b. Danvers, 30 May, 1806) and Mary Bass (Keen, b. 29 Dec., 1814, East Bridgewater) Richardson; m. 23 July, 1867, Nancy A. Wiggin, dau. of Henry and Sarah A. (Norton) Wiggin, b. Danvers. Ch.: Marietta, b. 18 June, 1868. Ernest F., b. 7 Apr., 1872.

Henry M., (H.)
m. 1 May, 1861, Co. H, 5th Inf.: dis. 31 July, 1861, ex. term; m. 2 Aug., 1862, Co. A, 23d Inf.; dis. 2 Dec., 1863, to reenlist; dis. 25 June, 1865.

b. Lynn, 8 July, 1841; son of William (b. Danvers, 30 May, 1806) and Mary Bass (Keem, b. E. Bridgeport, 29 Dec., 1814) Richardson.

Samuel P.,
m. 13 Mar., 1862, Co. M, 1st H. A.; dis. 16 Mar., 1864, to reenlist; died at Andersonville, Ga., 27 July, 1864.

b. Middleton, 1828; son of Amos Richardson; m. 29 April, 1850, Rebecca Jane, dau. of Moses Fairfield, b. Middleton. Ch.: Leon M. b. Middleton, 1858.

William H.,
m. 1 May, 1861, Co. H, 5th Inf.: dis. 31 July, 1861, ex. term; m. 28 Sept., 1861, Co. A, 23d Inf.; dis. 2 Jan., 1864, to reenlist; dis. 25 June, 1865.

brother of Henry H. Richardson; b. 7 Mar., 1839; m. 19 Apr., 1870, Mary J. L., dau. of Robert and Jessie (Murray) Brown, b. N. S., 1851. Ch.: Robert H., b. 30 June, 1870.

RICKER.
Charles W.,
m. 1 May, 1861, Co. A, 5th Inf.: dis. 31 July, 1861, ex. term.

RIGGS.
Edgar M.,
m. 1 May, 1861, Co. H, 5th Inf.; dis. 31 July, 1861, ex. term; m. 19 Aug., 1862, Co. F, 35th Inf., corp.: sergt.; prom. 2d Lt., 8 Sept., 1864: dis. 9 June, 1865, ex. term.

b. Derby, Ct., 1838; son of Clark and Mary (Morton) Riggs; m. 4 Mar., 1867, Mary E., dau. of Horace and Martha L. (Webb) Straw, b. 4 Jan., 1849. Ch.: Albert Horace, b. 19 June, 1867.

RILEY.
Michael,
m. 22 July, 1861, Co. C, 17th Inf.: dis. 2 Oct., 1863, disability; m. 22 Oct., 1864, V. R. C.: cred. to Haverhill; dis. 14 Nov., 1865.

Æt. 30 at enl.: b. Ireland; d. Haverhill; m. Bridget Grey. Ch.: Michael, b. 17 Oct., 1861.

ROACH.
Israel,
m. 19 Aug., 1862, Co. F, 35th Inf.; dis. 19 Aug., 1864, died at Andersonville, Ga., 19 Aug., 1864.

b. N. S., 1824; m. Almira Corning. Ch.: Almina Lizzie, b. 22 July, 1861.

ROBERTS.
Isaac N.,
m. 1 Nov., 1861, Co. K, 23d Inf.; hospital steward, 25 June, 1863; dis. 19 Oct., 1863, died at Newberne, N. C., 18 Oct., 1863.

b. Hamilton, 1832; son of Isaac W. and Charlotte Roberts; m. 1859, A. Augusta, dau. of Ichabod and Ann Sawyer, b. Danvers, 1832.

(Roberts Continued.)
John A.,
m. 22 July, 1861, Co. C, 17th Inf. ; dis. 31 Aug., 1862, disability : m. 25 Nov., 1863; Co. H, 3d H. A. ; dis. 30 Sept., 1865, ex. term.

b. Danvers, 28 Feb., 1844; son of John (b. Waterbury, Me., 30 Sept., 1816) and Mary Jane (Prince, b. Danvers, 16 July, 1819) Roberts; m. Emma Grover of Middleton. Ch.: Mary Emma, b. 13 Aug., 1873. Lives in Danvers Centre.

Stephen W.,
m. 29 July, 1863, Co. B, 2d H. A. ; dis. 3 Sept., 1865, ex. term ; sick in hospital at Newberne, N. C.

b. Alfred, Me., 1834; son of Edmund and Hannah (Webber) Roberts; m. 14 Oct., 1860, Minnie P. Raymond, b. Yarmouth, N. S., dau. of David and Mary (Trask) Raymond.

ROBINSON.
Matthew H.,
m. 5 July, 1861, Co. D, 1st H. A. ; dis. 8 July, 1864, ex. term. Æt. 22 at enl.; credited to South Danvers.

ROBERTSON.
Uriah,
m. 22 July, 1861, Co. C, 17th Inf.; sergt. 6 Aug., 1862; trans. to Co. E ; dis. 5 Jan., 1864, to reenlist : 1st sergt. : prom. 2d Lt., 7 Feb., 1865 ; 1st Lt., 1 June, 1865 ; dis. 11 July, 1865, ex. term as 2d Lt.

b. Eaton, N. H., 1835; son of Sam'l and Mary Robertson; m. 3 Nov., 1864, Lucy P., dau. of Putnam and Lydia A. Webb, b. Danvers. Ch.: Augusta Webb, b. 20 Aug., 1866, Geo. T., b. 20 Aug., 1869. A son, b. 22 Dec., 1872.
Bounty paid to Angeline Robertson.

ROGERS.
Lorenzo C.,
m. 1 Oct., 1862, Co. K, 8th

(Rogers Continued.)
Inf., corp.; dis. 7 Aug., 1863, ex. term.

b. New Boston, N. H., 19 Feb., 1819; m. 15 May, 1844, Lucy Ann Shackley, b. Shapleigh, Me., 15 Oct., 1825. Ch.: Frances Ellen, b. 19 July, 1844, Lucy Jane, b. 11 Oct., 1846, Simeon Alonzo, b. 3 June, 1848, Clarissa, b. 11 Sept., 1849. A child, b. 19 Dec., 1855. A child, b. 4 Sept., 1857.
Lives in N. H.

ROLAND.
Henry,
m. 5 Sept., 1864, 58th U. S. C. Inf.; enl. at Vicksburg, Miss. ; credited to Danvers.

Æt. 19; residence, Louisiana.

ROLLINS.
John W.,
m. 22 Aug., 1864, Co. A, 4th H. A. ; dis. 17 June, 1865, ex. term.

b. Essex, 27 July, 1837; son of John (b. Livermore, Me., 12 Mar., 1811) and Emily (Burnham, b. Essex, 1 Sept., 1813) Rollins: m. 26 Nov., 1862, Frances A. dau. of Artemas and Mary A. Wilson, b. Danvers, 1840. Ch.: Walter Alvin, b. 20 Sept., 1863, Frances Ellen, b. 30 Dec., 1866, Alfred Asa, b. 11 Feb., 1870, Sarah F., b. 22 Nov., 1871.

Jonas M.,
m. 19 Aug., 1862, Co. F, 35th Inf. ; dis. 20 Feb., 1863, disability.

b. Newbury, Vt.; æt. 32 at enl.; m. Samantha A. Clay. Ch.: Frank B., b. 3 Oct., 1866.
Lives in Danvers.

ROOME.
William J., junior,
m. 5 July, 1861, Co. I, 1st H. A.; 2d Lt., 9 Aug. ; 1st Lt., 22 Sept., 1861 ; dis. 2 Dec., 1862, resigned.

Æt. 22 at enl., and married; d. Peabody, 1893.

ROSENTHAL.

Jacob P.,
m. 24 Feb., 1865, Co. M, 4th Mass. Cav.; dis. 14 Nov., 1865, ex. term; credited to Lynn, " of Danvers."

b. Sept., 1838; d. Beverly, 27 Jan., 1894; resided in Danvers before and after the war; m. Ella dau. of Joseph N. Burchstead. Brother of John Rosenthal.

John,
m. 22 Aug., 1862, Co. B, 40th Inf., corp.; dis. 16 June, 1865, ex. term.

b. Greenville, Ct., 1844; d. Lynn, 9 Oct., 1881; son of Nathan and Elizb. Rosenthal; m. 30 Oct., 1866, Susan C., dau. of Richard Payne, b. Moultonborough, N. H. Ch.: Lester, b. 29 Sept., 1868.

Nathan,
m. 3 Sept., 1862, Co. F, 40th Inf.; dis. 13 Nov., 1862, disability; credited to South Danvers.

b. Germany, 1822; ("æt. 40" at enlistment) and married; d. Danvers, 18 Mar., 1868. Brother of John Rosenthal.

ROSS.

Amasa L.,
m. 22 Dec., 1863, Co. K, 2d H. A.; dis. 3 Sept., 1865, ex. term. Æt. 19 at enl.

George L.,
m. 19 Aug., 1862, Co. F, 35th Inf.; dis. 9 June, 1865, ex. term; credited to Shapleigh, Me.

b. Shapleigh, Me., 1838; son of Ivory and Eunice (Batchelder) Ross; m. 25 June, 1867, Augusta C. Peck, born Wenham. Ch.: Alice Edith, b. 24 July, 1874.

John Thomas,
m. 26 May, 1862, Salem Cadets; dis. 11 Oct., 1862, ex. term.

(Ross Continued.)

b. Ipswich, 5 Nov., 1831; son of Daniel and Elizb. (Perkins) Ross; m. 21 April, 1861, Frances E., dau. of Daniel and Frances Woodman, b. Danvers. Ch.: Frank Wentworth, b. 10 Dec., 1867.
Lives in Danvers.

William B.,
m. 23 Aug., 1864, Co. A, 4th H. A.; dis. 17 June, 1865, ex. term.

b. Shapleigh, Me., 1837; son of Ivory and Eunice (Batchelder) Ross; m. 1870, Jennie E. Hall, b. St. John, N. B.

ROWELL.

Gideon,
m. 22 July, 1864, Co. C, 5th Inf.; dis. 16 Nov., 1864.

b. Rockport, 1831; son of Enoch and Abigail Rowell; m. 19 Dec., 1855, Martha J. Skidmore, dau. of Stephen and Mary Skidmore. Ch.: Lillie P., b. 26 Oct., 1856. Walter G., b. 19 Dec., 1859. Albert Poole, b. 30 April, 1862. Warren Poole, b. 5 Feb., 1868. Sadie B., b. 12 July, 1870. Melvin, b. 18 April, 1875.
Lives Danversport.

RUSSELL.

Albert W.,
m. 12 Dec., 1861, Co. G, 11th Inf.; dis. 14 Dec., 1864, ex. term, from Co. D; wounded 2 July, 1863; credited to Salem.

b. Beverly, 23 Feb., 1843; son of Benjamin (b. Shapleigh, Me., 11 Sept., 1814), and Margaret (Needham, b. Danvers, 28 Nov., 1813) Russell; m. 1 May, 1869, Mary Jane Richardson. Ch.: Warren Herbert, b. 19 Oct., 1869. Clarence A., b. 22 Aug., 1871.

John (R.),
m. 1 Oct., 1862, Co. K, 8th Inf.; dis. 7 Aug., 1863, ex. term; m. 22 Aug., 1864, 29th unattached Co. H. A.; dis. 16 June, 1865, ex. term; cred. to Andover.

TOWN OF DANVERS.

(Russell Continued.)
b. Limerick, Ireland, æt. 30 in 1864, son of David and Honora (O'Connell) Russell; m. Mary Nell. Ch.: David, John, James, Margaret, Mary Ellen, Homer.

SANBORN.
Levi C.,
m. 25 May, 1861, Co. C, 2d Inf.; dis. 6 Jan., 1864, disability; credited to Lowell. Wounded in left arm at Battle of Gettysburg; m. 1 Sept., 1864, V. R. C.; credited to Lowell; dis. 30 Nov., 1865. Æt. 19 at enl.

SCAMPTON.
Frank,
m. 22 July, 1861, Co. C, 17th Inf.; dis. 29 Aug., 1862, disability (deceased at Danvers).

b. England, 1822; d. Danvers; ("died 15 Aug., 1862," town book); son of Joseph and Susannah Scampton m. Ellen Hill, b. England. Ch.: William, b. 13 Oct., 1850. Elizabeth Ann, b. 29 April, 1853, above b. in England. Susan, b. Danvers, 14 June, 1858. George Henry, b. Danvers, 7 Jan., 1861.

George,
m. 22 July, 1861, Co. C, 17th Inf.; dis. 6 April, 1863, disability.

Æt. 32 at enl.; b. Halifax, Co. York, England; m. 1st, Grace ———; m. 2d, Mrs. Wellman. Brother of Frank Scampton.
Now at Soldiers' Home, Togus, Me.

SEARS.
John Henry,
m. 1 Oct., 1862, Co. K, 8th Inf.; dis. 7 Aug., 1863, ex. term.

b. Danvers, 13 June, 1843; son of John Augustus (b. M'h'd, 26 Oct., 1814, and Henrietta Madeline (Kent, b. Boston, 21 Jan., 1821) Sears; m. 24 Nov., 1868, Lucinda Cutting Wallace, b. Danvers. Ch.: Henrietta Madaline, b. 17 May, 1869. Wallace Palmer. Anna Russell. John Resticaux, b. 14 Feb., 1876.
Lives in Salem.

SEVERANCE.
Joshua,
m. 2 Sept., 1861, 1st Co. S. S.; dis. 29 May, 1862, disability.

b. Orriston, Me., 1824; died No. Andover; m. Martha. Ch.: Coraestilia, b. 25 Nov., 1850.

SEXTON.
Patrick,
m. 22 July, 1861, Co. C, 17th Inf.; corp., 5 May, 1865; dis. 1 Jan., 1864, to reenlist; dis. 11 July, 1865.

Æt. 21 at enl.; removed to California.

SHACKLEY.
John,
m. 22 July, 1861, Co. C, 17th Inf.; dis. 1 Feb., 1863, disability; m. 5 Oct., 1863, Co. E, 2d H. A.

b. Lyman, Me., Apr. 21, 1828; died Beverly, 5 Nov., 1863, of consumption; son of John and Hannah Shackley; m. 3 July, 1851, Caroline A. Dodge, dau. of Robert and Hannah Dodge, b. Hamilton, 30 June, 1832. Ch.: Ellen Augusta, b. 29 April, 1852. Mary Frances, b. 4 June, 1854. Carmi, b. 17 Dec., 1861. John, b. 29 June, 1857.

William,
m. 13 June, 1861, Co. G, 11th Inf.; dis. 5 Jan., 1864, to reenlist; dis. 13 May, 1865, from Co. D, on account of wounds. Wounded 2 Oct., 1864.

b. Shapleigh, Me., 1831; m. 30 Jan., 1871, Mrs. Abby A. Cuken, b. Boston. Ch.: Clarence Aiken, b. 6 Sept., 1868. Ernest, b. 15 Jan., 1870. Lewis Henry, b. 18 July, 1874.

SHATTUCK.
George O.,
m. 14 Mar., 1862, Co. D, 1st H. A.; dis. 13 Dec., 1863, to reenlist; dis. 16 Aug., 1865, from Co. I.

(Shattuck Continued.)

b. Wenham, 1829; son of Ezra and Rebecca Shattuck; m. 1867, Priscilla B., dau. of Samuel and Priscilla Adams, b. Ipswich, 1842. Ch.: Mary Osgood, b. 5 Nov., 1868.

SHAW.
Alden C.,
m. 22 July, 1861, Co. C, 17th Inf.; dis. 20 Aug., 1861, at Lynnfield, rupture.

b. Yarmouth, N. S., 1838; son of Nathan P. and Lydia (Perry) Shaw; m. 1860, Hannah, dau. of Samuel and Mary A. Cann, b. Yarmouth, N. S. Ch.: Cyrus Edgar, b. 3 May, 1862. Bertha, b. 2 Aug., 1865. Mary C., b. 18 Feb., 1863.

Cyrus P.,
m. 18 May, 1861, Co. I, 8th Inf.; dis. 1 Aug., 1861, ex. term.

b. Yarmouth, N. S., 1841; brother of Alden C. Shaw; m. 4 Dec., 1865, Matilda A. Perry, b. Yarmouth, dau. of Sam'l and Hannah (Casby) Perry.

Joseph E.,
m. 22 July, 1861, Co. C, 17th Inf.; dis. 3 Aug., 1864, ex. term.

b. Nova Scotia, 1843; brother of Alden C. Shaw; m. 6 Feb., 1868, Caroline A., dau. of Joseph and Maria (Hatch) Leavitt, b. Danvers. Lives in Lynn.

SHEA.
John,
m. 26 Aug., 1864, Co. M, 3d H. A.; dis. 17 June, 1865, ex. term.

b. (about) 1822, Ireland; m. 21 Apr., 1845, Bridget Kenney, b. Ireland. Ch.: Edward, b. 25 Dec., 1847. John, b. 1 Apr., 1850. Thomas, b. 10 July, 1853.

Patrick F.,
m. 11 June, 1861, Co. F, 9th Inf.; wounded 1 July, 1862, at Malvern Hill, Va.; dis. 31 May, 1864; died of wounds

(Shea Continued.)

at Fairfax Hospital, Alexandria, Va. Æt. 20 at enl.

Thomas J.,
m. 21 Feb., 1862, Co. D, 17th Inf.; dis. 14 April, 1863, disability.

b. Ireland, 1835; m. Mary T. Hurley. Ch.: Lizzie, b. 26 Mar., 1872. Agnes, b. 5 Nov., 1874. Thomas. Lives in Danvers.

SHELDON.
Charles W.,
m. 5 July, 1861, Co. I, 1st H. A.; wounded 16 June, 1864; died of wounds at Petersburg, Va.; died 4 Aug., 1864.

Æt. 26 at enl. After severe and gallant fighting, the regiment had been withdrawn to rest and eat and there on slightly rising ground, Sheldon was mortally wounded.

SHELDEN.
William E.,
m. 5 July, 1861, Co. I, 1st H. A.; dis. 7 Dec., 1862; died at Andersonville, Ga. Æt. 27 at enl.

SHEPARD.
Charles A.,
m. 5 July, 1861, Co. I, 1st H. A.; dis. 29 Dec., 1863, to reenl.; dis. 31 July, 1865, ex. term, as sergt.

b. Utica, N. Y., 31 July, 1822; d. Danvers, 26 July, 1886; m. 28 Oct., 1848, Emma Kilgore, b. Wakefield, 24 Aug., 1826. Ch.: Chas. Phineas, b. 3 June, 1849. Helen Putnam, b. 15 Aug., 1851. Alice B., b. 1 June, 1853. Francis Albert, b. 8 April, 1858. Benj. K., b. 21 April, 1860.

SHIRLEY.
William H.,
m. 5 July, 1861, Co. I, 1st H. A., corp.; dis. 11 Dec., 1863, to reenlist; confined in Andersonville prison, 1 year; dis. 19 June, 1865, as sergt.

TOWN OF DANVERS. 55

(Shirley Continued.)
b. Salem, 1833; d. Danvers, 15 Jan., 1887; m. Mary Ann Hartley of Salem. Ch.: Wm. Alfred, b. Danvers, 2 Sept., 1860. Annie E.

SILLARS.
Malcolm,
m. 22 July, 1861, Co. C, 17th Inf.; reenl. 5 Jan., 1864, 17th Inf.; quartermaster sergt.; prom. 2d Lt., 4 July, 1864; prom. 1st Lt., 1 Sept., 1864; prom. Capt., 4 Aug., 1864; dis. 11 July, 1865, ex. term.
b. 17 Sept., 1837, Ryegate, Vt.; son of Donald and Margaret (McCall) Sillars; m. 2) Aug., 1861, Sarah Putnam Fuller, dau. of Daniel W., and Clarissa (Putnam) Fuller; d. 20 Nov., 1874. Ch. living: Henry M., b. 16 May, 1854. Walter A., b. 15 June, 1866. Alice, b. 24 July, 1870. He m. 2d, 10 Sept., 1876, Sarah E. McDermot, dau. of Charles and Mary (Donnely) McDermot. Ch.: Lizzie, b. 30 Oct., 1876. Malcolm, b. 8 Dec., 1878. Mary, b. 29 Mar., 1880. Helen M., b. 24 Jan., 1882. Chas. D., b. 6 Aug., 1883. Jas. McC., b. 8 Aug., 1885. Susan, b. 8 Nov., 1886. Alex M., b. 24 Jan., 1888. Wm. A., b. 15 Feb., 1889. Sarah E., b. 25 Dec., 1891. Jane b. 11 Mch. 1895.
Lives in Danvers.

William,
m. 22 July, 1861, Co. C, 17th Inf.; died at Baltimore, 4 Jan., 1862. Enl. from So. Danvers.
b. 12 Oct., 1844; buried at Danvers; brother of Malcolm Sillars.
He was the first one to die in the war from So. Danvers.

SKENE.
James,
m. 8 Aug., 1862; dis. 28 Dec., 1863, to reenl.: credited to Methuen; m. 29 Dec., 1863, Co. B, 1st H. A.; dis. 16 Aug., 1865, ex. term; cred. to Danvers. Æt. 28 at enl.

SLEEPER.
Charles F.,
m. 26 May, 1862, Salem Cadets; dis. 11 Oct., 1862, ex. term.

(Sleeper Continued.)
b. Danvers, 16 Mar., 1835; died Brooklyn, N. Y.; son of James (b. Brentwood, N. H., 1803) and Hannah (Felton, b. 30 Oct., 1800) Sleeper; m. 7 July, 1868, Ellen Maria, dau. of Haskett and Harriet (Blodget) Bixby. Ch.: James Fred'k, b. 6 Aug., 1869. Bessie May, b. 24 Apr., 1871. Lives in the West.

James H.,
m. 1 May, 1861, Co. A, 5th Inf., corp.; dis. 31 July, 1861, ex. term; m. 1 Oct., 1862, Co. K, 8th Inf., sergt.; dis. 7 Aug., 1863, ex. term.
b. Danvers, 21 Mar., 1828; brother of Chas. F. Sleeper; m. 2 Dec., 1849, Phebe Wilde Perkins, b. Topsfield, 21 Oct., 1822. Ch.: Emily Perkins, b. 20 July, 1850. Albert Cornelius, b. 2 July, 1852. Lives in Topsfield.

SLOPER.
Henry,
m. 1 May, 1861, Co. A, 5th Inf.; dis. 31 July, 1861, ex. term; m. 1 July, 1862, Co. B, 7th Inf., corp.; dis. 31 Dec., 1862, ex. term; m. 5 Oct., 1863, Co. E, 2d H. A.; dis. 3 Sept., 1865, ex. term. Æt. 31 at enl.

SMART.
Alfred E.,
m. 22 Dec., 1863, Co. K, 2d H. A.; dis. 23 May, 1865. Æt. 22 at enl.

Ancel C.,
m. 23 Aug., 1864, Co. M, 3d H. A.; dis. 17 June, 1865, ex. term. Æt. 18 at enl.

Joseph T.,
m. 3 Sept., 1861, 1st Co. S. S.; dis. 22 Aug., 1864; died Andersonville, Ga., 8 Sept.; reported as missing in action 25 Aug. 1864.
Æt. 31 at enl., unm.; died Salisbury, N. C., 22 Oct., 1864. It will be noticed the record of death differs.

SMITH.

Daniel,

m. 22 July, 1861. Co. C, 17th Inf.: died 27 Sept., 1862, at Newberne, N. C.

Aged 28 at enlistment; m. Ellen Perry. Brother of James Smith.

Daniel H.,

m. 5 July, 1861, Co. I, 1st H. A.; dis. 7 May, 1864; died at Andersonville, Ga. Æt. 26 at enl.

David,

m. 5 July, 1861, Co. I, 1st H. A.; dis. 9 Mar., 1864, to reenlist; dis. 29 Mar., 1865, disability.

b. Alfred, Me., 1831; son of Daniel and Patience Smith; m. 24 Aug., 1853, Mary E. Low, dau. of Ivory and Loisa C. Low, b. Alfred, Me., 1835. Ch.: Geo. F., b. 8 Feb., 1856. Chas. Edwin, b. 4 Jan., 1861. Dan'l H., b. 5 Jan., 1865. Lives in Danvers. He was wounded in left arm.

Edward,

m. 5 Sept., 1864, 58th U. S. C. Inf.; enl. at Vicksburg, Miss.; cred. to Danvers.

Æt. 18 at enl.; residence Donaldsonville, La.

George E.,

m. 8 Dec., 1863, Co. I, 1st H. A., sergt.: dis. 31 July, 1865, ex. term.

Æt. 21 at enl. Enlisted as of Wenham, 5 July, 1861; mustered same date; reenl. 8 Dec., 1863 to the credit of Danvers; but disputed and given to Wenham.

George O.,

m. 6 Aug., 1862, Co. C, 33d Inf., corp.; dis. 17 Mar., 1863, disability. Æt. 40 at enl.

Henry A.,

m. 28 Aug., 1861, Co. B, 19th

(Smith Continued.)

Inf.; dis. 28 Oct., 1861. disability: died 23 Nov., 1861.

b. 1842; son of George and Betsy Smith.

James,

m. 22 July, 1861, Co. C, 17th Inf.; 1st sergt., 11 Dec., 1862; prom. 2d Lt., 2 Aug., 1864; prom. 1st Lt., 1 June, 1865; trans. to Co. I; dis. 11 July, 1865, ex. term.

b. Simsbury, Conn., 8 Mar., 1838; son of John and Margaret (Sinclair) Smith; m. Miss Tufts of Peabody. Lives in Clay Centre, Clay Co., Kan.

James C. (S?),

m. 5 July, 1861, Co. I, 1st H. A.; dis. 8 July, 1864, prisoner of war.

b. Lancaster, England, 21 May, 1840; son of Michael (b. Lancaster, 12 Dec., 1807) and Mary Ann (Harrack, b. 24 Jan., 1807) Smith.

John,

m. 19 July, 1864, Co. D, 35th Inf.; sent to hospital 17 Aug., 1864; trans. to Co. D, 29th Inf. Never joined regiment.

Æt. 19 at enl., of Montreal, Canada.

John,

m. 16 July, 1864, Co. E, 33d Inf.; trans. 1 June, 1865, to Co. I, 2d Inf.: deserted 30 June, 1865.

Æt. 28 at enl.; b. St. Mary's, Canada West; resident of Danvers, credited to Boston.

John J.,

m. 16 July, 1864; Co. F, 33d Inf.; never joined regiment.

Æt. 22 at enl.; of Huntington, Penn.; credited to Danvers.

(*Smith Continued.*)

Robert,
m. 1 May, 1861, Co. A., 5th Inf.; dis. 31 July, 1861, ex. term; m. 16 Sept., 1861, 2d Co. S. S., sergt.; 2d Lt., 7 July, 1862; 1st Lt., 30 Jan., 1863; Capt.. 19 May, 1863; dis. 17 Oct., 1864, ex. term.

Lives in Painsville, Ohio.

Robert,
m. 22 July, 1861, Co. C, 17th Inf., sergt.; reenl. 5 Jan., 1864; dis. from Co. B, 1st sergt., 11 July, 1865; prom. 2d Lt., 1 June, 1865; 1st Lt. 16 June, 1865.

Æt. 27 at enl.; died in Kansas about 1880; brother of James, William and Daniel Smith, all of Co. C, 17th Inf.

William W.,
m. 22 July, 1861, Co. C, 17th Inf., 1st Lt.: prom. capt., 3 July, 1862; prom. major, 4 Aug., 1864: prom. Lt. Col.. 16 June, 1865; dis. 11 July, 1865, ex. term of service as Major.

b. Tarrifville, Conn., 1839; son of John and Margaret Smith: m. 1864, Caroline A., dau. of Joseph C. and Ruth A. Goldthwaite, b. So. Danvers, 1844. Ch.: Wm. Lyman, b. 1 May, 1866.
Lives in Topeka, Kas. State Senator; State Oil Inspector, &c.

SOUTHWICK.

William H.,
m. 22 Aug., 1863, Co. D, 2d H. A.: dis. 3 Sept., 1865, ex. term.

b. Peabody, 1837; son of Platts and Eliza Southwick; m. 4 Dec.. 1860. Nancy J. Jones, dau. of Theodore and Martha Jones. b. Bristol. Me.

SPALDING.

Albert,
m. 22 Dec., 1863, Co. K, 2d

(*Spalding Continued.*)

H. A.: dis. 3 Sept., 1865, ex. term.

b. Dracut, 15 June, 1847; son of Albert Jefferson (b. 1805) and Mary (Berry, b. Salem, 7 April, 1807) Spalding; m. 18 Oct., 1873, Flora A. Colburn, dau. of James S. and Sarah (Butterfield) Colburn.
Lives in Danvers.

Asa J.
m. 1 Oct., 1862, Co. K, 8th Inf.: dis. 7 Aug., 1863, ex. term.

Jacob C.,
m. 22 Aug., 1864, Co. A, 4th H. A.: dis. 17 June, 1865, ex. term.

b. Dracut, 24 Dec., 1842; son of Albert J. (b. 1805) and Mary (Berry) Spaulding.

SPINNEY.

Alexander,
m. 14 Aug., 1863, Co. C, 11th Inf.; dis. 18 Sept., 1864, died in N. Y. harbor.

SPOFFORD.

Edward C.,
m. 19 Aug., 1862, Co. F, 35th Inf., sergt.; dis. 18 May, 1863, to enable him to accept a commission tendered by Gov. of Missouri. Not found among Missouri troops. Credited to North Andover. Æt. 21 at enl.

STANLEY.

George W.,
m. 18 Jan., 1865, 38th Inf.: dis. 6 Mar., 1865, disability. Æt. 24 at enl.

STARKEY. (Sharkey.)

Edgar,
m. 6 Sept., 1861, Co. D, 22d Inf.; (2d Co. S. S.); music.; wounded 27 June, 1862; dis. 11 Nov., 1862, disability; enl.

(Starkey Continued.)
9 Sept., 1864, V. R. C.; cred. to Otis; deserted 2 Oct., 1864.

b. 1846.

STETSON.
Alonzo J.,
m. 1 Oct., 1862, Co. K, 8th Inf.; dis. 25 Nov., 1862, disability.

b. Green, Me., 5 Feb., 1838; son of Turner and Thankful (Lombard) Stetson; m. 2 Sept., 1862, Susan M. Stanley, dau. of Sands and Sarah (Hutchinson) Stanley. b. Salem, 5 Nov. 1840. Lives in Danvers. Commander Post 90.

Seth H. (S.,)
m. 19 Aug., 1862, Co. F. 35th Inf., corp.; dis. 20 Nov., 1862, disability.

b. Danvers, 27 May, 1839; son of Seth, jr. (b. Danvers, 3 Sept., 1808) and Mary Tucker (Haywood, b. Danvers, 9 Dec., 1813) Stetson; m. 15 Apr., 1858, E. P. Lang. Ch.: Herbert Howard, b. 20 Nov., 1859, Wm. David, b. 2 July, 1861. Frank Chase, b. 13 May, 1864.

William Hilbert,
m. 4 Aug., 1863, Co. C. 2d H. A.; corp., 17 Sept., 1863; dis. 3 Sept., 1865, ex. term.

b. Danvers, 7 Jan., 1834; son of Seth and Mary (Hayward) Stetson; m. Elizb. A. Wilson of Danvers; m. 2d Maria Fredrika Roache, of Danvers. Ch.: Mary Lavina, b. 30 Nov., 1860, Wm. Frederick, b. 8 Feb., 1878, Seth Hilbert, b. 3 June, 1879, Abbie Elizb., b. 4 May, 1881. Shoemaker. Lives in Danversport.

STEVENSON.
George W. (F.),
m. 5 July, 1861. Co. I, 1st H. A.; dis. 8 July, 1864. ex. term. Æt. 25 at enl.

STONE.
Frederick T.,
m. 22 Dec., 1863, Co. K, 2d

(Stone Continued.)
H. A.; dis. 3 Sept., 1865, ex. term.

b. Lynn, 30 Nov., 1847; son of Joseph (b. 19 Oct., 1816) and Martha Brown (Dow, b. No. Hampton, N. H., 13 June, 1818) Stone. "Of So. Danvers," cred. to Danvers.

STONEHALL.
John,
see Murray, Patrick.

STOWELL.
John,
m. 26 Aug., 1864, Co. M, 3d H. A.; dis. 17 June, 1865, ex. term. Æt. 26 at enl.

SULLIVAN.
Cornelius,
m. 8 Jan., 1862, Co. D, 11th Inf.; wounded 29 Aug., 1862; died 6 May, 1863, died of wounds received 3 May; credited to Boston. Æt. 18 at enl.

John,
m. 30 Nov., 1864, 5th Ill. Cav.; enl. at Vicksburg, Miss.; cred. to Danvers.

Æt. 28 at enl.; born Kerry Co., Ireland.

Philip,
m. 22 July, 1861, Co. C, 17th Inf.; dis. 3 Aug., 1864, ex. term.

Æt. 20 at enl.; went west.

SYLVESTER.
Henry S.,
m. 19 Aug., 1862, Co. F. 35th Inf., corp.; dis. 9 June, 1865, ex term, as corp.; credited to Gloucester. Æt. 21 at enl.

Seward P.,
m. 22 July, 1861, Co. G, 17th Inf.; dis. 3 Aug., 1864, ex. term.

(*Sylvester Continued.*)
b. Danvers, 3 Mar., 1843; son of Joshua (b. Winaset, 9 July, 1806) and Harriet L. (Noyes, b. Atkinson, N. H., 21 Nov, 1818) Sylvester.

TARLTON.
Walter F.,
m. 1 Oct., 1862, Co. K, 8th Inf.; dis. 7 Aug., 1863, ex. term; m. 15 July, 1864, Co. I, 6th Inf.; dis. 27 Oct., 1864, ex. term.

TEDFORD.
James C.,
m. 16 Nov., 1864, 2d Unatt. Co. Inf.; dis. 7 July, 1865, ex. term. Credited to Gloucester.

b. Yarmouth, N. S., 1843; son of Wm. and Mary Tedford; m. Danvers, 14 Oct. 1864, Emily, dau. of Joseph and Elizb. Ellis, b. Yarmouth, N. S., 1843.

Milford,
m. 5 July, 1861, Co. I, 1st H. A.; died Ft. Albany, Arlington Hts., 25 Feb., 1862.

b. Yarmouth, N. S., 1843; son of Alex Best and Ellen Tedford. Buried at Danvers.

THOMAS.
Edward W.,
m. 5 July, 1861, Co. I, 1st H. A.; dis. 29 Dec., 1863 to re-enlist; dis. 11 Aug., 1865.

Æt. 28 at enl.; b. Danvers, 6 July, 1833; son of Joseph (b. 4 Mar., 1796) and Mercy Carlton (Hadley, b. Andover, 23 Dec., 1810) Thomas; m. 1854, Amanda M., dau. of Betsey Messer, of Danvers.

John P.,
m. 20 Oct., 1863, Co. G, 3d H. A.; dis. 18 Sept., 1865, ex. term.

b. 4 May, 1842; son of Joseph (b. 4 Mar., 1796), and Mary Caroline (Hadley, b. 23 Dec., 1810, at Andover) Thomas.

Warren,
m. 10 July, 1863, Co. D, 32d Inf.; dis. 13 Dec., 1863, disability. Æt. 28 at enl.

THOMPSON.
John,
m. 15 July, 1864, Co. I, 6th Inf.: dis. 27 Oct., 1864, ex. term.

b. Springvale, Me., 1844; son of John and Mary Thompson; m. 17 Mar., 1869, Emma A., dau. of John and Emma Dudley.

John N.,
m. 1 May, 1861, Co. H, 5th Inf.; dis. 31 July, 1861, ex. term; m. 10 Sept., 1861, Co. B, 19th Inf.; wounded, as corp., 25 June, 1862. Died 17 Sept., 1862, at Ft. Ellsworth, Va. Æt. 30 at enl.

Joseph,
m. 15 July, 1864, Co. I, 6th Inf.; dis. 27 Oct., 1864, ex. term.

W. W.,
m. 16 Nov., 1864, 5th Ill. Cav.; enl. at Vicksburg, Miss.; credited to Danvers.

Æt. 18 at enl.; residence Clairborne, Miss.

TOOMEY.
Jeremiah,
m. 22 July, 1861, Co. C, 17th Inf.; dis. 3 Aug., 1864, ex. term.

Æt. 21 at enl.; d. in Chicago about 1870; brother of Patrick Toomey.

Patrick, 2d,
m. 22 July, 1861, Co. C, 17th Inf.; dis. 3 Aug., 1864, ex. term.

b. Ireland, 1837; d. Danvers, 8 June, 1873; son of Matthew and Honora Toomey; m. 1861, Ellen, dau. of Edmund and Bridget Cotter.

TOUGH.
Robert,
m. 22 Dec., 1863, Co. K, 2d H. A.; dis. 3 July, 1865, ex. term. Æt. 20 at enl.

TOWNE.
Daniel Austin,
m. 15 July, 1864, Co. I, 6th Inf.; dis. 27 Oct., 1864, ex. term.

b. 22 Dec., 1844; d., St. Louis, 26 Jan., 1879; son of Daniel and Paulina F. Towne; m. 3 Jan., 1870, Jennie D. Muchmore who m. 2d. in St. Louis, Wm. Alexander.

TRAINOR.
Patrick,
m. 22 July, 1861, Co. C, 17th Inf.; dis. 24 Dec., 1861; died Baltimore, Md., 24 Dec., 1861 (buried in Danvers). Æt. 19 at enl.

TRASK.
Alfred M.,
m. 3 Sept., 1861, 1st Co. S. S.; dis. 13 Nov., 1862, disability.

b. Danvers, 25 Jan., 1840; son of Alfred (b. Wendall, N. H., 7 Dec., 1811) and Mary J. (Blackley, b. Sandwich, N. H., 12 July, 1810) Trask; m. 24 Jan., 1861, Mary K., dau. of Joseph Eben and Elizb. A. (Jackson) Griffin, b. So. Danvers, 1843; m. Hattie M. Cuerg, b. Canada. Ch.: Edith Moulton, b. 21 July, 1875.

Charles P.,
m. 14 Oct., 1861, Co. G, 23d Inf.; dis. 3 May, 1865, ex. term; prisoner of war.

b. Beverly, 1843; son of Levi and Rebecca Trask; m. 30 Aug., 1872, Esther S. Richardson, dau. of James and Mary (Shillaber) Richardson, b. Salem, 1846. Ch.: Esther S., b. 9 Sept., 1873. Chas. J., b. 14 Oct., 1875.
Lives in Danversport.

Elbridge P.,
m. 22 Aug., 1864, 29th unattached Co., H. A.; 'dis. 16 June, 1865; credited to Andover. Æt. 34 at enl.

Levi,
m. 10 D 1861, Co. H, 19th

(*Trask Continued.*)
Inf.: dis. 18 April, 1863, disability.

b. Danvers, 2 May, 1811; son of Levi (b. 1838) and Mary (Grant) Trask; m. Rebecca Harris. Ch.: Chas., b. Roxbury, 24 Jan., 1829. Wm., b. 26 Aug., 1832. Eliza Jane, b. 25 Dec., 1834. Caroline, b. 13 Feb., 1837. Levi, b. 20 April, 1839. Geo. Levi, b. 27 Apr., 1846.

Levi A.,
m. 19 Aug., 1862, Co. F, 35th Inf.; dis. 9 June, 1865, ex. term.

b. Beverly, 1841; m. Elizb. C. Welding, b. Provincetown. Ch.: Willie Bradley, b. 20 June, 1866. Lizzie Ellen, b. 14 Mar., 1868. Carrie Morton, b. 9 May, 1871.

Samuel P.,
m. 23 July, 1864, Co. C, 5th Inf.; dis. 16 Nov., 1864, ex. term.

b. Danvers, 1 Feb., 1845; d. there 3 April, 1881; son of Elbridge (b. Beverly, 21 July, 1811) and Mary Herrick (Putnam, b. 23 Feb., 1812) Trask; m. 17 June, 1875, Eliza C. Mears, dau. of Wm. and Mary A. (Peabody) Mears, b. Essex. Ch.: a dau. b. 12 Dec., 1878.

TURNER.
Erdix T.,
m. 23 July, 1864, Co. C, 5th Inf.; dis. 16 Nov., 1864, ex. term.

b. Danvers, 19 Sept., 1843; son of Benj. (b. 9 Aug., 1805, at Lyme, N. H.) and Charlotte (Hamilton, b. Lyme, 14 Apr., 1812) Turner.

TWISS.
William F.,
m. 22 Aug., 1862, Co. B, 40th Inf.; dis. 19 Nov., 1864; died at Beverly, 19 Nov., 1864, while on furlough.

b. Londonderry, N. H., 11 Oct., 1831; son of Benj. (b. Beverly, 5 Sept., 1806) and Elizb. (Dwinnell, b. Londonderry, 6 Aug., 1805) Twiss; m. Mary F. Morgan, b. Manchester. Ch.: Clara Luella, b. 5 June, 1860.

TYLER.

Abel N.,
m. 7 Dec., 1863, Co. A, 23d Inf.; dis. 25 June, 1865, ex. term.

b. Danvers, 2 Mar., 1847; son of Abel Harvey (b. Bradford, 11 July, 1822) and Eliza (b. 9 Jan., 1805) Tyler; m. 25 Feb., 1866, Grace Ella, dau. of Stephen and Mary E. (Adams) Day. Ch.: Hattie Eva, b. 9 Oct., 1866.

UPTON.

Augustine,
m. 19 Sept., 1862, Co. E, 50th Inf.; dis. 24 Aug., 1863, ex. term; m. 2 Mar., 1864, Battalion U. S. engineers; dis. 2 Mar., 1867, ex. term; cred. to South Danvers, on second enl.

b. Melrose, 10 Dec., 1844; son of Augustus (of W. Peabody) and Asthenath (Phillips of Danville, Vt.) Upton; m. 12 Jan., 1875, Hattie A. Bodge, dau. of Nath'l and Esther A. (Flint) Bodge, b. Danvers, 27 Mar., 1848. Ch.: Nathalie Bodge, b. 28 Jan., 1887; m. 2d, 17 July, 1892, Amanda H. Marston of Pittston, Me.
Lives in Lynn.

Austin,
m. 3 Sept., 1861, 1st Co. S. S., corp.; dis. 16 Feb., 1864, to reenlist. Missing in action, 12 May, 1864, last seen at Spottsylvania. Prob. died in Confederate prison.

b. Danvers, 28 June, 1825; son of Capt. Eli and Matilda Upton.

USHER.

Daniel R.,
m. 5 July, 1861, Co. D, 1st H. A., dis. 8 July, 1864, ex. term; sent to hospital 30 June, 1864.

b. W. Cambridge, 1838; son of Daniel and Almira (Russell) Usher; m. 1866, M. Helen Berry, dau. of Daniel (b. Middleton, 8 Aug., 1808) and Mary May (Wright, b. Charlestown, N. H., 27 Dec., 1819) Usher. Ch.: Mira Porter, b. 18 June, 1873.
Lives in Danvers.

VERRY.

Herbert W.,
m. 1 May, 1861, Co. H, 5th Inf.; dis. 31 July, 1861, ex. term; reenl. 28 Sept., 1861, Co. A, 23d Inf.; reenl. 2 Jan., 1864; wounded at Whitehall, N. C., 1863.

b. Danvers, 21 Apr., 1839; d. at Worcester, 1893; son of Joseph D. (b Danvers, 15 Dec., 1814) and Sarah P. (Fuller, b. Middleton, 22 Mar., 1819) Verry. Left descendants.

John,
m. 10 Dec., 1861, Co. H, 19th Inf.; dis. 21 Dec., 1863, to reenlist; wounded 7 May, 1864; dis. 30 June, 1865; credited to So. Danvers.

b. Danvers, 1 Oct., 1844; son of Elijah (b. Salem, 16 Nov., 1801) and Sally (Twist, b. Danvers, 29 Dec., 1806) Verry.

Joshua,
m. 10 Dec., 1861, Co. H, 19th Inf.; dis. 21 Dec., 1863, to reenl.; died, a prisoner, 9 Dec., 1864, at Florence, S. C.; credited to So. Danvers.

brother of John; b. Danvers, 30 Sept., 1833.

Lewis,
m. 19 Aug., 1862, Co. F, 35th Inf.; dis. 24 Apr., 1863, disability.

b. Danvers, 14 Feb., 1827; d. there 3 Feb., 1882; son of Joseph 3d (b. Danvers, 15 June, 1788) and Polly (Dempsey, b. Danvers, 25 Jan., 1792) Verry; m. 21 Sept., 1849, Sarah A., dau. of Daniel M. and Harriet Guilford. Ch.: Lewis Alfred, b. 11 Dec., 1851. Edward Loring, b. 30 May, 1854. Albert A., b. 14 Oct., 1855. Caroline Harris, b. 9 Sept., 1858. Harriet Grover, b. 29 Apr., 1860. Irving F. and Bertha T., b. 16 Aug., 1865.

WAITT. (Waitte.)

Samuel A.,
m. 3 Sept., 1861, 1st Co. S. S.; dis. 29 Jan., 1862, disability.

(Waitt Continued.)
b. 27 June, 1833; son of Samuel (b. Danvers, 1 Mar., 1794) and Lydia (Woodbury, b. Gloucester, 19 Oct., 1779) Waitt; m. 27 July, 1857, Elizb. C., dau. of Henry and Ann Dodge, b. Hamilton.

WALLACE.
Henry D.,
m. 1 Oct., 1862, Co. K, 8th Inf., sergt.: dis. 7 Aug., 1863, ex. term.

WARD.
Angus,
m. 5 July, 1861, Co. I, 1st H. A.; dis. 4 Mar., 1864; died at Washington, D. C., 4 Mar., 1864.

b. Masenia, N. Y., 1834 (æt. "24" at enl.); son of Daniel and Sarah (Grant) Ward; m. Nancy B., dau. of Nathan, jr. (b. 8 Sept., 1803) and Elizb. B. (Batchelder, b. Danvers, 11 Aug., 1808) Cross. Ch.: Lelia Frances, b. 10 Feb., 1859, Sarah Elizh., b. 27 Oct., 1860. Ward Post 90, G. A. R., of Danvers, named in memory of William and Angus Ward.

William,
m. 5 July, 1861, Co. I, 1st H. A.; reenl. 7 Dec., 1863, died of disease on way home from paroled camp, 16 Mar., 1865.

Æt. 29 at enl. and married; brother of Angus Ward.

WATSON.
Ezra W.,
m. 22 July, 1861, Co. C. 17th Inf.; dis. 20 Nov., 1862, disability; m. 22 Dec., 1863, 2d H. A., Co. K, corp.: dis. 3 Sept., 1865, ex. term.

Æt. 24 at enl.; died Danvers, 30 May, 1875; m. Ella Burchstead. Ch.: De Forest W. Live in Tapleyville.

John,
m. 27 May, 1861. Co. C, 1st Inf.: deserted Dec., 1861; credited to Boston. Æt. 31 at enl.

WEBBER.
Albert D.,
m. 29 July, 1863, Co. B, 2d H. A.; dis. 3 Sept., 1865, ex. term, as corp. Æt. 21 at enl.

Marshall (Mendal S.),
m. 1 May, 1861, Co. A, 5th Inf.; dis. 31 July, 1861, ex. term.

William,
m. 1 Oct., 1862, Co. K, 8th Inf.: dis. 7 Aug., 1863, ex. term; m. 13 Feb., 1864, Co. A, 23d Inf., corp.; dis. 25 June, 1865, ex. term.

b. Beverly, 1847; son of John and Mary (Roberts) Webber; m. 1870, Adelaide Louisa, dau. of Hewitt and Lydia Burchstead, b. Danvers, 1847.

WEBSTER.
George,
m. 1 May, 1861, Co. H, 5th Inf.; dis. 31 July, 1861, ex. term.

WEEDEN.
John G.,
m. 5 July, 1861, Co. I, 1st H. A., corp.: dis. 8 July, 1864, ex. term.

b. North Berwick, Me., 1828; d. Danvers, 7 July, 1889; son of Edward and Ann Weeden; m. 11 Feb., 1854, Mrs. Martha A. Root, dau. of Oliver and Nancy Lee, b. Center Harbor, N. H., 1828. Ch.: Franklin Auburn, b. 21 July, 1858. A dau., b. 6 Oct., 1860. Forest Ambrose, b. 23 Feb., 1866. Alice Lee, b. 24 March, 1868. Ralph Gardner, b. 27 May, 1870.

WEEKS.
William H.,
m. 22 Dec., 1863, Co. K, 2d H. A.; dis. 3 Sept., 1865, ex. term.

b. Beverly, 7 Apr., 1846; son of Stephen L. (b. Porter, Me., 25 Dec., 1815) and Eunice (Odell, b. Beverly, 20 Aug., 1820) Weeks.

TOWN OF DANVERS.   63

WEIGAND.
Robert,
m. 5 July, 1861, Co. I, 1st H. A.: dis. 6 Dec., 1863, to reenlist: deserted 20 May, 1865. Æt. 26 at enl.

WEIR.
Alexander A. (G.),
m. 5 July, 1861, Co. I, 1st H. A., sergt.; dis. 12 Apr., 1864, disability. Credited to Boston. Æt. 24 at enl.

WELCH.
Charles E. M.,
m. 19 Aug., 1862, Co. F. 35th Inf.: dis. 17 Sept., 1862, killed at Antietam, Md.

b. Sanford, Me., 24 Oct., 1834; son of Solomon (b. Sanford, 16 Aug., 1816) and Martha R. (Shackley, b. 1 May, 1818 at Shapleigh) Welch; m. 24 Nov., 1858, Roxana (b. Alfred, Me.), dau. of Ivory N. and Louisa Dow. Ch.: Solomon and Martha, twins, b. 6 Mar., 1860. Georgianna, b. 15 Mar., 1862.

Edward F.,
m. 19 Aug., 1861, Co. C, 17th Inf.: dis. 6 Apr., 1863, disability; m. 12 July, 1864, V. R. C.; dis. 17 Nov., 1865.

b. Ireland; m. Feb., 1847, M'g't Monks. Ch.: Christopher, b. 24 Dec., 1848, at Salem. Edw., b. Danvers, 4 Sept., 1850. Thos., b. 27 Aug., 1852. Æt. 38 at enl.

George T.,
m. 16 Sept. 1861, Co. B, 26th Inf.; promoted Lt., 7 Sept., 1863, 98th U. S. C. T.; dismissed as 1st Lt., 98th U. S. C. T., 18 Mar., 1865.

b. Danvers, 1 May, 1840; son of Josiah (b. Shapleigh, Me., 29 Sept., 1814) and Mehitable (Hutchinson, b. Danvers, 18 Jan., 1819) Welch.

John Q.,
m. 22 Aug., 1864, Co. A, 4th H. A.; dis. 17 June, 1865, ex. term.

(Welch Continued.)
b. Shapleigh, Me., æt. 22 at enl.; died in Lynn; m. Janette Murphy. Ch.: Son, b. 9 Dec., 1859. Carrie Emma, b. 4 June, 1862. Myra Belle, b. 25 Sept., 1864. Dau., b. 27 Oct., 1866. Chas. W., b. 25 May, 1869. Mabel Etta, b. 12 Nov., 1871. Ernest Linwood, b. 19 Dec., 1874.

WELLS.
Charles F.,
m. 21 Oct., 1861, Co. C. 17th Inf., credited to Cambridge; dis. 18 Feb., 1864, to reenlist; corp. Co. B, 1 Apr., 1865; dis. 11 July, 1865, ex. term.

b. Danvers, 14 Sept., 1841; son of Moses (b. Shapleigh, Me., 22 July, 1821) and Clarissa (Ricker, b. Sanford, Me., 9 Feb., 1820) Wells; m. 28 Jan., 1867, Sarah J., dau. of Charles and Martha A. (Edgerly, b. 6 July, 1847, Dover, N. H.) Field. Ch.: Chas. L., b. 2 Feb., 1867. Frank Lester, b. 6 Jan., 1873. William, b. 6 Aug., 1875. Ralph Hudson, b. 31 Oct., 1879.
Lives in Danvers.

Edwin G.,
m. 21 Oct., 1861, Co. C, 17th Inf.: dis. 20 Oct., 1864, ex. term.

b. Watertown, 19 Nov., 1844; d. Greenfield; son of Nathan and Marion Wells.

John F.,
m. 22 July, 1861, Co. C, 17th Inf.: dis. 1 Jan., 1864, to reenlist; sergt. Co. B, 4 Mar., 1865; dis. 11 July, 1865, ex. term.

Æt. 24 at enl.; d. in Georgetown about 1870; brother of Nath'l K. Wells, q. v.; m. Lizzie Dale, of Georgetown. Ch.: Grace. Francis.

Nathaniel K.,
m. 13 Mar., 1862, Co. M, 1st H. A., corp.; dis. 17 Sept., 1864, died at Washington.

b. Boxford, 1839; son of John and Elizb. (Townes) Wells; m. 2 Jan., 1860, Mary J., dau. of Edw. and Sarah Whitten, widow of Abram Welch, b. Springvale, Me., 1837. Ch.: John Henry, b. 18 Oct., 1860.

WENTWORTH.

Fred A.,
m. 22 Dec., 1863, Co. K, 2d H. A., sergt.; dis. 27 July, 1865, ex. term.

b. Rumney, N. H., 1839; son of John L. and Louisa Wentworth: m. 31 May, 1865, Martha Ella, dau. of Joseph (jr. b. Danvers, 22 Mar. 1812) and Eliza Ann (Jackson, b. Charlestown, 17 Sept., 1818) Griffin.

WESCOTT.

John,
m. 5 July, 1861, Co. I, 1st H. A.; dis. 8 July, 1864, ex. term; taken prisoner at Smithfield, Va., by Confederate cavalry, 14 June, 1863; confined in Libby Prison, 18 to 24 June, 1863; then in Belle Isle, till July, 16, 1863. Paroled prisoner of war, 22 June, 1864.

b. Chester, N. H., 30 Jan., 1835; son of Joseph (b. Chester, N. H.) and Hannah (Hall of Plymouth) Wescott; m. 1855, Mehitable P., dau. of Caleb (b. 13 Mar., 1809) and Mehitable Felton (Proctor Russell, b. Danvers, 27 Sept., 1814). Ch.: Martha Evaline, b. 28 Sept., 1855. Asenath Proctor, b. 14 Feb., 1858. Ellen Marion, b. 1860. John Putnam, b. 1865. Annie Gertrude, b. 1868. Clarence Hermon, b. 1870. M. 2d, 1872, Sarah W. Trask, of Peabody.
Taken prisoner 22 June, 1864, in company with N. P. Fish, of Danvers, and carried to Libby Prison; thence to Danville, N. C., near which place they escaped and after an exciting tramp through a hostile country, upon one occasion a confederate officer was tricked into permitting the two federals to draw rations, finally reached friends in W. Va., and transportation home to Danvers.
Now resides in Lynn.

WEST.

Matthew C.,
m. 28 Sept., 1861, Co. A, 23d Inf.; wounded 8 Feb., 1862; dis. 22 Oct., 1862, disability.

WHIPPLE.

John F.,
m. 20 Feb., 1862, Co. L, 1st H. A.; cred. to Roxbury; dis. 20 Feb., 1864 to reenlist; m. 22 Feb., 1864; wounded 16 June, 1864, in left thigh; lost right arm by premature discharge of a cannon at Worcester, Mass., 10 Apr., 1865. Confined in City Point Hospital, also at Readville and Worcester, Mass.; dis. 3 July, 1865, disability.

b. Ipswich, 20 Aug., 1842; son of Daniel and Adeline (Stone) Whipple; m. 17 June, 1871, Cornelia E., dau. of John and Rebecca (Stanley) Hood, b. Danvers. Ch.: Guy M., b. 12 June, 1876
Now a resident of Danvers. Credited to Ipswich and Roxbury.

WHITEHOUSE.

Joseph G.,
m. 22 Aug., 1863, Co. D, 2d H. A.; dis. 3 Sept., 1865, ex. term.

b. Brookfield, N. H., 1833; d. Danvers, 14 Sept., 1892; son of David H. and Mary Ann Whitehouse; m. 1856, Venora C. Frost (b. Bridgton, Me.). Ch.: Loretta M., b. 13 Dec., 1862.

Jonathan,
m. 19 Aug., 1862, Co. F, 35th Inf.; dis. 21 Apr., 1864, trans. unattached company, V. R. C.; dis. 26 June, 1865.

b. Yarmouth, N. S., 1841, d. Danvers, 11 Aug., 1872; son of William and Ann Crowell; m. 30 Nov., 1861, Mehitable, b. Nova Scotia, dau. of Thos. and Ann (Shaw) Pearce.

WHITTIER,

James F. (L.) (T.),
m. 5 July, 1861, Co. I, 1st H. A.; dis. 8 July, 1864, ex. term.

b. Farmington, N. H., 1842; son of Osgood and Catherine Whittier; m. 14 Mar., 1865, Mary E., b. 4 Mar., 1847, dau. of Thos. (b. 10 Jan., 1826,

(*Whittier Continued.*)

at Tamworth, N. H.), and Lydia (Tyler, b. 4 Feb., 1826 at Benton, Vt.) Ch.: Lydia Ida, b. 12 May, 1869.

WHITNEY.
George T.,

m. 19 Aug., 1862, Co. F, 35th Inf.; dis. 12 Mar., 1865; died Annapolis, Md., of disease. Æt. 27 at enl.

WIGGIN.
George Abbott,

m. 6 Mar., 1865; Co. D, 62d Inf.; dis. 5 May, 1865, ex. term. Credited to Danvers.

b. 1848; d. Danvers, 8 Aug., 1893; son of Henry below; m. 11 Dec., 1868, Martha A., dau. of Peter and Sarah (Munsey) Roberts, b. Manchester, 1846.

Henry R.,

m. 22 July, 1861, Co. C, 17th Inf.; dis. 16 Jan., 1863, disability.

b. Salem, Oct., 1816; son of Chase and Susan (Trickey) Wiggin, of Salem; d. Danvers, 10 Aug., 1880; m. 15 Oct., 1845, Sarah Ann Norton. Ch.: John Henry, b. 21 July, 1846. Geo. Abbott, b. 29 Mar., 1848. Samuel. Warren. William. Abbie. Henrietta. Sarah. Sarah Ann, b. 27 Dec., 1858. He m. 2d, 12 May, 1859, Mrs. Mary Brown, dau. of Jeremiah and Abby (Low) Brown, b. Alfred, Me. Ch.: a son, b. 21 Dec., 1863; m. 3d, Harriet, dau. of Abraham and Hannah Mayhew, b. Haverhill, N. H. Ch.: Clarence, b. 7 Feb., 1869.

John H.,

m. 1 Oct., 1862, Co. C, 8th Inf.: m. 2d Unattached Co. H. A.

b. Danvers, 21 July, 1845; son of Henry, above; m. 1st, Mary Jane, dau. of Samuel and Mary Wilson; m. 2d, Mary E., dau. of Thos. and Marg't Haskell. Ch.: by 1st m.;

(*Wiggin Continued.*)

Nathan, b. 1868. Mary, b. 1870. By 2d m.: Sherman B. Lewis L. Harry W. Sarah N. Elizabeth Lorena. Lives in Danvers.

Joseph F.,

m. 22 July, 1861, Co. C, 17th Inf.; dis. 11 Mar., 1863, disability.

b. Salem, 1824; d. Danvers, 9 Feb., 1869; m. Mary A. Ashby. Ch.: Clara Elizb., b. 21 Oct., 1854. Hattie A., b. Salem. Brother of Henry Wiggin.

Oliver P.,

m. 19 Aug., 1862, Co. F, 35th Inf.; dis. 31 Jan., 1863, disability. Æt. 21 at enl.

WILEY.
Benj. F.,

m. 29 Aug., 1864, Co. G, 3d H. A.: dis. 14 June, 1865, ex. term: credited to Townsend.

Æt. 21 at enl.; b. Danvers Centre; Lives in Lynn. Brother of John F. Wiley.

John U.,

m. 2 Mar., 1864, U. S. engineer corps; dis. 2 Mar., 1867, ex. term.

b. Lynnfield, 1845; son of Benjamin and Elvira (Upton) Wiley; m. 3 Nov., 1872, Mary P. (b. Danvers, 1852) dau. of Eben'r and Emily (Sullivan) Goodale. Ch.: Florence May, b. Danvers, 29 Jan., 1875. Lives in Danvers.

WILSON.
Artemas,

m. 14 Feb., 1862, Co. D, 17th Inf.: dis. 13 Feb., 1865, disability.

b. Greenfield, N. H., Aug., 1816 (æt. "43" at enl.); d. there 24 Jan., 1880; m. 28 Nov., 1839, Mary Ann Wilkinson, b. Carlisle, 1 Jan., 1820. Ch.: Frances Ann, b. Greenfield, N. H., 22 Dec., 1840. Mary Ann, b. Greenfield, 24 Sept., 1842. George, b. Hancock, 8 Oct., 1844. Douglas, R., b. Greenfield, 23 July, 1846.

(*Wilson Continued.*)

Wm. Henry, b. Lowell, 10 July, 1894. Rathburn Elijah, b. Danvers, 8 June, 1851. John Moore, b. 13 Mar., 1854. Joseph Clinton, b. 29 May, 1861.

Douglass R.,

m. 22 Aug., 1864, Co. A, 4th H. A.; dis. 17 June, 1865, ex. term.

b. Bennington, N. H., 1821; d. Danvers, 30 June, 1891; son of Elijah and Sally (Rogers) Wilson; m. Ellen W. Moor, Ch.: Albert R., b. 6 Aug., 1855. David A., b. 16 July, 1857. Charles Francis and John Robinson, twins, b. 2 Feb., 1860. Geo. Edw., b. 12 July, 1868. Was in the Mexican war.

Douglas R., 2d,

m. 1 Oct., 1862, Co. K, 8th Inf.; dis. 7 Aug., 1863, ex. term; m. 20 Nov., 1863, Co. H, 3d H. A.; dis. 18 Sept., 1865, ex. term.

b. 23 July, 1846, at Greenfield, N. H.; d. Soldiers' Home, Chelsea, 29 Jan., 1894; son of Artemas (b. Greenfield, Aug., 1816) and Mary Ann (Wilkinson, b. 1 Jan., 1826, at Carlisle) Wilson; m. 27 Nov., 1890, Anzella B. Gray, dau. James and Eliza Richardson of Guysborough, N. S.

George A.,

m. 6 Oct., 1861, Co. G, 17th Inf.: dis. 7 Oct., 1864, ex. term.

Æt. 27 at enl ; died 25 June, 1882.

George C.,

m. 22 July, 1861, Co. C, 17th Inf.; dis. 4 Jan., 1864, to reenlist; dis. 11 July, 1865, ex. term, from Co. B, as musician.

b. Hancock, N. H., 8 Oct., 1844; d. Detroit; son of Artemas (b. Greenfield, 1816) and Mary Ann (Wilkinson, b. Carlisle, 1 Jan., 1820) Wilson.

WITHEY.

John,

m. 22 Aug., 1862, Co. B, 40th Inf., corp.; dis. 11 July, 1864, died at home.

b. Lynn, 1 Sept., 1814 (æt. "44" at enl.); son of John (b. N. H.,) and Sally (Ingalls, b. Lynn) Withey; m. Sally Boynton, Ch.: John P., b. Lynn, 1846. Geo. S., b. 1858. Ellen H., b. 1852. Samuel P., b. Lynn, 1846.

John P.,

m. 17 July, 1861, Co. D, 1st H. A., sergt.; dis. 18 Dec., 1863, to reenlist; dis. 23 June, 1865, disability.

b. Lynn, 1843; son of John and Sally (Boynton) Withey; m. 20 Sept., 1866, Louisa (b. York, Me.), dau. of Joseph and Clarissa (Littlefield) Grover, Ch.: Albert, b. 2 Mar., 1871.
Lives in Danversport.

Richard B.,

m. 1 Nov., 1861, Co. K, 23d Inf.; dis. 13 Oct., 1864, ex. term.

b. M'h'd, 21 July, 1836; son of John (b. Lynn) and Sally (Boynton, b. Salem) Withey; m. 1860, Ann B., dau. of Benj. G. and Susan W. Chaplin, b. Danvers. Ch.: Clara A., b. 31 Oct., 1860. Mary E. Benj. F., b. 13 Aug., 1867. L. F., b. 18 Nov., 1868. E. B. R. Arthur.
Resides in Danversport.

Samuel P.,

m. 22 Aug., 1862, Co. B, 40th Inf., musician ; dis. 16 June, 1865, ex. term.

b. Lynn, 1846; son of John above; m. 9 May, 1876, Annie M., dau. of Thos. and Mary (Lord) Walsh, b. Peabody.

WOOD.

Joseph,

m. 19 Aug., 1862, Co. F, 35th Inf.; dis. 17 Sept., 1862, killed at Antietam, Md., Æt. 24 at enl.

WOODBURY.

Albert,

m. 20 Nov., 1863, Co. H, 3d H. A.; dis. 3 Oct., 1864, disability.

b. Danvers, 21 Feb., 1836; died Danvers; son of Hezekiah (b. Gloucester, 12 Feb., 1807) and Eliza (Averill, b. 2 May, 1805, at Ulma, Me.) Woodbury; m. 21 Nov., 1861. Hannah E., b. Yarmouth, N. S., 1840. dau. of Allen and Ellen (Tedford) Bent. Ch.: Eliza Ellen, b. 23 Dec., 1862. Sadia A., b. 3 Aug., 1867. Mabel, b. 17 Jan., 1871. Althea, b. 17 Jan., 1873.

WOODMAN.

George,

m. 22 Aug., 1862, Co. B, 40th Inf.; dis. 1 June, 1864, killed at Cold Harbor, Va.

b. N. S., 1827; son of Robert and Leah Woodman; m. 30 Apr., 1854. Helen M., dau. of Hewit and Lydia Burchstead, b. Beverly.

Frederick A.,

m. 5 July, 1861, Co. D, 1st H. A.; dis. 8 July, 1864, ex. term; credited to Methuen.

b. Danvers, 5 Apr., 1832; died Danvers, 12 Feb., 1877; son of Daniel (b. Acton, Me., 13 Jan., 1800) and Fanny (Friend, b. Beverly, 22 May, 1804) Woodman; m. 27 May, 1866, Mira Green, b. England, dau. of Wm. and Jane (Tibbetts) Green. Ch.: Wm. A., b. 2 Nov., 1867.

WOODWARD.

Carleton,

m. 5 July, 1861, Co. I, 1st H. A.; dis. 14 Dec., 1863, deserted. Æt. 21 at enl.

WRIGHT.

Frederick,

m. 22 July, 1861, Co. C, 27th Inf.; dis. 9 Dec., 1861, disability; m. 15 July, 1864, Co. I, 6th Inf.; dis. 27 Oct., 1864, ex. term. Entered V. R. C.

b. England, 1832; son of John and Martha (Brunt) Wright; m. 19 Apr., 1863, Mrs. Eliza D. Wardwell, dau. of Thos. and Elizabeth (Dougherty) b. Ireland, 1822.

William A.,

m. 27 Nov., 1861, Reed's Rangers, sergt.; dis. 2 Jan., 1865, ex. term; credited to Marblehead; æt. 28 at enl.

YOUNG.

Charles A.,

m. 22 Aug., 1862, Co. B, 40th Inf.; dis. 1 June, 1864, killed at Cold Harbor, Va.

b. Danvers, 26 July, 1843; son of Benj. (b. Sanford, Me., 19 Nov., 1810) and Fanny C. (Hobbs, b. 10 June, 1819, at Sanford, Me.) Young.

NAVAL SERVICE.

ANDERSON.
James,
enl. on the Cumberland and was on board her when she was sunk by the Merrimack. Born about 1837, lives in Lowell.

BANKS.
John W.,
enl. on S. S. Keystone States; boatswain; was wounded in foot. Lives in Danversport.

BATCHELDER.
George G.,
enl. 20 Aug., 1861: dis. 5 Dec., 1862, from Potomac flotilla as paymaster's steward and appointed acting master's mate; revoked 29 Aug., 1864. Credited to Boston; born in Danvers, 1842.

BATSON.
Horace M.,
enl. at Boston as landsman, U. S. Gunboat Whitehead, m. 13 Aug., 1862 for one year; dis. 15 Aug., 1863, ex. term. Credited to Boston, Ward 11. Also served on the Hetzel.

b. Newcastle, N. H., 4 Nov., 1840; son of Nathaniel and Mary Olive (Locke) Batson of Newcastle; m. 3 July, 1867, Ellen Louise Tarleton. Ch.: Walter V., b. 20 July, 1872; Arthur D., b. 30 Nov., 1874; Roland, b. 1 July, 1884. Lives in Danvers.

BLAKE.
John Albert,
enl. at Boston, 14 July, 1863, as landsman, for one year; dis. 8 July, 1864. Served on New Ironsides. Credited to Danvers.

b. Danvers, 1843; m. Abigail Hyde. Lives in Lexington. Past Commander Post 90.

BRIDGES.
John H.,
enl. for three years, at New Bedford, 14 Sept., 1861; died on the Oreo, 9 July, 1862. Served on the Brandywine. Born Danversport, 1840. Credited to Boston.

CAIRD.
Alexander,
enl. at Boston, as landsman, 16 Feb., 1864, for one year. Credited to Boston. Served on the Massasoit. Dis. from the Dunbarton, 15 Feb., 1865. Born in Danvers, 1843.
See also Military service.

William, junior,
enl. at Boston, as landsman, 11 July, 1863, for one year. Credited to Danvers. Served on the Housatonic, Potapsco, Vermont. Dis. 25 Aug., 1864. On board Housatonic when rammed in Charleston harbor.

b. Danvers, 1842; lives in Chicago. Brother of Alexander Caird.

CAMERON.

John,
enl. at Philadelphia, 2 Aug., 1864; dis. from U. S. receiving ship North Carolina, 6 May, 1865.

b. Glasgow, Scotland, 2 Mar., 1847; d. in Danvers, Dec., 1870; unm.; son of John and Isabel Cameron. Resident of Danvers at time of enl.

CLYDE.

James,
enl. at Boston, as seaman, 22 May, 1862, for three years. Cred. to Milford. Born in Danvers, 1834. Served on Vermont.

COFFIN.

Enoch,
enl. at Philadelphia, as ordinary seaman, 2 May, 1864, balance of term of service in the army (i. e., 2 years, 7 mos., 24 days). Served on the Princeton; dis. from the Saratoga, 7 July, 1865. See Military service.

CROCKER.

Nelson,
enl. at Boston, 8 July, 1862, as 2d class fireman. Served on R. R. Cuyler. Credited to Boston. Born in Danvers, 1838. Dropped 8 May, 1864.

CUNNINGHAM.

William H.,
enl. at Boston, 15 Jan., 1862, for three years. Served on Vermont, Pawnee; dis. from Princeton, 23 Jan., 1865. Credited to Boston. Born Danvers, 1841.

FISHER.

Franklin W.,
enl. at Boston, 13 Aug., 1862, for one year. Served on Whitehead; dis. 21 Aug.,

(Fisher Continued.)
1863. Cred. Danvers, born there, 1842.
Lives at Danvers Centre.

FITZGERALD.

Florence,
enl. at Boston, as 1st class cabin-boy, 22 Aug., 1861, for three years. Gemsbok. Credited to Brookline; born in Danvers. Æt. 18 at enl. Deserted at Baltimore, Md., 8 June, 1862, from Gemsbok.

FOSTER.

George B.,
enl. at Boston, 12 June, 1862, as seaman; Genesee; dis. 13 Sept., 1864, as chief quartermaster and appointed acting master's mate; appointed acting ensign, 15 Nov., 1864; dis. as acting ensign, 3 Oct., 1865. Credited to Boston. Born in Danvers, 1827.

FULLER.

Joseph J.,
enl. at Boston, as ordinary seaman, 18 June, 1862; dis. 28 July, 1864 from Princeton. Served also on Genessee. Credited to Boston. Born in Danvers, 1840.

Son of Joseph Fuller; for family connections see Military Service. Lives in New London, Conn.

GROUT.

Edward B.,
enl. at Boston, 13 July, 1863, for one year, as landsman, &c. Atlantic Squadron; dis. 8 July, 1864, from New Ironsides. Cred. to Danvers; b. there, æt. 21 at enl.

HAYWARD.

Charles A.,
enl. at Boston, 13 July, 1863, for one year; dis. 8 July,

(Hayward Continued.)
1864; New Ironsides. Cred. to Danvers; born in Beverly, 1843.

HENDERSON.
David,
enl. at Boston as landsman, 5 Aug., 1862, for one year; on vessel. Ino; dis. 12 Sept., 1863. Credited to Cambridge. Born Danvers, æt. 19 at enl.

KANHAM.
Henry,
enl. at Boston, 22 July, 1864. for three years. Credited to Danvers (substitute). Born Sweden, æt. 22 at enl.

KENT.
George W.,
enl. at Boston, as carpenter, for three years, 15 Apr., 1861, on Minnesota; dis. as 2d class fireman, 14 Dec., 1861, from hospital at Washington, for disability. Credited to Ashburnham. Born Danvers, æt. 26 at enl.

LEAROYD.
Lewis E.,
m. 13 Aug., 1862, U. S. Gunboat Whitehead; dis. 21 Aug., 1863, ex. term. Credited to Danvers.

b. Danvers, 21 July, 1843; son of John A. (b. Boston, 11 June, 1808) and Sarah (Silvester, b. Andover, 5 April, 1810); m. 11 Oct., 1866, Adeline F. Woodbury, dau. of Daniel and Sophronia (Burnham) Woodbury. Ch.: Mabel W., b. Danvers, 11 Dec., 1870.
Lives in Tapleyville.

PARKER.
Benjamin F.,
enl. at Boston, 24 April, 1861. for three years, as ordinary seaman; dis. from Minnesota, 23 April, 1864. Credited to Egremont; born in Danvers; æt. 48 at enl.

PORTER.
Warren,
Commissioned at Washington, as acting ensign, 26 Oct., 1863; served on frigate Savannah, Magnolia, Honduras, Nita, Sunflower. Commissioned acting master, 8 Nov., 1864, while at Key West; dis. at Washington, 26 Aug., 1865. Appointed Commander of captured blockade runner Matagorda, 10 Sept., 1864; also, on 3 May, 1865, of U. S. S. Nita; 26 May, transferred to command of the Admiral's despatch Gunboat, cruising in the Gulf, which he held till close of war.
Credited to Danvers

b. 19 April, 1830, at Danvers; son of Warren (b. Danvers) and Ann (Welch, b. Plaistow, N. H.) Porter; married Sarah S. Holt, of North Reading. Commander of Essex Naval Veteran Assoc.

PRAY.
John H.,
enl. at Provincetown, 6 Aug., 1862, as first class boy, for one year. Served on Gemsbok and Vanderbilt; dis. from the latter, 31 Jan., 1864. No credit. Born in Marblehead, æt. 18 at enl.

Ruel Benton,
m. 22 July, 1861, Co. C, 17th Inf.; com. 2d Lt., 21 Aug., 1861. Provost marshal at Baltimore, Sept., 1861; appointed on staff of 1st Brigade. Col. Armory, at Newberne, N. C.; 1st Lt., 19 Dec., 1861; resigned 9 Aug., 1863, disability; m. U. S. Navy, 4 Mar., 1864, acting master's mate; prom. acting ensign, 30 Apr., 1864, reported at N. Y. U. S. ship Savannah, 4 Mar., 1864; confined in Norfolk

TOWN OF DANVERS. 71

(Pray Continued.)

Marine Hospital, Aug. and Sept., 1864; dis. 9 June, 1865, close of war; served on U. S. S. Savannah, Algonquin, Young America, Wilderness, Chicopee, Queen, Sarsacuss. b. April 18, 1838, Salem; son of Ruel and Mehitable (Kender) Pray; m. 28 Oct., 1860, Caroline E. Galloupe, dau. of Wm. and Sally R. Galloupe, b. Topsfield, 1834. Ch.: Charlotte Elizb., b. 21 May, 1861. Wm. G., b. 23 July, 1863. Claims the first man enlisted in Danvers on the evening of 16 April, 1861.

Thomas J.,
enl. at Boston, 26 Aug., 1861 for one year; dis. 15 May, 1862, as captain of fore-top, and appointed 16 May, 1862, acting master's mate. Resigned 29 June, 1864. Æt. 31 at enl., b. in Salem; credit first to Swampscott, second to Danvers. Served on Gemsbok.

PULSIFER.

Albert,
enl. at Boston, 21 Feb., 1865, as seaman. Served on Marblehead, Marion, Towanda, Santee, from the last named, he was dis. 27 Feb., 1868. Credited to Williamstown, Vt.; born in Danvers, æt. 25 at enl.

REYNOLDS.

John,
enl. at Portsmouth, N. H. No record. Brother of Wm. and James. Widow and son Thos., live in Danvers. Lost at sea.

SANFORD.

Alfonso,
enl. at Boston, 20 Aug., 1862, for one year; served on Miami; dis. 6 Sept., 1863. Credited to Danvers; born in Charlestown; æt. 23 at enl.

SCOTT.

James W.,
enl. at Boston, 30 May, 1861, for four years, marine corps; private; deserted from Portsmouth barracks, 24 Oct., 1861. Credited to Boston; born in Danvers; æt. 21 at enl.

SMART.

Ansel C.,
enl. at Boston, as first class boy, 22 May, 1863, vessel Cambridge; dis. 21 May, 1864. Credited to Danvers; born Burnstead, N. H., æt. 16 at enl.

SMITH.

Albert,
enl. at Boston, as second class fireman, 16 July, 1863, one year; dis. 26 Aug., 1863, claimed as a drafted man by Provost Marshal. Credited to Blackstone; born Danvers, æt. 21 at enl.

SOUTHWICK.

William H.,
enl. at Boston, 31 May, 1861, as seaman, for one year; dis. from Colorado, 30 June, 1862. Credited to Boston; born, Danvers, æt. 37 at enl.

TRASK.

Moses H.,
enl. at Boston, 23 Aug., 1861, for one year, vessel Gemsbok, deserted from Gemsbok, at Portland, Me., 29 July, 1862. Credited to Brookline; born in Danvers, æt. 39 at enl.

VERY.

Albert,
enl. at Boston, 4 May, 1861, as first class musician, for three years; dis. from Minnesota, 2 Apr., 1862. Credited to Danvers, born there, æt. 25 at enl.

MEN CREDITED TO DANVERS FROM NAVAL ENLISTMENTS.

Not natives or residents of Danvers.

BENSON, BENJAMIN, enl. 23 Oct., 1863; dis. 22 Oct., 1866. Born in Sweden.

BRADLEY, THOMAS, enl. 16 Jan., 1861. Born in Boston. (He was credited to Danvers by error.)

BROWN, JOHN, enl. 19 Oct., 1863; dis. 11 Mar., 1865. Born in Sweden.

CARROLL, JOHN J., enl. 3 Nov., 1863; dis. 11 May, 1864. Born in England.

CONNOLLY, ROGER, enl. 30 Oct., 1863; dis. as mate, 17 Sept., 1865. Born in Ireland.

DESMOND, JOHN, enl. 26 Nov., 1863. Born in Massachusetts.

DUNNING, HENRY P., enl. 19 Nov., 1863; dis. 4 July, 1864. Born in Harpswell, Me.

EASTON, JOHN, enl. 27 Jan., 1864; dis. 11 Dec., 1866. Born in Ireland.

EICHHORN, JOHN, enl. 22 Jan., 1864; was a Confederate prisoner. Born in Switzerland.

FERRELL, THOMAS J., enl. 11 Nov., 1863; dis. 17 Oct., 1866. Born in Syracuse, N. Y.

FOLEY, MARTIN, enl. 20 Nov., 1863; dis. 20 July, 1865. Born in Ireland.

GILLESPIE, FRANCIS, enl. 5 July, 1862; dis. 31 Dec., 1864. Born in Ireland.

GOULD, WILLIAM B., enl. at Boston, dis. 28 Sept., 1865. No place of birth given.

GRAHAM, JOHN F., enl. 23 Apr., 1863; dis. 22 Apr., 1864. Born in Boston.

GRAY, BENJAMIN F., enl. 13 Mar., 1862; deserted 31 Oct., 1864. Born in Portsmouth, N. H.

GLYNN, THOMAS, enl. 10 Oct., 1863; dis. 18 Aug., 1865. Born in Boston.

GRANEY, MARTIN, enl. 29 Oct., 1863; dis. 29 July, 1865. Born in Ireland.

HAIBON, ALBERT, enl. 28 May, 1861; dis. 30 June, 1862. Born in New York.

HAM, JOSEPH A., enl. 7 Oct., 1863; dis. 13 July, 1865. Born in Woolwich, Me.

HAPLEY, JOSEPH, enl. 26 Oct., 1861; dis. 20 Dec., 1864. Born in New York city.

TOWN OF DANVERS. 73

HARRISON, ROBERT, enl. 25 Oct., 1861 ; dis. 8 Oct., 1863. Born in New London, Conn.

KEARNEY, JOHN, enl. 26 Mar., 1863. Born in Boston.

MANN, RAY, enl. 13 Apr., 1863; transferred for dis. 31 May, 1864. Born in New Salem, N. H.

MARTIN, JOHN D., enl. 17 Apr., 1863. Born in Portland, Me.

MCDAVID, PATRICK, enl. 31 Mar., 1863 ; dis. 30 June, 1864. Born in Newfoundland.

MCGAFFERY, FLORINE, enl. 14 April, 1863; dis. 26 Jan., 1864. Born in Mt. Vernon, Me.

MCGARVEY, EDWARD, enl. 6 Apr., 1863 ; dis. 11 May, 1864. Born in Ireland.

MCGEE, JAMES, enl. 31 Mar., 1863 ; dis. 30 Mar., 1864. Born in Ireland.

MILLER, HENRY, enl. 11 Apr., 1863; dis. 13 June, 1864. Born in Philadelphia.

MOFFATT, THOMAS, enl. 4 Apr., 1863 ; dis. 2 Apr., 1864. Born in Boston.

MORTON, JOHN A., enl. 18 Apr., 1863 ; dis. 16 May, 1864. Born in Nova Scotia.

MOTT, PERKINS F., enl. 30 Mar., 1863. Born in Montville, N. Y.

MURRAY, JOHN, enl. 8 Apr., 1863 ; dis. 20 June, 1864. Born in Ireland.

NASH, FREDERICK, enl. 27 Mar., 1863 ; dis. 11 May, 1864. Born in England.

NASH, WILLIAM, enl. 25 May, 1863 ; dis. 13 July, 1864. Born in England.

NAUDIN, THEODORE F., enl. 11 Apr., 1863 ; deserted 21 Dec., 1863. Born in Bloomingdale, N. Y.

NICHAUS, JOHN, enl. 9 Apr., 1863 ; dis. 22 Apr., 1864. Born in Hamburg, Germany.

NICHOLS, EDWIN W., enl. 13 Apr., 1863 ; dis. 12 Apr., 1864. Born in Providence, R. I.

NOLAN, CHARLES, enl. 29 May, 1863 ; dis. 28 May, 1864. Born in Ireland.

NOLAN, CHARLES P., enl. 3 Apr., 1863. Born in Newcastle, Me.

NOLAN, DANIEL, enl. 15 June, 1863; dis. 6 Aug., 1864. Born in Ireland.

NOLAN, WILLIAM, enl. 28 May, 1863 ; dis. 13 July, 1864. Born in Damariscotta, Me.

NORWOOD, CHARLES N., enl. 9 June, 1863 ; dis. 26 July, 1864. Born in Hampden, Me.

NURSE, WILLIAM, enl. 1 Apr., 1863; deserted 4 Mar., 1865. Born in Scotland.

ADDITIONAL RECORDS,

INCLUDING DANVERS RESIDENTS WHO SERVED IN OUT OF STATE ORGANIZATIONS, AND PRESENT RESIDENTS NOT NATIVES NOR CITIZENS OF DANVERS PRIOR TO 1865.

ALLEY.

Edward Rogers,
m. 22 July, 1864, Co. E, 5th Inf.; dis. 16 Nov., 1864. Credited to Marlboro.

b. Danvers, 28 Sept., 1846; son of William (b. Salem, 14 Feb., 1814) and Susan Jane (Reed), b. Danvers, 11 May, 1864) Alley; d. at Marlboro, 9 Jan., 1895.

AMES. (Eames.)

Daniel Bradford,
m. 5 July, 1861, Co. I, 1st H. A.; dis. 28 Dec., 1864, disability.

On the rolls this man is given as aged 40, of Danvers on first enlistment. He is again given as Eames, aged 19, of North Bridgewater, and as enl. same organization, 12 Dec., 1863. "Out" is the same.

BATES.

Roswell D.,
m. 24 Mar., 1865, Co. C, 1st Batt., Me., Inf.; dis. 5 Apr., 1866.

b. Winthrop, Me. Past Commander, Post 90. Lives in Danvers.

BECKET.

Henry,
m. 9 Aug., 1862, Co. K, 17th Inf.; dis. 22 May, 1865, ex. term. Credited to Danvers.

Resided in Danvers; æt. 22 at enl. Lives Joliet, Ill.

BRAGDON.

George F.,
m. 28 Sept., 1861, Co. G, 23rd Inf.; wagoner; dis. 6 Aug., 1862, disability.

Aged 47 at enl.; "of Beverly, stonemason." On hospital rolls "Danvers." A George T. Bragdon, shoemaker, died in Danvers, 29 Mar., 1863, æt. 52, a native of Shapleigh, Me.; buried in Beverly. Left one child.

BURTON.

Jacob,
Additional family record. He was born 15 Aug., 1835; now lives Grand View, Jackson Co., Mo. Son of Stephen and Judith N. (Peaslee, not Clark) Burton; m. Abbie M. Elliott at Danversport. Ch.: James E., b. Peabody, 11 Nov., 1862. Alice P., b. 17 Dec., 1865. Asa, b. Woodville, N. H., 18 Nov., 1875. Eulan, b. 28 Oct., 1877. Helen A., b. 18 Apr., 1880.

CHICK.

Frank M.,
m. 6 Oct., 1864, Co. M, 2d Maine, Cav.; dis. 10 Oct., 1865, ex. term. Residence at enl. Shapleigh, Me.

Lives in Danvers.

COLCORD.

Benjamin F.,
m. 24 Aug., 1861, 3d Inf., N. H. V.; trans. 28 Oct., 1863, to U. S. Signal corps, dis. 24 Aug., 1864. Credited to Rochester, N. H.

TOWN OF DANVERS.

(Colcord Continued.)

b. Oldtown, Me., 22 May, 1836; son of Noah E. and Belinda (Canney) Colcord of Tuftonboro, N. H.; m. Annie S. Kirk of New Albany, Ind. Ch.: Melvin V., b. 6 Nov., 1879. Susan, b. 28 May, 1882. Now a planter at Beresford, Fla. Lives in Danvers.

COLEMAN.
David,

Additional record. He was b. in Cork, Ireland, Apr., 1800; d. 7 Apr., 1877; m. 1st, Bessie Fanning; m. 2d, Marg't O'Reilly. Ch., by 2d w.; Mary E., b. 10 Nov., 1845; m. Thos. R. McDermott, q. v. Thomas, b. 10 Nov., 1845, d. y. Julia A. Margaret. James D. Winifred T. Thomas F. Elizabeth.

COOK.
Benjamin F.,

m. 25 May, 1861, Co. B, 2d Inf.; dis. 21 Feb., 1863, disability.

b. Shapleigh, Me. Lives in Danvers.

CORLISS.
Benjamin M.,

m. 14 Oct., 1861, Co. G, 1st Maine Cav.; dis. 25 Nov., 1864. b. Hartford, Conn.

Lives in Salem; lived in Danvers about 1870-80.

CRANE.
Webster S.,

m. 29 Feb., 1864, Co. E, 31st Maine Inf.; dis. 15 July, 1865.

Now lives in Danvers; b. Edmunds, Me.

DAMON.
William T.,

m. 23 May, 1861, Co. A, 1st Inf.; dis. 23 May, 1864, as sergt.

Born in North Reading; lives in Danvers. Past Commander, Post 90.

DERBY.
Putnam T.,

m. 18 May, 1851, Co. D, 8th Inf.; dis. 1 Aug., 1861, ex. term. Credited to Salem.

Æt. 24 at enl. Co. I, 8th was the famous Salem Zouaves; Capt. Arthur F. Devereux, formerly Co. A, 7th M. M. Now lives in Danvers.

DOWDELL.
Charles,

Additional information. He was born in Dublin, Feb., 1841. Now lives in Danvers. His mother's maiden name was Russell. The correct dates of birth of children, are James, b. 23 Feb., 1866. John H., b. 14 Apr., 1867. Charles D., b. 16 July, 1869. Wm. F., b. 3 Mar., 1872. Jos. R., b. 29 Sept., 1873. He was in forty-four battles and skirmishes.

John,

Additional information. He was born 17 Mar., 1844, at Dublin. He was appointed corporal April, 1864; sergeant Sept., 1864. He was wounded twice, in 1864, face and knee. His wife's name is Catherine E. Loftus. Ch.: John Hancock, b. 22 May, 1887. Fred'k Bean, b. 15 Oct., 1889.
He says "after the battle of Cold Harbor, our regiment numbered 18 men and a sergeant. I was wounded in that battle. When I returned to my regiment at the battle of Reams Station, when the battle was over, I counted twenty-nine guns in our regiment." The regiment was armed with the Enfield rifle and consequently were constantly called upon for skirmishing duty.

EATON.
William Winslow, (M. D.,)

m. 27 June, 1862, asst. surgeon, 16th Me. Inf.; dis. 15 June, 1865.

b. Brunswick, Me., 26 May, 1836; son of William Eaton; m. 1865, Agnes H. Magoun of Brunswick. Lives in Danvers. Past Commander, Post 90.

ELLIS.
Reuben,
m. 19 Nov., 1864, Co. A. 32d Inf.; dis. 4 June, 1865.

b. Yarmouth, N. S.. 1844; son of John and Susan (Perry) Ellis; m. at Danvers, 8 June, 1864. Mary E. Raymond, b. Danvers, 1846. Buried in Danvers.

ENGLAND.
Edwin,
m. 8 June, 1861. Battery G. 2d U. S. Artillery: reenl. 22 Feb., 1864; dis. 22 Feb., 1867, ex. term.

On hospital rolls, reference to Danvers. His first enl. was at Boston; no credit; his second credit to New York. No further information.

FISHER.
Willard P.,
m. 13 Sept., 1862, Co. B, 42d Inf.; reenl.; final dis. 27 June, 1865, from 16th Lt. Batt'y.

b. Holliston; lives in Danvers. Past Com. Post 90.

GOODALE.
Lewis Ebenezer,
Additional record. He appears also as Ebenezer L.; m. 18 Dec., 1868. Sarah J., dau. of Robert and Margaret Finley.

GOULD.
John H.,
m. 22 June, 1861, Co. D, 12th Inf.; dis. 1 Apr. 1863, disability.

b. Danvers.
Lives in Danvers.

HALL.
Lorenzo,
m. 5 Sept., 1861, Co. H. 7th Conn.; dis. 4 Sept., 1864.

b. Mansfield, Conn.; lives in Danvers.

HAYNES.
Joseph W.,
m. 22 July, 1861, Co. A, 17th Inf.: dis. 8 May, 1862, disability.

b. Charlestown. Lives in Danvers.

HITCHCOCK.
Luman,
m. 25 Sept., 1861, Co. C, 20th N. Y. Inf.: dis. 29 Jan., 1866.

b. Blenheim, N. Y. Lives in Danvers.

LEWIS.
Walter R.,
m. 17 Apr., 1861, Co. I, 1st R. I. Inf.; dis. 1 Aug., 1861: reenl. R. I.

b. Charlestown, R. I. Lives in Danvers.

LITTLE.
Frank Henry,
m. 1 Sept., 1862, Co. E, 11th N. H. V. corp.; sergt.; 1st sergt.; dis. 13 July, 1865. O. W. dept.

b. Hampstead, 19 Oct., 1843; son of Nathaniel Hale and Almira (Tuksbury) Little of Hampstead, N. H.: m. Helen Matilda Dow of Atchinson, N. H. Ch.: Ernest Hale, b. 18 Apr., 1870; Frank Werter, b. 26 Aug., 1872; Helen Josephine, b. 3 Nov., 1873: John C. b. 29 June, 1875; Geo. Henry, b. 28 Nov., 1876; Emma Louisa, b. 24 Mar., 1878; Mary Eliz., b. 30 June, 1880; Hattie Atwood, b. 23 Dec., 1882; Henry Curtis, b. 12 Feb., 1885; Minnie Almira, b. 13 Oct., 1886; Jay Carleton. b. 22 July, 1891. Now a resident of Danvers Centre, Mass.

LOVEJOY.
Daniel W.,
m. 5 Jan., 1865, Co. H, 61st Inf.; dis. 16 July, 1865, as corp.

b. Andover. Lives in Danvers.

TOWN OF DANVERS.   77

(Lovejoy Continued.)
Walter S.,
m. 11 May, 1861, Co. F, 2d Inf., corp.; dis. 6 July, 1861: m. 3 Aug., 1861, Co. C, 19th Inf.; dis. 28 Aug., 1861.

b. 25 Aug., 1831, at South Danvers; son of Walter and Mary (Barrett) Lovejoy; m. Anna H. Mailey. Ch.: Mary Anna, b. 2 Aug., 1854; Edw. Franklin, b. 1 Mar., 1863. First enl. recorded as Wm. S. Lovejoy. Lives in Danvers.

McDERMOTT.
Thomas Riley,
m. 30 May, 1862, Co. H, 12th N. Y. Inf.; dis. 8 Oct., 1862; m. 30 June, 1863, Co. G, 12th N. Y. Inf.; dis. 30 July, 1863; m. 27 Nov., 1863, Co. E, 2d N. H. Inf.; dis. 14 June, 1865, on account of wounds. Taken prisoner at Harper's Ferry, 15 June, 1862. Wounded 30 June, 1864, at Petersburg.

b. Sligo, Ireland, 29 Sept., 1845; son of Patrick and Winifred (Manning) McDermott: m. Danvers, 10 Nov., 1868, Mary Ellen Coleman, dau. of David and Margaret (O'Reilly) Coleman, b. 10 Nov., 1845. Ch.: b. all in Danvers. Winifred C., b. 25 Oct., 1869; James M., b. 19 May, 1872; Thos. P., b. 2 April, 1874; Francis J., b. 5 July, 1876; Michael E., b. 25 Sept., 1878; d. 24 July, 1879; Edw. E., b. 17 May, 1880; d. 26 Jan., 1882; Mary V., b. 15 Aug., 1882; Annie J., b. 18 Dec., 1883. Past Commander, Post 90. Lives in Danvers.

MANNING.
Michael,
m. 18 Apr., 1861, Co. D, 11th Inf.; dis. 24 June, 1864. Musician.

b. Ireland, lives Danvers.

MANSFIELD.
Elbridge M.,
m. Sept., 1862, Co. C, 11th N. H.; dis. 12 June, 1865.

b. Lynn, Mass.; lives at Danvers Centre.

MORRISON.
George M.,
Enl. 14 Feb., 1865, Co. A, 1st Batt'y Arty.: dis. 20 Oct., 1865.

b. Safford, Me.; d. 31 July, 1887; buried in Danvers. He was a resident of Danvers prior to the war.

NIMBLETT.
John W.,
m. 29 Aug., 1864, 29th unattached Co. H. A.; dis. 16 June, 1865.

b. Salem, lives Danvers.

O'CONNELL.
Patrick Henry,
m. 5 July, 1861, Co. E, 14th Inf.; taken prisoner at Petersburg, Va., 22 June, 1864; dis. 10 Jan., 1865.

b. Ireland. Escaped from Confederate prison. Lives in Danvers. Past Commander, Post 90.

PAIGE.
George A.,
m. 20 Mar., 1865, Co. K, 14th Maine Inf.: dis. 28 Aug., 1865; of Canaan, Me.

b. Nova Scotia. Lives in E. Danvers. Never married.

PEABODY.
Henry A.,
m. 8 Sept., 1862, Co. B, 8th Inf.; dis. 7 Aug., 1863.

Formerly Danvers resident, now lives in Topsfield.

PERKINS.
John N.,
m. 21 Aug., 1862, Co. A, 48th Inf.; dis. 7 Aug., 1863, ex. term.

b. Newburyport. Lived at Danvers after the war.

PHILBRICK.
John C. H.,
m. 21 Aug., 1862, Co. F, 12th N. H.; dis. 21 June, 1865.

b. Epsom, N. H. Lives in Danvers.

PIERCE.
Charles Frank,
m. 1861, Co. E. 6th Inf.; dis. 16 Apr., 1862. Reenl.
b. Salem. Lives E. Danvers.

PILLSBURY.
Harvey H.,
m. 3 May, 1864, Co. C, 3d unattached Co., Mass.; dis. 5 Aug., 1864; credited to Amesbury.
b. Newburyport. Lives in Danvers. Past Commander, Post 90.

POTTER.
Henry H.,
m. 21 July, 1864, Co. D, 8th Inf.; reenl. 17 Sept., 1864, 2d H. A.; dis. 26 June, 1865. Credited to Topsfield.
b. Topsfield. Lives in Danvers. Past Commander, Post 90.

PRATT.
Samuel S.,
m. 23 May, 1861, Co. H, 1st Inf. sergt.; dis. 28 May, 1864, ex. term, as sergt.; Credited to No. Chelsea.
b. No. Chelsea. Past Commander of Post 90. Lives in Danvers.

PRAY.
Jeremiah H.,
m. 31 Oct., 1861, 1st Maine Cav., sergt.; dis. 1861.
b. Danvers, resident of Shapleigh, Me., at time of enlistment. Æt. 20. m. Dorothy Joy.

RICHMOND.
James W.,
m. 27 Sept., 1861, Co. B, 8th Conn.; dis. 15 Feb., 1863, disability.
Æt. 34 at enl. "of Enfield, Conn." Danvers resident. Now lives at Thompsonville, Conn.

SANGER.
George J., (Rev.)
m. 11 Nov., 1862, 42d Inf., Chaplain; dis. 20 Aug., 1863.
b. Framingham; lived in Danvers now lives in Essex.

SKIDMORE.
J. Warren,
m. 28 Feb., 1865, Co. E, 2d Mass. Cav.; dis. 20 July, 1865. Credited to Newburyport.
b. æt. 18 at enl. Lives at Danversport.

SPAULDING.
Dennison F.,
m. 12 Feb., 1862, Co. K, 7th Vermont; dis. 15 May, 1865.
b. Roxbury, lives in Danvers.

TIBBETS.
Charles,
m. 21 Oct., 1861, Co. H, 5th N. H. Inf.; dis. 6 Apr., 1863, on account of wounds.
b. Wolfboro, N. H. Lives Danversport.

TRICKEY.
William H., (Rev.)
m. 29 July, 1861, Co. G, 3d N. H. private; dis. 2 Aug., 1862 as major.
b. Exeter, Me. Lives in Danvers. Past Dept. Com. of N. H.

TURNER.
Edwin,
m. 19 Sept., 1862, Co. B, 5th Mass., corp.; dis. 2 July, 1863.
b. So. Scituate. Lives in Danvers. Past Com. Post 90.

WEST.
Charles F.,
m. 2 Feb., 1865, Co. I, 61st Inf.; dis. 2 Aug., 1865.
b. Boston. Lived in Danvers; moved 1894; now in Haverhill.

WELLS.
Dennis,
m. 25 July, 1832, Co. E, 23d Inf.; dis. 28 Sept., 1864; reenl. 16 July, 1865, V. R. C.; dis. 15 Jan., 1866.
b. Vincnia, Me. Lives in Danvers.

WOOD.

William H.,
m. 4 Dec., 1861, Co. K, 24th Inf.; dis. 23 Apr., 1863, disability. Credited to So. Boston.

(*Wood Continued.*)
b. Cornwallis, N. S., 12 June, 1818; d. Danvers, 23 Aug., 1894; son of William H. and Margaret (Butler) Wood: m. Martha A. Murton of Cornwallis, N. S. Ch.: Fernando, b. 19 Dec., 1859; Oriana F., b. 24 June, 1862; Wm. O., b. 23 Sept., 1864. Came to Danvers about 1889.

---

*In reply to a letter sent out by the Adjutant General, dated 9 Dec., 1865, seeking information as to the character and behaviour of discharged soldiers, etc., the following answer was returned from Danvers.

"The soldiers who have enlisted from this town have, on the whole, come back better men than when they entered the service. Up to this time none have been convicted of crime, and those who, before entering the army, were addicted to intoxication have some of them reformed, and almost all drink less. So far as we know they have gone to work immediately, and no families are in better circumstances than those of the soldiers."

(Signed) J. A. PUTNAM, for the Selectmen.

Brief Historical Sketches of Organizations of which Danvers Men Formed a Part.

1st Regiment Infantry.

Composed chiefly of the 1st Reg. M. V. M. and left camp the 15th of June, 1861; passed through Baltimore, the 17th of June and arrived at Washington the same day.

It was engaged at Bull Run, the 21st of July, 1861; at Williamsburg, Fair Oaks, Glendale, Malvern Hill, Kettle Run, 2nd Bull Run, Chantilly and Fredericksburg, in 1862, and at Chancellorsville, Gettysburg and Locust Grove, in 1863. In August, September and October it was on garrison duty in New York Harbor. Engaged in the Wilderness and Spottsylvania Court House in 1864. Mustered out the 28th of May, 1864.

This regiment lost 171 men killed, and 643 discharged for disability. At Chancellorsville, Stonewall Jackson was killed by his own men while reconnoitring, but the 1st Mass. claimed that on that very day a party of rebel officers approached their lines so closely, thinking them rebels, and under the conditions described by Jackson's party that they were enabled to open fire at close range. They claimed that Jackson was wounded by that fire.

This was the first three year volunteer regiment that reached Washington.

2nd Regiment Infantry.

Mustered in the 11th of May, 1861, and left the state the 8th of July, 1861, and that year was engaged at Jackson, Va. In 1862 it was at Mont Royal, Winchester, Cedar Mountain, Antietam and Fredericksburg, and in 1863 at Chancellorsville and Gettysburg, and like the 1st was ordered to New York City for the suppression of the draft riots, in the late summer of 1863. In 1864 it was a part of Sherman's army in his march through Georgia.

A great many of this regiment re-enlisted. Mustered out the 14th of July, 1865. Passed through Richmond the 11th of May, 1865, on the march home from the South, where they had taken part in Sherman's campaign in the Carolinas.

5th Regiment, M. V. M.

It was out for three months in 1861, taking part in the Battle of Bull Run, and upon the call for troops for nine months, volunteered as an organization and went into camp at Wenham. In Oct., 1862, it was ordered to Newbern, N. C., where it took part in the various engagements, as Kingston, Whitehall, Goldsboro, and performed much arduous service.

July 28, 1864, the regiment was again mustered into the United States' service and left for Washington. During its first term of service, Col. Lawrence was in command. Col. Pierson, of Salem, was in command during the two later campaigns. Quite a large number of Danvers men went out in the first three month's campaign.

6TH REGIMENT. M. V. M.

This was the second regiment to leave the state on the call for troops, and in passing through Baltimore on the 19th of April, was attacked by a mob.

It was also out for nine months in 1862 and 1863 and stationed at Suffolk, Va., and again in 1864 for 100 days when it was stationed at Fort Delaware, Md.

8TH REGIMENT, M. V. M.

This was one of the first regiments to respond to the call for troops in April, 1861. The Salem Light Infantry left Salem in the morning of the 18th and under the command of Gen. Benj. F. Butler arrived at Annapolis on the 21st of April, where was lying the old frigate, Constitution, which was manned and carried to N. Y. The regiment was on duty about Washington and Baltimore.

In 1862 upon the call for nine months men, the Eighth responded and went into camp at Wenham, and in November sailed for Newbern, N. C., where the regiment was repeatedly called upon for sharp work in reconnoitring, etc., besides having many of its companies detached upon garrison duty. Leaving Newbern in June, they were detained at Baltimore and attached to the Army of the Potomac, but were finally mustered out Aug. 7, 1863.

In 1864 they performed garrison duty at New Bedford. Co. K of this regiment, Capt. Albert G. Allen, was a Danvers company.

9TH INFANTRY.

This regiment was mostly composed of men of Irish parentage. It arrived in Washington the 29th of June, 1861, and was engaged in the battles before Richmond, and in 1862 at Fredericksburg and in 1863 at Chancellorsville, Gettysburg, and Mine Run. During the winter of 1863-64 the regiment were looking after the rebel raiders, especially Mosby and the Black Horse Cavalry.

In 1864 it took part in the battles of the Wilderness, Spottsylvania, Shady Oak, Cold Harbor, etc. Mustered out on the 21st of June, 1864. Loss, 174 killed.

10TH INFANTRY.

It left the state the 25th of July, 1861. It was engaged in the battles before Richmond, and at Fredericksburg in 1862. In 1863 it took part in the battles of Chancellorsville, Gettysburg and Rappahannock Station. In 1864 at the battle of the Wilderness, the regiment lost one third of its force in killed and wounded on the first day. During the succeeding engagements it was constantly in action. It was ordered home in June and mustered out on the 8th of July, 1864. Lost 110 killed.

11TH INFANTRY.

It was mustered in the 13th of June and left the state the 24th of June, 1861. It was at the battle of Bull Run, and in 1862 in the battles before Richmond, second Bull Run and Fredericksburg. In 1863 it was in the battles of Chancellorsville, Gettysburg and Locust Grove.

In 1864 it was in the battles of the Wilderness, Spottsylvania and North Anna.

In June those whose term of service had expired, returned to Boston, and the remainder were strengthened by men from the 1st and 16th regiments. The regiment was engaged at Cold Harbor, Petersburg, and several other lesser battles. Discharged the 14th of July, 1865.

12TH REGIMENT.

It was raised by Col. Fletcher Webster who fell in battle. It left the state the 23rd of July, 1861, and was engaged at the battles of Cedar Mountain, 2nd Bull Run, Antietam and Fredericksburg in 1862, and at Fredericksburg and Gettysburg in 1863.

In 1864 it was a part of Grant's army in his campaign against Richmond. It was engaged in the Wilderness, Spottsylvania, North Anna, Cold Harbor, Petersburg, etc. Mustered out the 8th of July, 1864.

13TH INFANTRY.

It left Massachusetts the 30th of July, 1861. It was engaged in the battles of 2nd Bull Run, Antietam and Fredericksburg in 1862 and at Fredericksburg and Gettysburg in 1863. It was engaged at Spottsylvania and North Anna, Cold Harbor and Petersburg. During this campaign the regiment numbered on duty but about 150 men. Discharged the 16th of July, 1864.

17TH INFANTRY.

This regiment was recruited at Lynnfield and was composed, with the exception of one company each from Suffolk and Middlesex, of Essex County men. Co. C was almost entirely composed of Danvers men. Mustered in July 22, it left the state under the command of Lt. Col. Fellows, 23 Aug., 1861, but was soon after joined by its colonel, Capt. Amory, U. S. A.

During 1861 the regiment was stationed near Baltimore and in Accomac Co., Va., but in the spring of 1862 was ordered to Newbern, N. C., where it engaged in its first battle of consequence, viz., at Kinston and Goldsboro, behaving with great gallantry.

At Goldsboro, Co. C, commanded by Capt. Fuller, did good work on the skirmish line. In the expedition to relieve Washington, N. C., the regiment had to retire with the loss of several men as it was impossible to face the great odds brought against them. The second attempt was successful. During the remainder of the year the regiment was constantly on the alert and took part in several small engagements. On Feb 1, 1864, while supporting the 132d N. Y. Inf., near Bachelder's Creek, Col. Fellows, with 7 officers and 58 men were captured.

In July, Co. C was stationed at Brice's Creek.

July 16, the men whose term expired July 21, embarked for home and the remainder of the regiment was consolidated into companies A, B, and C, under command of Capt. Henry Splaine. This battalion was mustered out 11 July, 1865. In Mar., 1865, 450 recruits from the 2d H. A. were transferred to the 17th.

At the battle of Wise's Forks near Kinston, 7th to 10th March, the regiment did gallant work and contested against overwhelming numbers every inch of ground.

On the 24th March, junction was made with Gen. Sherman and line of march for Raleigh taken up. The regiment reached home July 19, 1865.

23RD INFANTRY.

It left the state, the 11th of Nov., 1861, and was encamped for a time at Annapolis, Md. In Jan., 1862, the regiment sailed for Roanoke Island and took part under Burnside in his campaign. In March they landed at Newbern and took part in the operations about there in 1862 and were in the battles of Kingston, Whitehall, Goldsboro, Wilcox's Bridge and Winton in 1863.

April 26th, 1864, they embarked at Portsmouth for York river and joined Gen. Butler, but in May were detached to reenforce the army of the Potomac and took part in the battles of Cold Harbor and Petersburg. In September they embarked again for Newbern. Those whose terms expired were mustered out the 28th of Sept., 1864. The balance of re-enlisted men and recruits the 25th of June, 1865.

The 23rd took an active part in the so-called second battle of Kingston, see the 17th Inf.

There were quite a number of men from Danvers in the various companies of this Regiment.

35TH INFANTRY.

Mustered into the service the 21st of Aug., 1862, and left the state the next day. This regiment participated in the battles of Antietam, Fredericksburg, Jackson, Spottsylvania, North Anna, Cold Harbor, Weldon R. R., South Mountain, Vicksburg, Petersburg. and many other engagements.

The regiment had a large number of foreigners sent to it while in the field, which caused jealousy and some bad feeling. This feeling passed away in time and the report of the commanding officer is that these men behaved well. Mustered out the 9th of June, 1865.

There was quite a large number of Danvers men in this regiment.

14TH REGIMENT INFANTRY AFTERWARDS 1ST HEAVY ARTILLERY.

This was organized almost entirely from Essex County and was frequently alluded to in '62 as the "Essex County Regiment." It was mustered in at Fort Warren the 5th of July, 1861 and on the 7th of August left for Washington. Co. I of this Regt. was a Danvers company.

The regiment did garrison duty at Ft. Albany and Ft. Runyon, before Washington. On the 1st of Jan., 1862, by orders of the War Dept., the regiment was changed to 1st Mass. Heavy Artillery regiment and the additional men required to bring it up to the standard immediately sent forward. Until the 26th of Aug., the regiment did garrison duty in the forts before Washington but were on that day ordered to Manassas.

On the 28th a number of the regiment were taken prisoners by the enemy, but paroled. During the remainder of the year and the next year the regiment was actively engaged in guarding the defenses before Washington, etc. In June, 1863, Co. L was ordered to Winchester and lost its captain, and 44 men were taken prisoners, thirty-six of whom rejoined the company, Oct. 14.

On the 15th of May, 1864, the regiment marched to join the army of the Potomac, and for the remainder of their term of service were actively engaged at the front participating in the battles of Spottsylvania, North Anna, Tolopotomy, Cold Harbor, Petersburg, Strawberry Plain, Deep Bottom and other engagements. Mustered out the 16th of Aug., 1865. I Company of this regiment were the Putnam Guards, a company almost entirely composed of Danvers men. The company went into camp June 24, 1861, at Fort Warren. Judge A. A. Putnam of Uxbridge, has published an interesting and valuable account of the formation and early history of this organization of which he was the first commander.

2ND HEAVY ARTILLERY.

The companies composing this regiment were mustered in at various dates between Sept , 1863 and Jan , 1864. During its term of service the regiment was stationed in North Carolina, Newbern, etc., and Virginia, and the greater part of the regiment was never engaged in battle.

Companies G and H, about 275 men, were captured at Plymouth, N. C., and were confined in Andersonville. But thirty-five rejoined the regiment. Mustered out the 3rd of Sept., 1865.

3RD REGIMENT, HEAVY ARTILLERY.

This regiment was composed of the 3rd, 6th, 7th, 8th, 9th, 10th, 11th, 12th, 13th, 14th, 15th and 16th unattached companies of heavy artillery, of which the first eight were originally raised for, and for a time were on duty in the coast defenses of this state, but in the fall of 1864 were sent on to Washington and remained on duty in the defences of that city. They were mustered out the 18th of Sept., 1865.

The 13th Co. Unattached Heavy Artillery, Co. L of the 3rd Reg. were on detached duty as engineers. This company was mostly recruited from the Springfield Armory and received great praise.

The Following List is that of Names of Men about whom the Committee have not satisfactory evidence to include in the foregoing lists.

Italics indicate that such a name is not found on the rolls at the Adjutant General's Department.
*Given in town reports 1861-5, as a Danvers man.
†Occurs in former report to the town.

*Baker, ———, " credited to Salem."

*Bradbury, Josiah, " credited to Essex."

‡*Bradbury*, William, said to have been a member of 23d regiment, M. V. M.

Brennan, J W., corp. Co. D, 59th Inf. Gave his residence as Danvers on hospital roll. There was a John W. living in Danvers prior to the war. John W. Brennan, corp. Co. H, 59th, appears on the rolls, as of Harvard.

*Britton, Lewis, " credited to Sharon." There was a Lewis Britton in town, 1865, who married Maria Wilson.

Butler, Pierce, m. 5 July, 1861, Co. A, 1st H. A.; reenl. 25 Nov., 1865; dis. 22 Jan., 1865, died at Ipswich, 22 Jan., 1865. Æt. 20 at enl. He seems to be an Ipswich man, and was credited to Ipswich.

Byrnes, James, m. 11 Dec., 1863, Co B, 17th Inf.; lost at sea, off Sandy Hook, on way to rejoin regiment, 7 June, 1865. Æt. 37 at enl. and married. He was a resident of West Peabody, and was credited to South Danvers.

Clarke, John H., cannot be identified.

*Coleman, Benjamin F., m. 26 May, 1862, Salem Cadets; dis. 11 Oct., 1862. Credited to Salem. Æt. 27 at enl.

Collemy, Charles. buried in Danvers; his grave is yearly decorated by G A. R. Post 90.

*Collemy, Levi F., " credited to Haverhill." A Levi T., was a resident of Danvers in 1863. His wife was Mary Hutchinson.

Fischer, Charles G., gave while in hospital his residence (or that of relatives?) as North Danvers. He was sergt.-major, Co. G, 35th Inf.; but no such person appears on the roll. There was a Charles Gilman Fisher, born in Danvers, 29 Apr., 1849, son of Charles R. and Sophronia Fisher.

‡Forrest, William S., m. 30 Sept., 1862, Co. G, 31st Inf.; dis. 27 July, 1863. Credited to Oxford; m. 22 Dec., 1863, Co. K, 2d H. A., corp.; dis. 3 Sept., 1865. Credited to Oxford. Æt. 42 at enl. He appears to be an Oxford man.

‡Freeze, George A., m. 22 Dec., 1863, Co. K, 2d H. A.; dis. 3 Sept., 1865, ex. term. Of East Saugus, credited to Saugus. Æt. 31 at enl.

*Hayward, George, æt. 28 at enl. Not returned by enrolling officer.
Henderson, Edward, "conscript." Æt. 29 at enl. He was dropped at Long Island.
*Hennessey, Thomas, "New York Regiment."
*Howell, James. He was a Danvers man, and is thought to be a member of a G. A. R. post in Boston.
‡James, William H., m. 12 Oct., 1861; Co. F, 23d Inf.; dis. 12 Nov., 1863, disability; m. 19 Oct., 1864, V. R. C. Credited to Salem. Probably of Topsfield.
Knights, Charles A., not returned by enrolling officer.
*McLoud (McLeod, Alfred), "credited to Salem." Now of Haverhill.
*Morrison, ———, "credited to Salem."
Morrison, George M., born in Safford, Me.; enl. 14 Feb., 1865, in Co. A, 1st Batt'y Art.; dis. 20 Oct., 1865; d. 31 July, 1887. Buried in Danvers.
*Nelson, Henry, "Co. I, 19th Inf." Not found on rolls of that organization.
*Pearsons, Moses T , "credited to Newbury."
*Peterson, John, "reenl. 1st H. A." There was a John J. Peterson in the 1st Batt'y H A. Credited to Duxbury.
*Splane, Edward, "40th N. Y. Vol."
‡Trask Ira F., m. 5 July, 1861, Co. I, 1st H. A.; reenl 29 Jan., 1864; dis. 16 Aug., 1865, ex. term. Credited to Wenham. He does not seem to have been a Danvers resident.
‡Wentworth, Enoch J. He obtained a bounty, but appears never to have been mustered. Is said to reside in Ipswich.

The Monument Erected to the Soldiers and Sailors in the Last War.

In 1868 steps were taken to arrange for the erection of a monument with tablets inscribed with the names of the soldiers and sailors of Danvers who fell in the war. After various votes in the two annual town meetings following, it was finally decided in July, 1870, to erect the monument in front of the town house.

The cost was $6,298.20 of which sum Hon. Edwin Mudge contributed the larger part of his two years salary as representative to the General Court.

The monument was dedicated 30 Nov., 1870. It is of Hallowell granite, thirty-three and one quarter feet high. The following names are inscribed upon the tablets:

Major, Wallace A. Putnam.   Lieutenant, James Hill.

Hector A. Aiken	Daniel H. Gould	Alfred Porter
Henry F. Allen	Samuel S. Grout	Robert W. Putnam
James Battye	Ambrose Hinds	Isaac N. Roberts
Edwin Beckford	Levi Howard	S. P. Richardson
Isaac Bodwell	James J. Hurley	S. A. Rodgers
Sylvester Brown	Thomas Hartman	Israel Roach
James H. Burrows	Abiel A. Horne	Daniel Smith
Lewis Britton	James H. Ham	Henry A. Smith
John H. Bridges	Everson Hall	Wm. E. Sheldon
William H. Croft	Charles Hiller	Chas. W. Sheldon
Simeon Coffin	T. C. Jeffs	John Shackley
H. Cuthbertson	Wm. W. Jessup	Frank Scampton
Thomas Collins	James W. Kelley	Cornelius Sullivan
Wm. H. Channell	Moses A. Kent	Patrick F. Shea
Charles W. Dodge	James E. Lowell	Joseph T. Smart
Geo. H. Dwinell	Samuel A. Lefflau	Edward Splane
Moses Deland	Joseph Leavitt	Milford Tedford
Wm. C. Dale	Charles H. Lyons	Patrick Trainer
Geo. A. Ewell	Charles E. Meader	Wm. F. Twiss
Geo. W. Earl	John Merrill	John N. Thompson
Reuben Ellis	T. A. Musgrave	Austin Upton
Geo. A. Elliott	James Morgan	Angus Ward
Wm. S. Evans	Michael McAuliff	Joseph Woods
Nathaniel P. Fish	Wm. Metzgar	C. E. M. Welch
Benj. M. Fuller	Allen Nourse	George Woodman
Ephraim Getchell	Wm. H. Ogden	John Withey
E. I. Getchell	Wm. H. Parker	Nathaniel K. Wells
William F. Gilford	Geo. W. Peabody	Geo. T. Whitney
John Goodwin	J. Frank Perkins	Joseph F. Wiggin
C. W. C. Goudy	Geo. W. Porter	Charles H. Young
Alonzo Gray	Samuel M. Porter	

The photographs from which the accompanying illustration of the monuments was made are from Frank Cousins' collection of historic views.

LEXINGTON MONUMENT,
PEABODY.

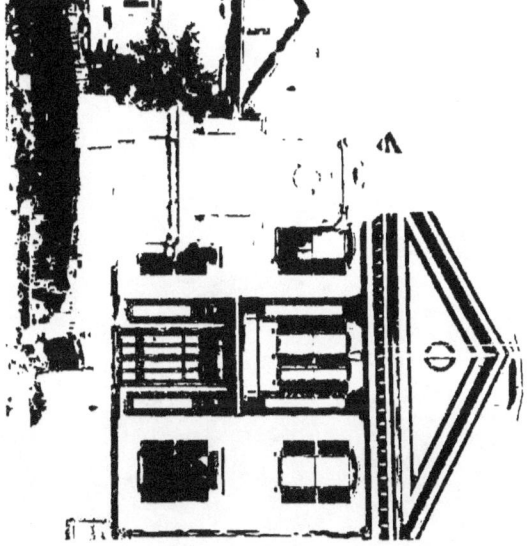

WAR OF 1861 MONUMENT,
DANVERS.

APPENDIX.

EARLY MILITARY ORGANIZATIONS AND SERVICE.

Danvers as a separate district dates only from 1752, but the territory now embraced within its limits and much of the towns of Peabody and Beverly, was early designated as Salem Farms and later as Salem Village, although that part of the present town wherein the first substantial improvements were begun by John Endicott in 1633, was not a portion of Salem Village, but of the old parish in Salem.

The earliest settlers in Danvers may be presumed to be Richard Waterman, a hunter, and a certain "Mr." Freeman, both of whose estates were soon afterward incorporated in the estate of John Putnam. Waterman came over in 1629 as a hunter; of Freeman very little is known except that he was a very early settler near Beaver Brook. Waterman's land was near Davenport's Hill.

John Endicott was the first to improve a farm in the present limits of the town. He set to work as early as 1633 to clear the "Orchard Farm," granted him in the preceding year. From that time on the grants in the "Farms" are of frequent occurrence and were immediately occupied by the more energetic. Thus John Putnam, first on the Plains, and then at Beaver Brook, and Daniel Rea and others, Davenport, Gardner and Reed, noted military leaders of their day, found Danvers a promising field for farming operations and lived here a great part of their time.

So rapid was the settlement and opening up of roads and the country that soon demands were made by the settlers for a separate parish, which question was continually agitated till settled favorably in 1672.

In the early Indian wars, men were drawn from this district to an extent which shows a considerable population of a military spirit. The General Court ordered, in April, 1631, that every captain should train his company on Saturday in every week, and various precautions were taken that the colonists should not expose themselves to the danger of attack by Indians. In November, 1632, monthly training days were appointed, but, five years later, eight trainings a year were considered sufficient.

In 1636, 13 Dec., the military companies were divided into three regiments of which the third was composed of the men of Saugus (now Lynn), Salem, Ipswich and Newbury, of which John Endicott was appointed colonel and John Winthrop, jr., lieutenant colonel It was also ordered that in the future each regiment should each year elect a colonel and lieutenant colonel, and that the several towns should each choose for the positions of captains and lieutenants of the several companies, some principal man, all whom were subject to confirmation by the council.

Capt. (William) Trask was appointed muster master for the East or Essex Regiment. It was during the year 1634, at one of the trainings, that the cross in the colors was cut out. In this were concerned Davenport and Endicott. The colors at that period consisted of a green field with a white union having upon it the red cross of England. On the 25 Aug., 1636, ninety volunteers agreed to go against the Pequots. They were divided into four companies, one of which was commanded by Ensign Davenport and the whole commanded by Endicott. The results of this expedition were the destruction of much corn and property of the Indians and the loss of two soldiers, killed. They returned about the 14th of September.

The following year the military company at Salem was officered by Capt. William Trask, Lieut. Richard Davenport, and Ensign Thomas Beede; and Trask and Davenport, with Salem's quota of 28 men for the Pequot war, joined the Massachusetts force under Stoughton. The expedition returned Aug. 26, having lost none killed, although having had a severe encounter with the Indians in a swamp at Fairfield. After that there were no affairs of consequence to call for military action till the breaking out of the terrible war known as King Philip's War, although on the 20th Aug., 1664,* 200 volunteers were called for to serve against the Dutch, and again 10 Dec., 1673, a levy from each county was made, and ordered to hold themselves in readiness to serve against the Dutch. The fort at Salem was put in a state of repair. The quota of Essex was 100 foot soldiers and thirty troopers, all of which were to be commanded by Daniel Dennison. Geo. Corwin had 8 Oct., 1662, been appointed captain, Thomas Putnam (of the Village) lieutenant, and Walter Price, cornet of the Troop of horse in "Lynn, Salem, etc."

Upon the petition of "Sergeant Major General" Endicott, Wm. Hathorne, Capt. Robert Bridges, and other gentlemen of Lynn and Salem, a military company, to be called the "Military company of Salem and Lynn" was chartered 14 May, 1645. This company on parade made a dashing appearance. In time interest flagged, but in Oct., 1678, a successful attempt was made to reorganize and William Brown, jr., was appointed captain, John Putnam, formerly corporal in the training band, was chosen lieutenant.

Upham says that among the signers to this petition were Anthony Needham, Peter and Ezekiel Cheever, Thomas Flint, Thomas and Benjamin Wilkins, Thomas and Jacob Fuller, John Proctor, William Osborne, Thomas Putnam, jr., and others of the Farms. Each of the officers of this troop were wealthy and took much pride in the display of fine uniforms and trappings.

Again Upham in his admirable history of Salem Village says, "Another marked feature of this people was their military spirit.

---

*This year Walter Price was captain, George Gardner, lieutenant, and Zerubabel Endicott, ensign of the Salem company.

Authority was early obtained from the General Court to form a foot company. All adults of every description belonged to it, including men much beyond middle life—its officers were the fathers of the Village. Every title of rank, from corporal to captain, once obtained, was worne ever after through life." Jonathan Walcott, a deacon of the church was its captain. Nathaniel Ingersoll also a deacon, was successively corporal, sergeant, lieutenant. Thomas Putnam, clerk of the parish, was sergeant. " It was almost as much thought of as the church, officered by the same persons, and composed of the same men. It was a common practice, at the close of a parade, before 'breaking line,' for the captain to give notices of prayer, church or parish meetings."

KING PHILIP'S WAR.

At the opening of the war the colonial militia was quite efficiently organized. The Essex regiment consisted of thirteen foot companies, and one cavalry company. There were 73 organized companies in the Massachusetts colony, besides the " Three County Troop " made up of men of Suffolk, Middlesex and Essex. The highest military office was Major-general and held by Daniel Dennison of Ipswich. The highest regimental officer was a Sergeant-major.

The local companies were not sent on active service out of their towns, but men were impressed from them and placed under officers especially selected by the Council. Each company of foot had a captain, lieutenant, ensign, sergeants, clerk, corporals, and drummer. Cavalry companies had a cornet in place of ensign and a trumpeter, and quartermaster, no drummer. Foot companies were composed of 70 men, horse 50. On special service it was more.

Upon the commencement of the war, the old matchlock musket was in use but was exchanged for the flint-lock as being more serviceable. There were no bayonets, but each company had a certain number of " pikemen." In the campaign culminating in Feb., 1675-76, and in which the memorable assault was made on the Narragansett fort, 19 Dec., 1675, the following men from Capt. George Curwen's company of troopers served in Capt. Prentice's troop of horse, Stephen Haskel, Thomas Putnam, jr.,* Charles Blinkoe, John Richards, Thomas Howard, Nathaniel Ballard, jr., William Dodge, jr., John Edmonds, William Merriam, Thomas Flint, Sr.†, also Joseph Hutchinson and Henry Kenney.‡

---

*Thomas Putnam, son of Thomas, and grandson of John. He is the sergeant Thomas, whose daughter Ann was one of the unfortunates concerned in the Witchcraft delusion a few years later. He married Ann Carr. He was b. 12 Mar., 1652-3 and died 24 May, 1699.
†Thomas Flint, son of Thomas and Ann Flint. It is said he was wounded at the fight in the swamp against the Narragansetts. He married Hannah Moulton who died 30 Mar., 1673, and again 15 Sept., 1674, Mary Dounton. He died 24 May, 1721, æt. about 76.
‡Henry Kenny served under Capt, John Whipple of Ipswich in June, 1676, near Springfield.

The names of Kenny, Hutchinson, Howard, Putnam and Flint are those of Danvers men.

The following names of men who served under Capt. Nicholas Page, in his company of troopers are familiar to Danvers ears, Joseph Proctor, Nathaniel Ingersoll, William Osborn, Joseph Needham, Francis Coard (Caird?), Benjamin Wilkins, John Whipple* (lieut.), Daniel Wilkins. As no places of residence are given we do not here attempt to identify the families to whom they belonged. This troop accompanied Major Thomas Savage in an expedition against Mt. Hope, June to Sept., 1675.

In Mar., 1675-6, a levy of 48 men from Essex Co., and 40 from Norfolk Co., was made to reenforce Major Willard at Groton. These men were placed under command of Capt. Joseph Cook of Cambridge. They arrived at Groton the 14th of March, shortly after the destruction of that place.

BLOODY BROOK.

When Capt. Thomas Lothrop and 71 of his men, almost entirely from the county of Essex, were slain by the Indians at Bloody Brook, 18 Sept., 1675, the consternation throughout the county was general.

Lothrop was among the rate payers of the parish at Salem Village when it was set off from Salem, but his residence was in the present town of Beverly.

Upham says "No man was ever more identified with the history of Salem Farms." He was constantly engaged in military service either against the Indians or the French. The following names of inhabitants of the Farms are found among the list of slain at Bloody Brook.

Thomas Bayley,	Thomas Buckley,
Edward Trask,	Joseph King,
Josiah Dodge,	Robert Wilson,
Peter Woodbury,	James Tufts,
Joseph Balch,	Thomas Smith,† sergt.

Among the names of men under the command of Major Samuel Appleton in the Narragansett campaign occur those of Israel Hen‚ick (Herrick), Thomas Abbey, John Rayment (Raymond), Robert Leach, Samuel Hebbart, Stephen Butler, Samuel Verry, which are all to be found on our early records. As usual in these rolls no places of residence are given, but the company was largely drawn from Essex County.

Among the noted commanders in King Philip's War, was Capt. Joseph Gardner of Salem. He was the son of Thomas and Mar-

---

*Commanded a company of troopers in the next campaign in the spring of 1676.

†Born in the Village, but at this time a resident of Newbury.

garet Gardner and was a man of much importance in the early history of Salem. The company he commanded was composed of men, residents of Salem and vicinity. Among the men of his company who may be claimed for Danvers are William Hathorne, his lieutenant and successor in command,

Joseph Houlton, jr.,   Eleazer Lyndsey,
Thomas Flint,   Thomas Bell,
Thomas Kenny,   *Charles Knight*,
John Stacey,   Isaac Reed.

Capt. Gardner was killed during the battle at the fort and those in italics wounded. The story of the attack and capture of the fort of the Narragansetts and the effectual blow it dealt to Philip has been told again and again. There is no room to repeat it fully here.

The force, commanded in part by two men identified with our town, Gardner and Davenport, and composed largely of men from our county, in the heart of winter, 19 Dec., penetrated the fastnesses of the Indians and in the face of a fearful fire attacked the fort of the enemy. The Massachusetts troops were in the van. Says one historian "in all military history there is not a more daring exploit. Never, on any field, has more heroic prowess been displayed."

Davenport, mentioned above, was the son of Capt. Richard and Elizabeth (Hathorne) Davenport and was born in Salem Village. He was dressed when he fell in a full buff suit. He and Gardner "were both the idols of their men." For some time Davenport had been living in New York. He married Elizabeth, daughter of James Thatcher.

Capt. Richard Davenport has been already mentioned in connection with a command in the Pequot war, and the cutting out of the cross in the flag. He was afterward commandant of the Castle, Boston Harbor.

Besides the men already mentioned as having served in this campaign, Upham gives the following, taken from records in the State archives, who were present at the Narragansett fight, as from Salem Village and its farming neighborhood, viz.

John Dodge,   William Raymond,
William Dodge,   Thomas Raymond,
Joseph Herrick,   Thomas Putnam, jr.,
Thomas Abbey,   Robert Leach,
             Peter Prescott.

Grants of land known as the "Narragansett Townships" were made to the survivors and heirs of the soldiers in the Narragansett expedition. To these grants are due in part the very large migration of the younger sons of Danvers families during the early years of the 18th century.

While the campaign against the Narragansetts was taking place, the garrisons on the Connecticut River were placed under the command of Capt. Jonathan Poole of Reading. Among the men in his command were Joshua and Elisha Fuller, George Eborne, Thomas Bishop, Edward Bishop, William Rayment, Zechariah Herrick, Benjamin Collins, Joseph Jacobs, Caleb Ray, William Stacey, John Dunton.

These men served under Poole at various dates from Oct., 1675 to Oct., 1676. No places of residence are given on the rolls and that the above are names common on our records, and that a large number of Reading men appear on the rolls, is the principal excuse for giving them in this connection.

Jonathan Kettle and Joseph Needham served under Capt. Joseph Sill in June, 1676, John Tarball, and Caleb Ray, in Aug., 1676.

Among the recruits who joined the army after the Narragansett fight was a company from Essex county under Capt. Nicholas Manning of Ipswich. Anthony Needham was lieutenant. On the company rolls occur the names of Richard Scott, John Ballard, Stephen Henrick (Herrick). Thomas Raymond, Richard George. Richard Norman, Thomas Fuller, William Rayment, Joseph Collins, some of whom were undoubtedly from Salem Farms.

A careful examination of the rolls relating to King Philip's War will reveal many names which have their counterparts on our early records, but the data to locate them, as has already been noticed, is extremely hard to obtain. There is an extremely valuable book, prepared by the Rev. George M. Bodge which tells the story of the whole war and gives lists of the soldiers; it is entitled "Soldiers in King Philip's war."

During the years immediately preceding the Witchcraft delusion, there were depredations by the Indians on the frontier.

FRENCH WARS.

The Colonies of Great Britain and France for the whole period of their existence under separate governments, were engaged in continual wars, some of much more consequence than others. The Indian wars during the 18th century were instigated nearly always by the French.

The first of the series of the French and Indian Wars opened in 1689; the last closed in 1763. King William's War, so called, 1689-1697 is memorable for the attack upon Haverhill. Sir William Phips led an expedition from Boston, which captured Port Royal in 1690.

In 1689 (1 April), John Bishop, and Nicholas Reed*, a servant of Edward Putnam, and in 1690. Godfrey Sheldon† were killed by Indians, in the outskirts of Salem. "Thomas Alsob, Edward Crocker, George Ingersoll killed at Casco Bay," on the 4, 5, 6 July respectively.‡ In June, 1693, William Tarbell, a soldier, was killed at the Eastward. In Aug. and October, 1689, Billerica and

---

*21 Sept. he was eighteen years of age.
†3 July he was twenty-four years of age.
‡Church Records.

Newbury were attacked, and in 1698 a destructive assault was made on Haverhill.

The next of the series is known as Queen Anne's War, 1702-13. The French and Indians destroyed Deerfield and the Colonies recaptured Port Royal, which was re-named Annapolis. An expedition against Quebec ended in disaster. Eight men from the Village were impressed to help man the "Flying Horse," of Salem.

The rolls of this war contain Danvers names, but as Danvers was then a part of Salem it is impossible to glean with accuracy. Most of the men recorded below, it will be seen, are enrolled after 1710.

On the 3rd July, 1706, a garrison was stormed at Dunstable, and Holyoke, son of Edward Putnam of Salem Village, was killed, as well as three other soldiers, and on the 29th Aug., 1708 the French and Indians destroyed Haverhill. Upon this alarm the military companies of Salem, including a company of foot and troop of horse from the village hastened to the rescue of the inhabitants and pursued the flying Indians for some distance. Rev. Joseph Green, pastor of the church, seized his gun and joined with his parishioners in the pursuit.

King George's war, 1744-48 is chiefly remarkable for the capture of the famous French stronghold of Louisburg, by Sir William Pepperrell, whose name was well known in Danvers. The capture of this fort was by a land force wholly of New Englanders, but unfortunately the rolls are not complete and such men as went from Danvers are credited to Salem.

The last war of the series usually called the French and Indian War, 1754-63, is the one chiefly with which these records have to do as the armies raised were the largest so far attempted and the drafting from militia regiments was accurately recorded. Thus we have a source of information extremely valuable, making it possible to give definite information concerning the men of Danvers who served in the French Wars. The individual records will be found, alphabetically arranged under the head of "French War Soldiers."

The following summary of events by years will enable the reader to see about what service the various soldiers were engaged in.

1755.

The expedition against the French forts in Nova Scotia was successful. One of the results was the eviction and transportation of 7,000 Acadians from their home to the colonies. About 1,000 of these unfortunate people were settled in Massachusetts.

Two thousand Provincials under John Winslow and Gen. Monckton of the British army took part in this expedition. The same year 3,000 men mostly from Massachusetts and Connecticut and some from New Hampshire under the command of Sir William Johnson were engaged about Lake George. The battle of the 8th of September near Fort Edward resulted in the rout of the French and the capture their commander, Dieskau. Col. Ephraim Webb of Massachusetts was killed.

Further west Gov. Shirley, with a force composed of his own and Sir William Pepperell's regiment, unsuccessfully attempted to capture Fort Niagara on Lake Ontario. The troops returned and went into winter quarters at Albany.

1756.

Gen. Winslow led an expedition against the French at Lake George. This expedition accomplished nothing. Lord Loudoun succeeded Shirley in command in July, 1755.

1757.

Loudoun got as far as Halifax in an expedition against Louisburg. Montcalm, the French leader, captured Fort William Henry, the 9th of Aug., commanded by Col. Monroe. Two thousand men surrendered. Many Danvers men, it will be seen, were there. A horrid massacre was attempted by the Indian allies of the French on account of which the paroled prisoners (18 months), felt that they were free to enter the service again in 1758, and did so in great numbers.

Upon the intelligence of this disaster, 20,000 militia rushed to arms in New England and were placed under the command of Sir William Pepperell who went to Springfield to protect the Western frontier.

This alarm was nearly as generously responded to by the men of Essex Co. as that of the 19th of April, 1775, but no fighting occurred and the term of service was very short.

Seven thousand men were drafted from the "train bands" in Massachusetts, being every fourth free holder training. Gen. Abercrombie, on the 8th of July, attacked Ticonderoga by assault and lost 2,000 men, of whom 500 were from New England. After this assault he retired to Lake George.

1758.

Col. Bradstreet of Mass. and 3,000 men (about 1,000 from Massachusetts) captured Ft. Frontenac on Lake Ontario. Few were killed by the enemy, but a number died of disease. Sir Jeffrey Amherst besieged Louisburg with 3,000 regulars and some provincials. Col. Gridley was there. It was captured the 26th of July.

1759.

Amherst took Crown Point, Ticonderoga, etc., but failed to effect a junction with Wolfe before Quebec. Wolfe had captured Quebec alone the 13th of Sept., 1759.

1760.

10th of Sept., Montreal surrendered. Treaty of Peace, Feb., 1763.

A few words concerning some of the commanders and the companies from Danvers will not be amiss.

During the last French War, companies were raised for the various expeditions against Crown Point, Nova Scotia, or for further service. The men enlisted for those purposes, except that in the last years Amherst enlisted his men "for the complete reduction of Canada." There were several popular leaders in and near Danvers. Capt. William Flint of Reading had a number of men from the outskirts of Danvers in his company. His lieutenant was Eleazer Lyndsey, whose father died in Danvers and owned farms in both Lynn and Salem Village. James Pool was ensign. They were attached to Col. Ichabod Plaisted's regiment, and served from May to December, 1756, at Crown Point.

That same year Capt. Andrew Fuller of Middleton enlisted in his company no less than sixteen Danvers men. They were stationed at Ft. William Henry in October. Joseph Swain, a son of Capt. John of Reading, and the minister at Wenham, was their chaplain. John Calef of Ipswich, afterward famous as a Loyalist in the Revolution, was their surgeon. Both the lieutenant, James Jennison, and the ensign, James Collins, were Danvers young men.

Again in 1758 we find Fuller's company with a large representation from Danvers with Israel Hutchinson as lieutenant, and Richard Skidmore, "old skid" the famous drummer, on the rolls.

Israel Herrick of Boxford in his company of Rangers always had several Danvers men to rely upon. He was engaged on the Eastern frontier, that is in and about Maine.

John Tapley of Salem was captain of a company which was at the surrender of Fort William Henry. Twelve Danvers men were in his company at that time.

In 1759, Israel Davis of Danvers commanded a company which went to Louisburg and remained in the service till 1761, and a large number of his townsmen were in this company.

Many Danvers men, impressed for the war, were however placed in companies raised in other parts of the county. The average age of the men serving from Danvers could not have been much above 21 years, so that it is not to be wondered at the spirit prevailing in 1775, and the knowledge acquired by these men in the French War was used to great advantage in the Revolution.

Soldiers in French and Indian War, 1756-1763.

ABBY, EZEKIEL,
Capt. Andrew Fuller's Co., Col. Bagley's Reg. March to Nov., 1758.

BAKER, OSMAN,
Capt. Israel Herrick's Co., enl. 30 Apr., 1757. Eastern frontier.
b. Beverly, 1734; cooper.

BELL, BENJAMIN,
Capt. John Tapley's Co., 12 Feb. to 8 Nov., 1757. In capitulation at Ft. William Henry. Also served in 1758. Enl. 6 Apr., 1759 under Capt. John Clark for invasion of Canada.
Served 7 April, 1 Nov., in Capt. Davis' Co.: dis. 14 April, 1761.
b. 1736; son of Samuel Bell, who d. 1759, leaving w. Elizabeth and sons Joseph, Samuel, Daniel, and Benjamin.

BROWN, ASA,
Capt. Andrew Fuller's Co., Feb. to Dec., 1756. Crown Point.
b. Danvers, 1736; of Salem, 1756; blacksmith.

BUTLER, RICHARD,
Capt. Israel Herrick's Co., raised for the reduction of Canada, 2 May to 12 June, 1758.

BUXTON, JONATHAN,
enl. 2 Apr., 1759, Col. Plaisted's Reg.
b. 1741, son of Jonathan Buxton.

BUXTON, WILLIAM,
Capt. Flint's Co., 1755.

CARRELL, PATRICK,
Capt. Andrew Fuller's Co., Col. Bagley's Reg.; Mar. to Nov., 1758.
See Revolutionary Soldiers.

CLEMONS, JOHN,
Capt. Samuel Flint's Co., 1755.

CAMPBELL, ALEXANDER,
Capt. Samuel Flint's Co., 1755.

CLARRIDE, LEWIS,
Capt. Samuel Flint's Co., 1755.

CLINTING, JOHN,
Capt. Andrew Fuller's Co., Col. Bagley's reg.; Mar. to Nov., 1758.

COBURN, JOHN,
Capt. Samuel Flint's Co., 1755.

COLLINS, (JEAMS) JAMES,
Ensign in Co. of Capt. Andrew Fuller, 18 Feb., to 1 Dec., 1756, for Crown Point. Ens. in Capt. John Tapley's Co., 12 Feb. to 17 Nov., 1757, at Fort William Henry.
b. Marblehead, 1732; potter.

CROWELL, JOHN,
Served in Nova Scotia, 1756; enl. 2 Apr., 1759, Col. Plaisted's Reg.
b. 10 Apr., 1733; m. Sarah Fowls, who was b. 23 Apr., 1734. Ch.: John E., b. 10 Oct., 1757. See Revolutionary soldiers.

CUNNINGHAM, SAMUEL,
Capt. Andrew Fuller's Co., Feb. to Dec.. 1756. Crown Point.
b. Townsend. 1738.

CURTIS, WILLIAM,
Capt. Samuel Flint's Co., 1755. Capt. Andrew Fuller's Co., Col. Bagley's Reg., Mar. to Nov., 1758.

DAVIS, CHARLES,
enl. 27 Mar., 1759, Capt. Davis' Co.: dis. 14 Apr., 1761. Canada expedition.

DAVIS, ISRAEL,
Capt. in Col. Bagley's regiiment, 31 Mar. to 1 Nov., 1759. Served at Louisburg; dis. 6 May, 1761.

DAVIS, NATHANIEL.
enl. as sergt., 21 Mar. to 24 Oct., Capt. John Tapley's Co.

DUSTAN, ASA,
Capt. Samuel Flint's Co., 1755.

DWINNELL, CHARLES,
Capt. Samuel Flint's Co., 1755. Capt. Andrew Fuller's Co., Plaisted's Reg., Feb. to Dec., 1756. Crown Point. At Fort William Henry, 11 Oct., 1756. In Capt. Moses Parker's Co., 1760.
b. France, 1732; of Boston 1756: cord-wainer.

EDEY, DANIEL.
enl. 2 Apr., 1759, Col. Plaisted's Reg.
b. 1740; servant of Samuel Putnam:

EMERSON, EDWARD,
Lt. in Capt. Davis' Co., Col. Bagley's reg., 31 Mar. to 1 Nov., 1759; at Louisburg; dis. 24 Dec., 1759.

ENDICOTT, JOHN,
Capt. in Col. Plaisted's Reg., 1757, at Lake George. Major in Col. Joseph Frye's Reg., Mar., 1759 to May, 1760.
son of Samuel and Anna (Endicott) Endicott, b. Danvers, 29 Apr., 1713; d. 1783; m. 18 May, 1738, Elizb. Jacobs, who d. Aug., 1809, æt. nearly 91. She it is who impatient at Col. Pickering's delay in marching, 19 Apr., 1775, asked him if he did not hear the guns at Charlestown. Ch.; John, b. 1739; Elizb., b. 1741, d. y.; William, b. 1742; Robert, b. 29 Oct., 1756.

EUSTIS, NATHANIEL,
sergt., Capt. Samuel Flint's Co., 1755.

FELTON, *Edwin* ?,
enl. 6 Apr., 1759, Col. Plaisted's Reg.
son of Jonathan Felton, b. 1740.

FELTON, NATHAN,
Capt. Israel Herrick's Co., Canada, 2 May to 29 Oct., 1758.

FISK, JONATHAN,
enl. 29 Feb.; dis. 8 Dec., 1760, in Capt. Moses Hart's Co.

FLINT, SAMUEL,
Captain in Col. Plaisted's Reg., 1755. Crown Point Expedition. See also under Revolutionary Soldiers.

FLINT, THOMAS,
clerk, Capt. Samuel Flint's Co., 1755.

FORD, JAMES,
Capt. Samuel Flint's Co., 1755.

FOSTER, JOSEPH,
Capt. Israel Herrick's Co., 2 May to 29 Oct., 1758, raised for the reduction of Canada.

FULLER, ANDREW (of Middleton),
Lieut. in Capt. Samuel Flint's Company, 1755, Col. Plaisted's Reg.
b. 1718; husbandman.

GILLINGHAM, JAMES,
enl. 17 Mar., 1760. served in Capt. Israel Herrick's (of Boxford) Company.
b. 1739.

GLOYD, DANIEL,
Capt. Samuel Flint's Co., 1755.
Capt. Andrew Fuller's Co., Feb. to Dec., 1756, for Crown Point. Same Co., Mar. to Nov., 1758; enl. 1759, for Canada Expedition.
b. Danvers, 1736. Of Beverly, 1755-1756; of Danvers, 1758; of Beverly, 1759; servant to Samuel Leach, 1755.

GOLDTHWAITE, JONATHAN,
Capt. Andrew Fuller's Co., Feb. to Dec., 1756. Crown Point. At Lake George, 1757. Enl. 2 Apr., 1759, Canada Expedition, Capt. Davis' Co.; dis. 14 Dec., 1760.
b. Danvers, 1737; blacksmith of Salem, 1756.

GOLDTHWAIT, SAMUEL,
Capt. John Tapley's Co.; enl. 12 Feb.; died 20 Oct., 1757.

GOLDTHWAIT, THOMAS,
Capt. Samuel Flint's Co., 1755; Capt. Andrew Fuller's Co., Feb. to Dec., 1756. Crown Point.
b. Volunston, 1738-9; potter.

GOODALE, AMOS, "of Salem."
Capt. Andrew Fuller's Co., Col. Bagley's Reg., Mar. to Nov., 1758.
svt. to Benj. Russell, 1758.

GOODALE, JAMES,
Capt. Endicott's Co., Col. Plaisted's Reg., at Lake George, 1757.

GOODALE, JOHN,
Capt. Andrew Fuller's Co., Col. Bagley's Reg., Mar. to Nov., 1758.
son of Abraham Goodale.

GREENE, FRANCIS,
Capt. John Tapley's Co., 12 Feb. to 10 Aug., 1757, Ft. William Henry.
svt. to Benj. Goodhue.

GUILFORD, BENJAMIN,
Capt. Andrew Fuller's Co., Col. Bagley's Reg., Mar. to Nov., 1758.
See Revolutionary Soldiers.

GILFORD, WILLIAM,
Capt. John Tapley's Co., 12 Feb. to 8 Nov., 1757. In capitulation at Ft. William Henry. Enl. 23 Mar., 1759, Capt. Davis' Co.; dis. 14 Dec., 1760.
See Revolutionary Soldiers.
son of William and Mary Gilford.

GYLES, SAMUEL, (no residence) sentinel in Capt. Shadrack Walton's Co., and Reg.; enl. 17 July, 1722; died 9 Nov., 1722.
son of John Gyles.

GILES, JONATHAN,
Capt. John Tapley's Co., at Fort William Henry, 17 Mar. to 17 Nov., 1757.

HALL, JOHN,
served from 2 Apr., 1760 to 13 Apr., 1761 in Capt. Davis' Co. at Louisburg.

HALLEY, GERSHOM,
Capt. Samuel Flint's Co., 1755.

HART, EBENEZER,
Capt. Samuel Flint's Co., 1755.

HAYWARD, ARCHELAUS.
Capt. Israel Herrick's Co.; enl. 30 Apr., 1757. Eastern frontier, Capt. Andrew Fuller's Co., Col. Bagley's Reg., Mar. to Nov., 1758.
servant of Gilbert Tapley. 1757; son of Paul Hayward. bapt. 9 Oct., 1737.

HAYWARD, DUDLEY,
Capt. Andrew Fuller's Co., Col. Bagley's Reg., Mar. to Nov., 1758.
bap. 11 Aug., 1734; son of Paul Hayward.

HAYWARD, NICHOLAS
Capt. Herrick's Co., Rangers, Eastern frontier, 2 May to 30 July, 1757.
b. Salem, 1737; housewright.

HAYWARD, SAMUEL,
Capt. Benj. Johnson's (of Woburn) Co., 11 Sept. to 17 Dec., 1755.

HOWARD, DANIEL,
enl. Apr., 1759, for Expedition against Canada.
b. 1740.

HOWARD, SAMUEL,
Col. Richard Saltonstall's Co. and Reg., 15 Mar. to 23 Oct., 1757, at capitulation of Ft. William Henry, 9 Aug., 1757.

HUTCHINSON, EBENEZER,
Capt. Andrew Fuller's Co., Col. Bagley's Reg., Mar. to Nov., 1758.
svt. of Richard Whittredge.

HUTCHINSON, GEORGE,
Capt. Samuel Flint's Co., 1755, at Lake George, 1758; enl. 2 Apr., 1759, Col. Plaisted's Reg.
b. 1 Nov., 1730; d. in Lyndeborough, N. H.; son of Ambrose and Ruth (Leach) Hutchinson; m. 1st, 8 June, 1745, Elizb. Bickford; m. 2d, Susan Bevins. They had 12 ch.

HUTCHINSON, ISRAEL,
sergt. in Capt. Israel Herrick's Co. Rangers, 19 Apr. to 6 Oct., 1757. Eastern frontier in Maine. Lt. in Capt. Andrew Fuller's Co., Col. Jona. Bagley's Reg., Lake George and Ticonderoga, 13 Mar. to 7 Aug., 1758. Captain 1759. Said to have scaled the heights of Abraham with Wolfe, at the head of his company.
See Revolutionary Soldiers.
b. Salem Village (1729, muster roll) bapt. 12 Nov., 1727; son of Elisha and Genger (Porter) Hutchinson; m. 1st, 1748, Anna, dau. of Robert Cue of Wenham; m. 2d, Mehitable, widow of Archelaus Putnam. Ch. by Anna; Genger, b. 23 June, 1749; Anna, b. 26 Mar., 1751; Elizabeth, b. 10 Apr., 1752; Elisha, b. 25 May, 1755; q. v. Rev. Soldiers. Ch. by Mehitable, Israel, b. 27 Sept., 1760. See Rev. Soldiers.

HUTCHINSON, JONATHAN,
killed in battle, 2 Sept., 1758, at Lake George.
b. Danvers, bapt. 26 Oct., 1740; son of Jonathan and Elizb. (Ganson) Hutchinson. The family had removed to Andover in 1750.

HUTCHINSON, SAMUEL,
Capt. Samuel Flint's Co., 1755; recruit; served 31 Aug. to 10 Nov., 1756, under command of James Carr of Woburn.

HUTCHINSON, SAMUEL, JR.,
Capt. John Tapley's Co. at Ft. William Henry, 17 Mar. to 17 Nov., 1757.

JENNISON, JAMES, called Samuel on another roll.
Lt. in Co. of Capt. Andrew Fuller. Col. Plaisted's Reg. Crown Point, 18 Feb. to 1 Dec., 1756.
b. Salem, 1734; merchant; widow Abigail Jennison died 1764, leaving Ch., Samuel, Wm., and Mary, w. of Thomas Giles.

KING, JOHN,
Capt. Israel Herrick's Co., raised for reduction of Canada. 2 May to 29 Oct., 1758.
son of John King.

KINNEY, ANDREW,
With Capt. Herrick at Penobscot, 1759.

KINNEY, JOSIAH,
Capt. Andrew Fuller's Co., Col. Bagley's Reg., Mar. to Nov., 1758.

LARKING, WALTER,
enl. 2 Apr., 1759 in Col. Plaisted's Reg.
b. 1736.

LEATHERBY, JOHN,
Capt. Samuel Flint's Co., 1755.

LEECH, JOHN,
ensign, Capt. Samuel Flint's Co., Col. Plaisted's Reg., 1755; died 30 Oct., 1755.

LEGROW, } PHILIP.
LEGRAW, }
Capt. Samuel Flint's Co., 1755. Capt. Andrew Fuller's Co., 1756.
b. Jersey, 1731; of Andover, 1756; sailor.

LYNDSEY, ELEAZER,
Lt. in Co. of Capt. William Flint of Reading, Col. Ichabod Plaisted's Reg.; m. 7 May, 1756.

MARSHALL, SAMUEL,
Capt. Samuel Flint's Co., 1755; enl. 6 Apr., 1759, for Canada Expedition, Capt. Davis' Co.
b. 1731.

MARSTON, SAMUEL,
Capt. Samuel Flint's Co., 1755.

MASURY (Magery), SAMUEL,
Capt. Samuel Flint's Co., 1755; was at Lake George, 1757; enl. 23 Mar., 1759, for invasion of Canada. Sergt. in Capt. Davis' Co., 23 Mar. to 1 Nov., 1759.
b. Danvers, 1732.

MASURY (Majory), JONATHAN,
Capt. Samuel Flint's Co., 1755; died 26 Nov., 1755.
servant to J. Preston.

MECHAM, JAMES,
Sergt. Capt. Samuel Flint's Co., 1755; died 24 Nov., 1755.

NEWELL, NATHANIEL,
Capt. Andrew Fuller's Co., Col. Bagley's Reg., Mar. to Nov., 1758.

NURSE, DANIEL,
Capt. Samuel Flint's Co., 1755; private in Co. of Capt. Andrew Fuller, Feb. to Dec., 1756. Crown Point, prom. corp., Oct.
Corp. in Capt. John Tapley's Co. at Ft. William Henry, 16 Mar. to 24 Oct., 1757.
b. Danvers, 1734; cordwainer.

OAKMAN, JOHN, of Salem,
Capt. John Tapley's Co., 12 Feb. to 8 Nov., 1757. In capitulation of Ft. William Henry. Capt. Andrew Fuller's Co., Col. Bagley's Reg., Mar. to Nov., 1758; enl. Apr., 1759, for Canada.
svt. of David Britton, 1758; b. 1739; son of Samuel and Rebecca.

PITCHER, JOHN,
Capt. Samuel Flint's Co., 1755. Capt. Andrew Fuller's Co., Feb. to Dec., 1756, for Crown Point. Capt. Andrew Fuller's Co., Col. Bagley's Reg., Mar. to Nov., 1758 at

TOWN OF DANVERS. 105

(Pitcher Continued.)

Lake George; enl. Apr., 1759, for Canada Expedition.
b. Danvers. 1729 or 1731.

PORTER, BENJAMIN,

Capt. Stephen Whipple's Co., Col. Jona. Bagley's Reg., 2 May to 2 Nov., 1758.

PRINCE, NATHAN,

Capt. John Putnam's Co. Capt. Fuller's Co., Col. Bagey's Reg., Mar. to Nov., 1758.
son of Dr. Jona. and Mary (Porter) Prince: b. 21 June, 1738; d. s. p. 22 Nov., 1759.

PROCTER, JONATHAN,

enl. Apr., 1759, for Canada Expedition. Served 23 Mar. to 1 Nov., 1759, Capt. Davis' Co.; dis. 2 May, 1760.
b. 1738.

PUTNAM, ALLEN,

Capt. Israel Herrick's Co., enl. 30 Apr., 1757. Eastern frontier.
b. Salem, 1734; son of Henry Putnam; housewright.

PUTNAM, AMOS,

surgeon in Col. Jona. Bagley's Reg.; enl. 28 Nov., until 31 Mar. Was at Fort Wm. Henry, '56.
b. Sept., 1722; d. 26 July, 1807; son of John and Rachel (Buxton) Putnam; m. 18 Mar., 1743, Hannah Phillips of Danvers; m. 2d. 13 Aug., 1759, Mary Gott of Wenham. Ch.: Jas. P., b. 21 Apr., 1745. Hannah. b. 18 Sept., 1749; m. Nathan Putnam, see Revolutionary Soldiers. Elizb., b. 8 Mar., 1753.

PUTNAM, DANIEL, "of Salem,"

Capt. John Taplin's Co., Col. Jona. Bagley's Reg., 1758.

PUTNAM, EZRA,

sergt., prom. ensign 31 Oct., 1755. Capt. Samuel Flint's Co., 1755. Was an officer at taking of Cape Breton. See Revolutionary Soldiers.

(Putnam Continued.)

b. Salem Village, bapt. 8 June, 1729; d. Marietta, Ohio, 19 Mar., 1811; m. 21 June, 1750; Lucy, dau. Col. David Putnam. Ch.: Betty, b. 18 Mar., 1751. Nehemiah, b. 14 Oct., 1753. Lucy. b. 4 Jan., 1757. Ezra. b. 5 July, 1759, see Revolutionary Soldiers. Deborah, b. 19 Jan., 1761. David, b. 10 July, 1767. John.

PUTNAM, HENRY,

Capt. Andrew Fuller's Co., Feb. to Dec., 1756. Crown Point. At Lake George, 1758; enl. 2 Apr., 1759, Col. Plaisted's Reg.; sergt. in Capt. Davis' Co., at Louisburg, 2 April to 1 Nov., 1759; dis. 17 Nov., 1760.
b. Danvers, 1736; son of Henry and Hannah Putnam.

PUTNAM, ISRAEL, GEN., of Pomfret, Conn. Served in the French and Indian and Spanish Wars. See Revolutionary Soldiers.

PUTNAM, JEREMIAH,

Capt. Andrew Fuller's Co., Feb. to Dec., 1756 at Crown Pt. Capt. Andrew Fuller's Co., Col. Bagley's Reg., Mar. to Nov., 1758; enl. 6 April, 1759 in Col. Plaisted's Reg.
b. Danvers, 31 Oct., 1737; son of Jonathan and Sarah (Perley) Putnam.

PUTNAM, JOHN,

Corp. in Capt. Sam'l Flint's Co., 1755: d. 30 Nov., 1755.

PUTNAM, JONATHAN,

Capt. Fuller's Co., Col. Bagley's Reg., Mar. to Nov., 1758.
bro. of Jeremiah; if so, b. 30 Dec., 1740; d. Nov., 1762.

PUTNAM, UZZIEL,

Corporal in Capt. Samuel Flint's Co., 1755.
b. 1735; died in New Salem; m. —— Ganson; son of Amos and Hannah Putnam. Ch.: Daniel. Samuel. Joseph. Uzziel. Mary.

RAY, PETER (no residence).
Capt. Paul Mascarene's Co. at Annapolis Royal. 1710-11.

REA, CALEB,
surgeon, Col. Jona. Bagley's Reg., 13 Mar. to 2 Nov., 1758.

REED, DANIEL,
Capt. Nehemiah Richard's Co. in Col. Joseph William's Reg., 2 May to 1 Nov., 1758, raised for reduction of Canada.

REED, ISAAC,
Capt. Samuel Flint's Co., 1755; enl. 2 Apr., 1759, Capt. Davis' Co., Col. Bagley's Reg.; dis. 14 Dec., 1760.

RIX, SAMUEL,
Capt. Samuel Flint's Co., 1755.

ROGERS, WILLIAM,
enl. 2 Apr., 1759, Col. Plaisted's Reg.; served from 6 Mar. to 5 Dec., 1760 in Capt. Israel Herrick's Co.
servant of Edmund Putnam; b. 1742.

RUSSELL, JONATHAN,
Capt. Andrew Fuller's Co., Col. Bagley's Reg., Mar. to Nov., 1758.

SAFFORD, JOSHUA,
Capt. Andrew Fuller's Co., Col. Bagley's Reg., Mar. to Nov., 1758.
svt. of Thos. Giles.

SHELDON, SAMUEL,
In Capt. Moses Parker's Co., 1760.
Not known positively to be a Danvers man.

SHELDEN, WILLIAM,
m. 7 May, 1756, in Capt. Wm. Flint's Co., Col. Plaisted's Reg., for Crown Point. In Capt. Moses Parker's Co., 1760.

SILVER, DANIEL,
Capt. Andrew Fuller's Co., Col. Bagley's Reg., Mar. to Nov., 1758.

SKIDMORE, RICHARD, of Middleton,
enl. as drummer 13 Mar.; dis. 9 Dec., 1758, Capt. Andrew Fuller's Co.; dis. 1 Nov., 1759. Capt. Davis' Co.; dis. 15 Apr., 1761. Was in expedition against Havana, 1740.

SMITH, FRANCIS,
Capt. Samuel Flint's Co., 1755.

SMITH, PETER,
Capt. Samuel Flint's Co., 1755.

SMITH, THOMAS,
Capt. Samuel Flint's Co., 1755.

SPENCE, GEORGE, of Beverly, 1756,
sergt. in Capt. Samuel Flint's Co., 1755. Capt. Andrew Fuller's Co., at Ft. Edward, 26 July, 1756.
b. London, 1734; tailor.

STACEY, JOHN,
Capt. Andrew Fuller's Co., Feb. to Dec., 1756. Crown Point. Taken prisoner prior to October.
b. Ipswich, 1736; joiner.

STAFFORD, JOSHUA,
enl. 29 Feb.; dis. 8 Dec., 1760. Capt. Moses Hart's Co.

STONE, ROBERT,
Capt. Andrew Fuller's Co., Col. Bagley's Reg., Mar. to Nov., 1758; enl. 6 Apr., 1759. Capt. Davis' Co., Col. Bagley's Reg.; dis. 9 Nov., 1760. Robert Stone " of Salem, æt. 27", enl. Apr., 1759, for Canada Expedition.

STONEING, GEORGE,
Capt. Andrew Fuller's Co., Feb. to Dec., 1756. Crown Point; ditto Mar. to Nov., 1758, at Lake George; enl. 2 Apr., 1759, Col. Plaisted's Reg.; enl. 2 Apr., 1759, Capt. Davis' Co., Col. Bagley's Reg. at Louisburg. Served 6 Mar. to 6 Dec., 1760 in Capt. Nathan Bailey's Co.
b. Danvers, 1730; prob. son of George Stoneing of Danvers who d. July, 1752, leaving a son Samuel who m. Mary, and died 1761.

SWINNERTON, JOB,
sentinel in Col. Shadrack Walton's Co. and Reg.
In Capt. Jacob Tilton's Co., 17 July to 14 Nov., 1722.

TAYLOR, ELIPHALET,
in Capt. Samuel Flint's Co., 1755. Capt. Andrew Fuller's Co., Col. Bagley's Reg., Mar. to Nov., 1758.

TOWN, JONATHAN,
In Capt. Moses Parker's Co. Perhaps a Danvers man.

TOWN, SAMUEL,
Capt. John Tapley's Co. at Ft. William Henry, 17 Mar. to 17 Nov., 1757.

TOWN, SOLOMON,
Capt. Israel Herrick's Co., enl. 28 Apr., 1757. Eastern frontier. Capt. Andrew Fuller's Co., Col. Bagley's Reg., Mar. to Nov., 1758. With Capt. Herrick at Penobscot, 1759; enl. 25 Feb., 1760. Served 5 Mar. to 5 Dec., 1760, in Capt. Israel Herrick's Co.
son of Daniel Town, b. Topsfield. (Middleton), 1739; housewright.

TOWN, THOMAS,
With Capt. Herrick at Penobscot, 1759.

TOWN, WILLIAM,
Capt. John Tapley's Co., 12 Feb. to 8 Nov., 1757. In capitulation of Ft. William Henry. Sergt. in Capt. Andrew Fuller's Co., Col. Bagley's Reg., Mar. to Nov., 1758.

TRASK, JONATHAN,
Capt. Andrew Fuller's Co., Feb. to Dec., 1756. Crown Point, prom. sergt. Oct.
b. Salem, 1727.

TUKESBURY (Dukesbury), JOHN,
At Lake George, 1758; enl. 2 Apr., 1759, for expedition against Canada, in Capt. Davis' Co.; dis. 24 Dec., 1759.
b. 1738.

TWIST, BENJAMIN,
Capt. Andrew Fuller's Co., Col. Bagley's Reg., Mar. to Nov., 1758.
son of Joseph Twist.

UPTON, DANIEL,
Capt. Andrew Fuller's Co., Col. Bagley's Reg., Mar. to Nov., 1768.
b. North Reading, 19 Aug., 1731; d. prev. 1759; son Wm. and Lydia (Burnap) Upton. Ch.: b. Danvers, Daniel, b. 1755; d. 1765. Huldah, b. 1757.

VERRY, BENJAMIN,
at Lake George, 1758; enl. Apr., 1759, for Canada Expedition. Corp. in Capt. Davis' Co., 2 Apr. to 1 Nov., 1759; dis. 17 Nov., 1760.
b. 1733.

VERRY, ISAAC, of Salem,
Capt. John Tapley's Co., Col. Bagley's Reg., 1758. There were also in the same organization, Samuel Verry "of Salem": Joseph Verry, Jr., who enl. Apr., 1759; and Joseph Verry, who enl. 6 Apr.,

(*Verry Continued.*)
1759. He was dis. 17 Nov., 1760, from Capt. Davis' Co. at Louisburg.

VERRY, SAMUEL,
in Capt. Samuel Flint's Co., 1755. See above.

WHIPPLE, JOB,
Corp. in Capt. Paul Mascarene's Co., Sir Charles Hobbs' Reg. of N. E. troops, 10 Oct., 1710 to 10 Oct., 1711 at Annapolis Royal.

WHIPPLE, JOB,
Capt. Israel Herrick's Co.; enl. 28 Apr., 1757; eastern frontier. Enl. Apr., 1759 for Canada. See also Revolutionary Soldiers.
servant to Israel Hutchinson, 1757; b. Danvers, 28 May, 1739; brother of Matthew; housewright.

WHIPPLE, MATTHEW,
Capt. Andrew Fuller's Co.; enl. 22 Apr., 1756, for Crown Point; prom. sergt. 26 June.
b. Danvers, 28 Feb., 1726-7; son of Joseph and Sarah (Swinnerton) Whipple; m. Sarah Putnam of Bedford. Ch.: Mathew, b. 20 Mar., 1754. Benj., b. 5 Sept., 1756. He is called "sailor" on muster roll. Mrs. Whipple, m. 2d. Samuel Herrick of Reading.

WHIPPLE, STEPHEN,
Capt. John Tapley's Co., 12 Feb. to 8 Nov., 1757. In capitulation of Ft. Wm. Henry. In Capt. Andrew Fuller's Co., Col. Bagley's Reg., Mar. to Nov., 1758.
svt. of Phineas Putnam.

WHITMORE, NATHANIEL, JR.,
enl. 6 Apr., 1759, for Canada Expedition. He was with Capt. Davis at Louisburg.
b. 1739; son of Nathaniel Whitmore.

WHITTEMORE, JONATHAN,
Recruit; served 31 Aug. to 10 Nov., 1756, under James Carr of Woburn.

WHITECAR (Whittaker) ABRAM,
Capt. Andrew Fuller's Co., Col. Bagley's Reg., Mar. to Nov., 1758. Enl. 2 Apr., 1759, Col. Plaisted's Reg.
b. 1736.

WOODBERRY, ANDREW, of Beverly, Capt. Andrew Fuller's Co., Feb. to Dec., 1756. Crown Point.
b. Ipswich, 1737; joiner.

WOODMAN, BENJAMIN,
enl. 2 Apr., 1759, Capt. Davis' Co.

WOODMAN, NATHANIEL,
in Capt. Samuel Flint's Co., 1755.

WYAT, ABRAHAM, of "Salem." Capt. John Taplin's (*sic*) Co., Col. Bagley's Reg., 1758.

WYATT, NATHAN,
Capt. Andrew Fuller's Co., Col. Bagley's Reg., Mar. to Nov., 1758. Lake George. Enl. 29 Mar., 1759, Col. Plaisted's Reg.
b. 1734.

After the conquest of Canada, the militia of Essex County was organized into seven regiments, the Danvers companies being placed in the 1st regiment with those of Salem, Lynn, Beverly and Middleton. In Jan., 1766, Danvers had two militia companies, with officers as follows :

1st company,
Elisha Flint, captain,
Archelaus Putnam, lieutenant.
Oliver Putnam, ensign.

2d company,
John Epes, captain,
John Proctor, jr., lieutenant.
Francis Epes, ensign.

The Troop of Horse connected with the regiment was officered as follows:
Daniel Mackey, captain,
John Wilkins, lieutenant,
Cornelius Tarbell, cornet,
John Putnam, quartermaster.

In April, 1766, the second company was officered as follows:
Thomas Porter, captain,
Joseph Southwick, lieutenant,
Benj. Procter, ensign.

Unless as I suspect this was a new company and the one formerly known as the 2d became the 3d.

In 1771, the 1st Essex Regiment was commanded by Col. William Brown and the three Danvers companies were officered as follows:

1st company,
Caleb Low, captain,
Ezekiel Marsh, jr., lieutenant,
John Dodge, ensign.

2d company,
Not commissioned.

3d company.‡
Jeremiah Page, captain,
Enoch Putnam, lieutenant.
Elias Endicott, ensign.

William Proctor was captain of the Troop of Horse.

At the outbreak of the Revolution, Samuel Flint commanded one company of the militia; Samuel Epes the other company of militia; the remaining six companies which responded to the Lexington Alarm were "Alarm Companies" or "Lists" and "Minute Men." Upon the alarm that Col. Leslie was marching to Salem, 26 Feb., 1775, to destroy stores, the minute men of Danvers quickly responded, and had not the British retraced their steps after crossing the North River, the first battle of the Revolution would have been fought at Gardner's Hill. The rolls of these eight companies numbering in all 303 men* are given below.

---

‡For interesting facts regarding this organization see Revolutionary Soldiers under Jeremiah Page.

*The names of the Lexington Alarm Men, who saw no further service are not repeated in the lists of Revolutionary soldiers given on pages 111 et seq.

"LEXINGTON ALARM." 19 April, 1775.

Muster Roll of Alarm Company in Danvers commanded by Capt. John Putnam, who marched in defence of the country, on the 19th April, 1775.

JOHN PUTNAM, *Captain.*

Gilbert Tapley, *Lieut.*
George Small, *ensign.*
Francis Nurse, *Sergt.*

Cornelius Tarbell, *Sergt.*
Skelton Sheldon, *Sergt.*
John Walcott, *Corp.*

Asa Putnam. *Clerk.*

Privates.

Samuel Cheever	James Prince, jr.	George Kelley
Caleb Clarke	Daniel Prince	(Anthony) Buxton
Peter Cross	Jona Russell	Israel Cheever
Jona. Cutler	John Russell	James Swinerton
Samuel Marble	John Rea	Benj. Russell, jr.
Nathaniel Pope	John Swinerton	Enos Putnam
Eleazer Pope	George Wiat	James Phillips Putnam
Amos Putnam	Samuel White	John Oaks
Phineas Putnam	Eb Holt	Joseph Putnam

NOTE.—This company marched 40 miles except the last seven men who are credited with but thirty miles. All are credited with two days service.

Muster Roll of Company in Danvers commanded by Capt. Jeremiah Page, who marched in defence of the country, on the 19th April, 1775.

JEREMIAH PAGE, *Captain.*

Jos. Porter, *1st Lieut.*
Henry Putnam, *Sergt.*

Richard Skidmore, *Sergt.*
Samuel Stickney, *Corp.*

Privates.

James Putnam	Elisha Hutchinson	Nathan Porter
Benjamin, jr.	Asa Stickney	Samuel Whittemore
Daniel Bootman	Matthew Whipple	Nathaniel Putnam
David Bootman	Enoch Thurston	Peter Putnam
John Nichols, jr.	Phillip Nurs	Samuel Fowler
John Brown	Robert Endacott	Samuel Dutch
Jethro Putnam	David Felton	Benj. Kent
Jeremiah Putnam	Daniel Verry	Ebenezer Jacobs, jr.
William Fenno	David Verry	Samuel Page
John Wood	Arch'l Rea, jr.	Stephen Putnam
Michael Webb	James Goady	Joseph Smith
Benjamin Kimball		

NOTE.—This company marched 40 miles and are credited with two days service.

TOWN OF DANVERS. 111

Muster Roll of Alarm Company in Danvers, commanded by Capt. Edmund Putnam, who marched in defence of the country, 19th Apr., 1775.

EDMUND PUTNAM,‡ *Captain.*

Benjamin Balch, *Lieut.*   Tarrant Putnam, *Ensign.*

Sergeants.

Benjamin Putnam*   Samuel Clarke*
Benjamin Porter†   Joseph Jackson

Privates.

John Nichols   Samuel Andrews   Nathaniel Webb
Archelaus Dale   Patrick Carrell   Benj. Porter, jr.*
Archelaus Rea   Aaron Putnam*   Wm. Hilbord
John Sheldon

*Marched 30 miles. †Marched 36 miles. ‡This company with the exceptions noted above marched 40 miles and with the exception of Benjamin and Aaron Putnam are credited with two days service. The two above excepted with one days service.

A Muster Roll of the men who marched under the command of Capt. Asa Prince, on ye 19th April, 1775, in defence of ye country.

ASA PRINCE, *Captain.*

Ezra Putnam, *Lieut.**   Jeremiah Hutchinson, *Ensign.*

Sergeants.   *Corporals.*

Benj. Gardner*   Elijah Wilkins
Arch. Bachelor*   Moses Prince
Ezekiel Cooper   Joseph Putnam
Benj. Peabody   Aquilla Wilkins

Privates.

Benj. Gilford   Asa Brown   Enos Wilkins
Israel Putnam   Israel Curtis, jr.   Arch'l Kinney
Samuel Whipple   James Johnson   Richard Thomas
Wm. Berry   Peter Porter   Richard Thomas
Samuel Wiot   Ab'l Dempsey   John Flint, jr.
Amos Dwinnell   Phineas Putnam   John Fuller
Levi Howard   Andrew Gray   Francis Peabody, jr.
John White   James Buxton   John Wright
Joshua Wiot   Stephen Nichols, jr.

In addition to the above the following names are scratched off the roll, Andrew Elliot, Joseph Nichols, Stephen Nichols, jr.

NOTE.—These men with the exception of the last nine, marched 50 miles. The nine excepted marched 55 miles. The company is credited with two days service. Those starred among the officers also marched 55 miles.

A Muster Roll of Capt. Sam'l Flint's of ye militia, in the regiment whereof Timothy Pickering jr., Esq., was Col., and who marched on the 19th Apr., last past, in consequence of the alarm made on said day, dated at Danvers, Dec. 20, 1775.

SAMUEL FLINT, *Captain.*

Daniel Putnam, *Lieut.*   Joseph Putnam, jr., *2d Lieut.*
Israel Putnam, *Ensign.*

Sergeants.   *Corporals.*

Asa Upton   Wm. Putnam, jr.
Abel Nichols   Joseph Dwinnell
Thomas Anderson   Joshua Dodge
Amos Tapley   Jona. Sheldon

Privates.

William Goodell	Simon Mudge	Eleazer Goodall
Benj. Russell, 3d	Wm. Whittredge	Amos Buxton, jr.
Matthew Putnam	Eben'r McIntyer	Peter Putnam
John Hutchinson, jr.	Josiah Whittredge	Reuben Barthirck
Aaron Tapley	John Kittle	John Preston
John Hutchinson	Benj. Nurs	James Burch
Jethro Russell	Levi Preston	Daniel Lakman
Stephen Russell	Aaron Gilbert	Michael Cross
George Small, jr.	Nathaniel Smith*	Israel Cheever
Nathaniel Pope, jr.	Jona. Russell	Israel Smith
Joseph Tapley	Daniel Russell	Eleazer Pope, jr.

NOTE.—*Went to Ipswich with prisoner. This company with the exception of Smith marched 40 miles. He marched 60; and all are credited with two days service.

A Muster Roll of the officers and men who marched on the 19th April, 1775, under command of Samuel Epes, Col. Pickering's regiment.

SAMUEL EPES, *Captain.*

Benj. Jacobs, 1st *Lieut.*   James Osborne. *Sergt.*
Gideon Foster, 2d *Lieut.*   Jona. Tarbel, *Sergt.*
Fras. Symonds, 2d *Lieut.*   Benj. Doughty, jr. *Sergt.*

Corporals.   *Drummers.*

Aaron Osborn   Wm. Tarble
John Epes   Abra. Reddinton
Andrew Curtis
Isaac Twiss

Privates.

Israel Osborn	Jona. Procter	Nathaniel Fitts
Nathan Upton	Timothy Felton	Wm. Frost
Robert Stone, jr.	Eben'r Felton	Newhall Wilson
Abel McIntier, jr.	Asa Felton	Jona]Wilson, 3d
Richard Phillips	Thos. Andrews	Barth'w Motton
Joseph Whitemore	Joseph Osborne, 4th	Hab Lynse
John Wilson, jr.	Daniel Reed	Eben Motton
Samuel Small	Jona. Southwick	Jona. Ridney
Benj. Epes	Thomas Day	John Collins
Joseph Epes	James Goldthwait	Jacob Reed
Nathaniel Goldthwait	Samuel Cook, jr.*	Abijah Reed
Daniel Motton	James Epes	Thos. Bond
John Reed	Wm. Southwick	John Getchel
Daniel Marsh, jr.	John Southwick, 3d	Solomon Wyman
Wm. Goldthwait	George Twiss	Samuel Stone
Marble Osborn	John Southwick, 4th	James Stone
Joseph Osborne, 3d	John Curtis	Joseph Twist
John Jacobs	Job Wilson	Stephen Twist
Thomas Gardner, jr.	Robert Wilson, 3d	Wm. Perkins
Silvester Osborn	Isaac Wilson, 3d	Benj. Dealand, jr.*
Amos King	Joshua Motton	Henry Jacobs, jr.*
Jonathan Nurse	Joseph Ingalls	George Southwick, jr.*
Jona. Felton	David Newhall	Eben'r Goldthwaite*

*Marched 20 miles. The rest marched 45 miles. All are credited with two days service.

A Muster Roll of a Minute Company under command of Capt. Israel Hutchinson.

ISRAEL HUTCHINSON, *Captain.*

Eben Francis,* *Lieut.*   Enoch Putnam, 2d *Lieut.*
John Woodbury,* *Ensign.*

TOWN OF DANVERS.

<table>
<tr><td>Sergeants.
Aaron Cheever
Job Whipple
Asa Brown*
Thomas Francis*</td><td></td><td>Corporals.
James Friend*
Samuel Goodridge
Eliphalet Perley
Francis Smith*
Nathaniel Oliver</td></tr>
</table>

Privates.

Eben Andrews	Samuel Baker	Nathan Putnam
James Burley	Samuel Fairfield	Wm. Towns
Samuel Chase	Benj. Porter, 3d	Wm. Warner
Nat Duston	Jona. Sawyer	Perley Putnam
James Porter	Henry Dwinnell	Benj. Shaw
Tarrant Putnam, jr.	John Francis	Wm. Batchelder
Thomas White, jr.	Wm. Freetoe	Jotham Webb

All of Danvers except those starred.

From Beverly.

Elisha Dodge	John Bachellor, jr.	John Smith
John Dodge	Reuben Kinston	Wm. Woodbury
Asa Herrick	Benj. Shaw, jr.	Nathan Cleves
John Jones	Gideon Woodbury	Joseph Raymond
Jona. Perkins	Gideon Batchelor	Daniel Twist
Samuel Woodbury, jr.	Nathaniel Dodge	Andrew Elliot
Wm. Dodge, jr.		

A Roll of Capt. Caleb Lowe's company belonging to Danvers, who marched on the 19th of April last, against the British Troops.

CALEB LOWE,† *Captain.*
Ezekiel Marsh, jr., §*Lieut.*   John Dodge, 2d *Lieut.*

Privates.

Thomas Gardner§	John Brown‡	Joseph Stacey
Stephen Needham	John Upton	Ezekiel Marsh††
Benjamin Needham	John Marsh§	Robert Shillaber
Hezek Dunklie§	Jona. King	John Molton
Ezra Trask	Jona. Trask	Thomas Whiterage§
Benjamin Morton§	Eben'r Spraguett	Zachariah King§
Abel McIntier	Doctor Joseph Osgood†	

---

*From Beverly. The Beverly men marched 54 miles. The rest 50 miles. All are credited with two days service.
††Marched 15 miles. †Marched 50 miles. ‡Marched 35 miles. §Marched 30 miles. With the above exceptions, the company marched 40 miles. No time specified.

MILITIA COMPANIES OF DANVERS DURING THE REVOLUTION.

In the possession of Mrs. Elizabeth Putnam, widow of Captain Andrew Putnam of Danvers, are a number of ancient papers among them several lists of militia organizations in Danvers during the Revolution, which we print below. Mrs. Putnam is a granddaughter of the John Preston† to whom these papers belonged.

†Since printing the list of French War soldiers, the fact that Levi Preston of Danvers was a soldier has been discovered. His record is given below.
PHILLIP PRESTON served in the second Louisburg campaign as is shown by the following extract from his brother John Preston's diary. "June 10, 1745, my brother listed for Cape Britton. Sailed from Boston, June 26, and arrived at Louisburg harbor July 6, and wrote me a letter dated July 7. I received it July 27. Aug. 13, he was brought home sick."
Phillip Preston the subject of the above note died Apr. 14, 1748.
He was the son of John and Elizabeth (Voden) Preston, and was born Mar. 6, 1719. He married Ruth, dau. of Thomas and Elizabeth (Whipple) Putnam.

Those names starred have been scratched in the original.

The first company in Danvers, Nov. ye 26, 1776.
Nathaniel Pope, James Smith, James Prince, George Small, jr., Peter Putnam, Eleazer Pope, Capt. Samuel Flint*, Hon. Samuel Holton, William Goodale, Ebenezer Goodale, Walter Smith, Samuel Endicut, Joseph Tapley, Lt. Jeremy Hutchinson*.
Lieut. Joseph Putnam.
Second company. Every fifth man.
Ebenezer Sprague, Robert Sheliber, Daniel Jacobs, jr., Nathaniel Fitts, Aaron Osborn.
Second company.
Robert Willson, 3d, Jonathan Felton, Zachariah King, Ebenezer Southwick, jr., Benjamin Willson, Joseph Whittermore, Lt. John Endicott, Isaac Willson, jr., Ensign John Dodge, Major Samuel Epes, Isaac Southwick, jr.
Third company.
Deacon Edmund Putnam, Joseph Endicott, Ensign Stephen Putnam, Lt. Archelaus Putnam, Nathaniel Brown, David Prince.
Fourth company.
John Needham, Asa Felton, Ebenezer Larribee, Nathaniel Putney, Ebenezer Moulton, Benjamin Procter.
On the reverse.
One colonel, two lieutenant colonels, three majors, twenty or thirty drummers and fifers, ninety odd serjeants, 740 rank and file.
A List of Capt. Wm. Townes' company, Oct. ye 22, 1778. John Preston, April, 1779.

Sergeants.
Joseph Putnam,* William Goodell, Benjamin Nurse, Matthew Putnam.

Corporals.
Joseph Dwinel, Benjamin Russell, Levi Preston, Daniel Verry.

The Training Band.
Danvers, Oct. 22, 1778.

Amos Buxton	Joseph Crose	Timothy Fuller
Asa Brown	Nathan Crose	Eleazer Goodell
Ebenezer Brown	Ezekiel Chever*	William Giffard*
William Berey*	William Cheever*	Moses Gilford
John Crowel*	Nathan Chever	William Gifford*
Israel Chever, jr.	Joshua Dodge	Moses Goodall*
John Crowel, jr.*	Elijah Flint	Aaron Gilford

TOWN OF DANVERS. 114*

John Holtt*	Israel Putnam, jr.*	Amos Sheldon*
Job Holtt*	Israel Porter	John Swinnerton, jr.*
Levi Hayward*	Elisha Putnam	Francis Smithe*
John Hutchinson	Eleazer Pope, jr.	Jonathan Sheldon*
Nich. Hayward*	Nathaniel Pope, jr.*	Ebenezer Sawyer*
John Holman	Jasper Pope*	Israel Smith
William Holt*	Joseph Putnam, sr.	Joseph Standley
Enoch Jarvice	Joseph Prince	Francis Sheldon
Ebenezer Larebee*	Daniel Putnam, jr.	Joseph Tapley*
Ephraim Larebee	Timothy Putnam	Asa Tapley
Simon Mudge	Timothy Patch*	William Tarbel*
Elijah Moulton*	James Prince	Enoch Thurston*
Thomas Moulton*	Joseph Pope	Ely Upton
Benjamin Nichols	John Rea	Daniel Verey
Ely Nurse*	Jethro Russell	Wm. Whitredge
James Nichols*	William Russell	Issiah Whitredge*
James Putnam	Ely Russell*	Joseph White
Eleazer Putnam	John Russell*	Richard Whiteredge, jr.
Levi Preston	John Swinnerton	Jonathan Wolcott*
Moses Preston*	Elisha Swinnerton*	Joshua Wiatt*
Peter Putnam	Bartholomew Smith, jr.	Samuel White, jr.
William Putnam	George Small, jr.	Solomon Wilkins
John Kettell, lieut.		

In another book apparently of latter date occur the same names as above with some additions which appear below. This list appears to be a clean copy of the above.

ADDITIONAL NAMES ON SECOND LIST.

William Flint, Jacob Goodale, Ebenezer Hutchinson, Benjamin Nichols, Zephaniah Pope, Jonathan Russell, Jethro Russell, jr., Daniel Shelden, John Smith, George Wiatt, jr.

Preceding the revised list is an "Alarm List" as follows.

Thomas Andrew, Joseph Brown, Israel Chever, Samuel Chever, Caleb Clarke, Peter Crose, Michael Crose, Samuel Endicott, Benjamin Gilford, James Goodale, Robert Hutchinson, Lt. Jeremy Hutchinson, Levi Hayward, Samuel Marble, Capt. John Putnam, Capt. Asa Prince, Lt. Daniel Putnam*, Lt. Joseph Putnam, Ensign Oliver Putnam, Nathaniel Pope, Eleazer Pope, James Prince, James Phillips Putnam, Phinehas Putnam, Benjamin Russell, jr., John Russell, George Small, James Smith, James Swinerton, Walter Smith, Skelton Shelden, Nathaniel Smith, Gilbert Tapley, Ezra Upton, Asa Upton, George Wiatt, John Walcott.

On another list of the same company dated July, the same names occur and in addition Israel Chever, jr. The Joseph Putnams are further distinguished as "3d" and "4th." On the "Alarm List" are placed Deacon Asa Putnam, Enos Putnam, Lt. John Stacey, Stephen Smith and Samuel Wiatt. Gilbert and Amos Tapley are both styled Lieutenants.

A return of Capt. Willm. Townes' company.
  1 Subaltearn
Clerk 1
Sergts. 4
Rank and File 63   Alarm List 30
Continental   Continental Servis 3
Absent in the State Servis 4
Priveteering 4
  Danvers, December ye 8, 1778. The above is a Return of the Training Band and Alarm List of the First Company in Danvers.

Amos Tapley, 2d Lt., under date of May 9th and Oct. 17th, 1777, gives to John Preston receipts for money toward hiring men for three years service in the continental army.

Privateers from Danvers.

During the Revolution, the Jupiter, Harlequin, Gen. Greene, and many other privateers and vessels of war, besides merchant vessels were built at Danversport. Four twenty gun ships were built in the Revolution. The anchors of the celebrated frigate Essex were made at the Iron Works. (*Hanson*, p. 111). It will be also recalled that the stern post of the Essex was a part of the tree which stood in the field opposite the Collins house to which tree the British soldiers who were camped there in 1774, were tied for flogging, when occasion arose.

The name of but one of the privateersmen has been obtained, as follows:

Hines, Wm., entered on board the sloop (General) Gates, (a privateer) 10 July, 1778, at Salem, bound on a cruise to the eastward toward the Gulf of St. Lawrence. Was Master's Mate on said Sloop, which was captured in July, 1778, by British frigate Triton, carried to Quebec, afterwards taken to England, lodged in Forton Prison near Portsmouth, England, in which he died on the 14th day of June, 1781, after a 3 years captivity.

Gen. Gage in Danvers.

Gen. Gage then the Royal governor of Massachusetts took up his residence in the Collins house, 5 June, 1774. On the 21st July, two companies of the 64th Reg. Royal troops arrived and encamped opposite the mansion. The British returned to Boston, 5 Sept., 1774. During this period the Page mansion was occupied in part, as an office and headquarters.

In a field on the south side of Sylvan Street, in the rear of the residence of I. P. Andrews, Esq., are the unmarked graves of several British soldiers.

List of Revolutionary Soldiers.

Allen, Jacob,
enl. 8 May, 1775, 3 mos., Capt. Gideon Foster's Co., Col. Mansfield's Reg.; on coast rolls, 19th Reg., Capt. Baker's Co., Oct. 27, 1775; enl. 1777 for 3 years, Continental Army.

Allen, Isaac, of New Gloucester, recruit 29 Aug., 1776, for Capt. Mayberry's Co., Col. Eben Francis' Reg. at Dorchester. Enl. 27 Oct., 1777 for Danvers; served 3 yrs. Continental Army, Capt. Turner's Co.; trans. 1780 to Scott's Light Inf. Co., Col. Jackson's Reg.
Claimed by both New Gloucester and Danvers, awarded to New Gloucester.
There was a pensioner of this name residing in Essex Co., æt. 76, 13 Aug., 1833. He was prob. the Isaac Allen of Gloucester who enl. 1776 in Capt. Bradbury Saunders Co.: dis. 31 May, 1776.

Andrew, Thomas.
Lexington Alarm, Capt. Eppes Co. Enl. 29 Apr., 1777, Capt. Silas Adam's Co., Titcomb's Reg.; enl. 25 Aug., 1777; dis. 30 Nov., 1777, Capt. Flint's Co., Col. Johnson's Reg.

prob. b. 20 Oct., 1736, and son of Thos. and Sarah (Jacobs) Andrew; m. Sarah. Ch.: Anna, b. 11 Nov., 1762; Hannah, b. 9 Oct., 1764.

Andrews, Ebenezer,
enl. 4 May, 1775; reenl.: on coat roll, 26 Oct., 1775, Capt. Francis' Co., Mansfield's Reg.

Ayers, Jonathan, of Buxton, enl. 1777 for 3 yrs., Continental Army.

Balch, (Rev.) Benjamin,
Lieut. in Capt. Edmund Putnam's Co., Lexington Alarm: was Chaplain of Col. Ephraim Doolittle's Reg., 8 mos. service, siege of Boston. Drafted May or June, 1778 to serve as a private in Continental Army, when he petitioned in vain for a release. Was appointed chaplain on frigate Alliance, and afterward enl. 28 Oct., 1778, as chaplain, on frigate Boston.

born Dedham, 12 Feb., 1743; d. Barrington, N. H., 4 May, 1815; son of Thos. and Mary (Sumner) Balch; H. C., 1763; m. 1764, Joanna O'Brien, born in Scarboro. At outbreak of Revolution lived in Danvers, having come from Mendon, where he was settled from 1768 to 1772. Settled in Barrington in 1784. Ch.: Thos., b. 2 Oct., 1765; q. v. Benj., b. 5 Jan., 1768; d. 10 Apr., 1809, q. v. Mary, b. 11 June, 1770, d. 30 Aug., 1855. John, b. 4 Sept., 1772; d. 5 Aug., 1843. Wm., b. 17 Jan., 1775; d. 31 Aug., 1842. Geo. Washington, b. 16 Oct., 1777; d. 21 June, 1826. Horatio Gates, b. 3 July, 1780; d. 1850. Joanna, b. 3 July, 1780. Martha, b. 19 Jan., 1783; d. Feb., 1866. Jeremiah O., b. 31 July, 1785; d. 5 Nov., 1875. Hannah, b. 20 July, 1791. Joseph, b. 7 Nov., 1794; d. 22 June, 1797.

BALCH, BENJAMIN. JR.,
appears on pay roll of the Alliance, same date as father and brother.
b. Dedham, 5 Jan., 1768; d. unm., at sea, 10 Apr., 1800; son of Rev. Benj. Balch.

BALCH, THOMAS,
Powder boy on frigate Alliance in Capt. Paul Jones' squadron, and received a pension for disabilities. Also served on frigate Boston, Capt. McNeil. Enl. 1780, on privateer Hannibal, of 25 guns, Capt. Jere. O'Brien of Marblehead, and that year was taken prisoner and confined in Jersey prison ship at New York. After his exchange enl. at Boston on the U. S. frigate Alliance, Capt. James Barry, and served on her as a marine until her return to Boston, Dec., 1781.
b. Scarboro, Me., 2 Oct., 1765; d. Waterloo, N. Y., Jan., 1839; son of Rev. Benj. Balch; m. 10 Nov., 1793, Elizb. Kingman, b. 16 Aug., 1774; d. Barrington, 21 Apr., 1802. Ch.: Joanna, b. 5 May, 1794; d. Oct., 1863. Benj., b. 2 May, 1796; d. 28 Jan., 1869. Dolly, b. 10 Sept., 1799; d. 28 July, 1870. He m. 2d, 6 Dec., 1803, Judith (Swain) Perkins, b. 10 Aug., 1773. Ch.: Elizb., b. 4 Feb., 1805. Lucy C., b. 22 Dec., 1807. Lucretia, b. 16 Dec., 1814; d. 4 Feb., 1833.

BARRETT, JOSEPH,
Quarter gunner on U. S. Frigate Decatur, in the fight with the Guerrierre.
There was a Joseph Barrett a seaman on the brigantine Massachusetts, commanded by John Fiske; enl. 22 Feb., 1777; and was serving in Oct., 1777.

BARKER, PETER,
arrived at Fishkill, 27 June, 1778; m. 9 Aug., 1778, at Fishkill for 9 mos., Continen-

(*Barker Continued*.)
tal Army. Received a pension; resided in Essex Co., 7 Sept., 1820; transferred to N. H. Agency, 4 Mar., 1820.
In 1778, æt. 22, 5 ft., 9 in. hgt; light hair and eyes, dark complexion.

BARKER, RICHARD,
m. 9 Aug., 1778, at Fishkill; served 9 mos., Continental Army; enl. 12 July, 1781 for 3 yrs., Continental Army.
at Hospital, New Windsor, Feb. 1783.

BARNAM, ELIJAH.
enl. 1777, 3 yrs., Continental Army.

BATCHELDER, GIDEON,
enl. 1775, corp.; prom. sergt. Capt. Low's Co., Col. Mansfield's (19th) Reg.; coat roll 21 Oct., 1775.
prob. son of John (who d. 1753) and Jemima Batchelder, b. (æt. above 14 in 1753).

BEARY, BENJAMIN,
enl. 1777 for 3 years in Major's Co., 12th Reg., Continental Army; served 6 mos., 6 days; taken prisoner.
There was a Benj. Berry, 2d, of Essex Co., a pensioner, who d. 31 Dec., 1830, æt. 87.

BELL, DANIEL,
enl. 1 Dec., 1779, 3 yrs., drummer, Capt. Daniel's Co., 6th Reg.; promoted; enl. 1778 (æt. 16, 5 ft., sandy complexion), and forwarded to Capt. Putnam at Fishkill in Dec.
b. 8 Oct., 1762; d. 28 July, 1810, at Danvers, painter; m. 28 Oct., 1784, Hannah Verry, b. 25 Sept., 1758; d. 9 Sept., 1839. Ch.: Hannah, b. 28 May, 1785. Samuel, b. 8 June, 1786; d. Harvard, 24 Mar., 1811. Mary, b. 2 Dec., 1787. Sarah, b. 13 Oct., 1790. Daniel Calder, b. 4 Sept., 1793. Geo. F., b. 20 Apr., 1801.

BELL, DAVID,
  enl. 1777, during war. Capt. Daniel's Co., 6th Reg.. Continental Army ; served 14 mos.

BELL, JOSEPH,
  enl. 22 July, 1775, Capt. Foster's Co., Col. Mansfield's Reg. ; on coat rolls 27 Oct., 1775. Capt. Baker's Co., 19th Reg.: enl. 16 Jan., 1777, for 3 yrs., Continental Army, Capt. Sam'l Foster's Co., Col. Greaton's (2d) Reg.: reported deserted prior to 25 Aug., 1777; credited to Salem.
  Joseph Bell and Mary Soomes, m. 29 Oct., 1754.

BIRCH, JAMES,
  enl. 4 May, 1775, Capt. Eben'r Francis' Co., Mansfield's Reg. ; said to be of Topsfield ; on coat roll, 26 Oct., 1775; enl. 8 Feb., 1777, for 3 yrs. Light Inf. Co., 13th Reg., Continental Army ; served 36 mos.
  son of James Burch of Topsfield (died before 1770), b. 1755; int. of m. with Sarah Gale, 13 Dec., 1788, who m. 2d. 20 Oct.. 1808. Moses Hoyt.

BOND, THOMAS,
  Lexington Alarm, Capt. Eppes' Co. ; enl. 8 May, 1775, for 3 mos., Capt. Foster's Co., Col. Mansfield's Reg.: also Capt. Baker' Co., 19th Reg., 6 Oct., 1775 ; enl. 1777 for 3 yrs., Continental Army.

BRAY, ZACHARIAH,
  enl. 5 July, 1780 for 6 mos.: dis. 5 Jan.. 1781 (2d Reg.?).

BROWN, JOHN,
  enl. 20 Mar., 1777, for Bennington Expedition, Capt. Page's Co., Col. Francis' Reg.: also in Capt. Flint's Co., Col. Johnson's Reg.

BROWN, THOMAS,
  enl. 25 Aug., 1777 ; dis. 14 Dec., 1777, Capt. Flint's Co., Col. Johnson's Reg.

BUFFINGTON, ZADOCK,
  Capt. in Col. Johnson's Reg., 1777.
  Son of James Buffington. Lived in Salem most of his life.

BUKLEY, JAMES,
  enl. 4 May, 1775, Capt. Francis' Co., Col. Mansfield's Reg.: 1 Aug., 1775.*

BURNS, THOMAS," a transient,"
  enl. 1777 for 3 yrs., Continental Army.

BUXTON, JAMES,
  Lexington Alarm, Capt. Asa Prince's Co. Enl. 4 May, 1775, Capt. Prince's Co., 19th Reg.; on coat roll, 21 Dec., 1775; returned home from Albany, a member of Capt. Stephen Wilkin's Co., Col. Wigglesworth's Reg. Enl. as ensign, 1 Jan., 1777, 11th Reg. and was appointed Lieut.,Capt. Samuel Page's (7th) Co., 11th Reg.: 7 Nov., 1777, at West Point; prom. Adj., Apr., 1780 : prom. Capt. 28 Feb., 1781. Appointed Capt. in 10th Mass., 1 Jan., 1782.

BUXTON, PETER,
  enl. 15 July, 1780 for 6 mos.: dis. 15 Aug., 1780.
  æt. 44 yrs.; 6 ft., 1 in. Negro.

BUXTON, PRINCE,
  enl. 29 May, 1775, Capt. Gallusha's Co., 25th Reg.; in service Oct., 1775.

---

*Dates following the number or names of regiments as in this case, show that the man was in the service at that time.

CALLAHAN, JOHN, "a transient,"
enl. 1777, for 3 yrs., Continental Army.

CANNADA, SILAS,
enl. prior to Sept., 1776, in service, 24 Dec., Capt. Gilman's Co., 4th Reg.: enl. 10 Mar., 1777 for 3 yrs., Capt. Page's Co., 11th Reg., Continental Army; dis. 10 Mar., 1780 from Tupper's Reg.

laborer, d. Danvers; Adm. on estate, 26 Apr., 1785.

CARPENTER, URIAH,
enl. 29 Mar., 1781, for 3 yrs., Continental Army.

CARROLL, JOHN,
enl. 21 July, 1776, reenl. 1 Aug., 1776, Capt. James Gray's Co., Col. Marshall's Reg.; dis. 1 Nov., 1776; reenl. Nov., 1776; in service 3 Dec., 1776.

CARRIEL, PATRICK,
Lexington Alarm. Capt. Edmund Putnam's Co.: enl. 1 July, 1776, Capt. Gray's Co., Col. Marshall's Reg.; reenl. 8 Aug., 1776, in service 3 Dec., 1776, same Co.: enl. 10 Sept., 1777, for 3 yrs., Capt. Hatfield White's Co., 5th Reg.: served 24 mos.: died 10 Sept., 1779.

brickmaker; adm. to his widow Amme Carroll, 5 Aug., 1800; m. 13 Dec., 1759, Amma Porter. She died 1810 or 11. Ch.: John, b. 22 Aug., 1762, Wm., b. 17 Apr., 1764, Michael, b. 25 Jan., 1766, Margaret, b. 25 Mar., 1768; bap. middle parish, So. Danvers.
He was in French War, 1758.

CARRIEL (CARROLL), WILLIAM,
enl. 26 Feb., 1781, for 3 yrs., Continental Army.

prob. son of Patrick Carriel, above; m. 18 May, 1788, Hannah Page.

CARSON, JAMES,
enl. 20 Mar., 1777, for Bennington Expedition; marched 8 Apr.: Capt. Samuel Page's Co., Col. Francis' Reg.

CHASE, JOHN, of Brunswick,
enl. 1777, for 3 yrs., Continental Army.

CHANDLER, ASA,
enl. 6 Oct., 1775, Capt. Baker's Co., 19th Reg.

prob. Asa Chandler of Andover.

CHENEY, ENOCH, of Methuen,
m. 9 Aug., 1778, at Fishkill, 9 mos., Continental Army.

COOPER, EZEKIEL,
enl. 1775; sergt. Capt. Prince's Co., 19th Reg.: 6 Oct., 1775.

m. 23 Oct., 1766, Hannah Smith.

COLLINS, JOHN,
sergt. in Capt. Baker's Co., 19th Reg., 1 Oct., 1775.

m. Margaret. Ch.: Mary, b. 14 Aug., 1766, Jedidiah, b. 17 Aug., 1768, John, b. 3 Aug., 1771, Betsey, b. 8 Apr., 1780.

COLYER, JONATHAN,
enl. 1775, Capt. Prince's Co., 19th Reg.; in service 6 Oct., 1775.

COOK, DANIEL,
enl. 1777, for 3 years, Continental Army.

CREER, THOMAS,
enl. 20 Mar., 1777, for Bennington Expedition, Capt. Page's Co., Col. Francis' Reg.

CRISPIN, RICHARD,
enl. Capt. Baker's Co., 19th Reg.: 1 Oct., 1775.

m. 4 June, 1778, Mehitable Moulton, jr. A Wm. Crispin of Salem, living 1789, was m. 15 June, 1755, to Margaret Swazey, jr.; perhaps he a son of Richard who m. 15 Feb., 1731-32, Mary Hamilton.

CROWEL, JONATHAN, (prob. JOHN),
enl. 1775, Capt. Putnam's Co., 19th Reg.; in service 6 Oct., 1775.

CROWELL, JOHN,
enl. 25 Aug., 1777; dis. 14 Dec., 1777, Capt. Flint's Co., Col. Johnson's Reg.; enl. 1778 and in Dec. sent forward to Capt. Putnam at Fishkill, Continental Army.
son of John and Sarah (Fowls) Crowell; b. Danvers, 10 Oct., 1757; m. 4 Sept., 1777, Betty Masury. See French War Soldiers.

CURRIER, JONATHAN, of Bow,
m. 9 Aug., 1778, at Fishkill, 9 mos., Continental Army.

CUTLER, JOSIAH,
recruit for Capt. Gardner's Company, Continental Army, at Fishkill, Dec., 1778.

CURTIS, JOHN,
enl. 1775-76, Capt. Gay's Co., Col. Francis's Reg.; 2 days service, marched 31 miles.
m. 30 Nov., 1777, Mary Collins.

DALE, EBENEZER,
enl. 1775, Capt. Prince's Co., 19th Reg.; 6 Oct., 1775.
b. Danvers, 7 Mar., 1730-31; d. 1772, son of John, (d. Danvers, 13 Apr., 1763) and Abigail (d. Danvers, 22 Apr., 1777) m. Rebecca. Ch.: Eben'r, b. 25 Dec., 1755 (this may be the one whose record is given above). Anna, b. 27 Sept., 1757. Thos., b. 19 Aug., 1759. Samuel, b. 23 July, 1761. Rebecca, b 27 Apr., 1764. Eben Dale, m. Abigail Cutler, of Beverly, pub. 5 Dec., 1780. Ch.: Ebenezer, b. 13 Oct., 1781. Martha, b. 23 Oct., 1784.

DALE, SAMUEL,
recruit, 1778, for Continental Army at Fishkill, 9 mos.
b. Danvers, 23 July, 1761, son of Ebenezer and Rebecca Dale, above.

DAWN, JAMES, "a transient,"
enl. 1777, for 3 years, Continental Army.

DEANE, SAMUEL,
m. at Fishkill, 1778, 9 mos., Continental Army.

DEMPSEY, ABRAHAM,
enl. 1775, Capt. Prince's Co., 19th Reg.; 6 Oct., 1775.
b. Danvers, 17 Feb., 1756; son of Isaac (b. Danvers, 30 Aug., 1728, son of Christopher and Elizh.) and Ruth (d. 11 Apr., 1761) Dempsey.

DERBY, CHARLES,
enl. 1777 for 3 years, Continental Army.
b. Danvers, 7 Sept., 1756; son of Samuel and Hannah Derby; m. Tabitha Getchel. Ch.: Hannah, b. Marblehead, 26 July, 1781. Lucretia, b. 4 Aug., 1783. Sally, b. 14 July, 1786.

DEVERIX, CATO,
enl. 25 Aug., 1777; dis. 14 Dec., 1777, Capt. Flint's Co., Col. Johnson's Reg.

DODGE, FRANCIS,
enl. 25 Aug., 1777; dis. 14 Dec., 1777, Capt. Flint's Co., Col. Johnson's Reg.

DODGE, WILLIAM,
enl. 1775, Capt. Gallusha's Co., 25th Reg.; Oct., 1775; enl. 1777, during war, 2d Co., 9th Reg., Continental Army.

DOLE, JOSEPH,
enl. 1776, Capt. Gray's Co., Col. Marshall's Reg.; 15 July, 1776.
Adm. on his estate, 11 July, 1783 to widow Ruth. He a shipwright; m. 19 Dec., 1765, Ruth Endicott; she d. 7 Sept., 1828, æt. about 90.

DOW, NATHAN,
enl. 1778; sent to Fishkill, Dec., 1778 to join Capt. Putnam's Company, Continental Army; reported at Spring-

(*Dow Continued.*)
field, 18 Aug., 1779 as a recruit (9 mos.) for Capt. Putnam's Co., Col. Thorndike's Reg., æt. 24 : 5 ft., 8 in., dark complexion : enl. 15 July, 1780, for 6 mos. ; enl. 27 Nov., 1780, 3rd Reg. Art'y, Capt. Shaw's Co. for 3 years.

DUSTON, NATHANIEL,
enl. 4 May, 1775, Capt. Francis's Co., Col. Mansfield's Reg.; 1 Aug., 1775.

DWINNELL, AMOS,
enl. 1775, Capt. Prince's Co., 19th Reg.; 6 Oct., 1775.
b. Topsfield, 1754; son of Zechariah Dwinnell of Ipswich and Topsfield, who d. 1757.

DWINNELL, GEORGE,
enl. 1775, Capt. Putnam's Co., 19th Reg. : 6 Oct., 1775 : enl. 15 July, 1776, Capt. Gray's Co., Col. Marshall's Reg.
m. 1 Apr., 1773, Susanna Sheldon.

DWINNELL, HENRY,
enl. 1775, Capt. Putnam's Co., 19th Reg.; 6 Oct., 1775.
Henry Dwinnell of Newbury m. Lydia Curtice of Danvers, 16 June, 1779.

DWYER, JOHN,
enl. 13 Mar., 1777, for Bennington Expedition, Capt. Page's Co., Col. Francis's Reg.; "a transient," enl. 1777 for 3 years, Continental Army.

EATON, WILLIAM,
enl. 27 June, 1781 for 3 yrs., Continental Army.

ELLIOTT, RICHARD,
enl. July, 1780 for 6 mos. Continental Army, æt. 17, 5 ft., 5 in., dark complexion., Received pension 1836.
d. Danvers, 1849; perhaps the Richard who m. 10 Mar., 1802, Polly

(*Elliott Continued.*)
Macintire and had Richard, b. 17 Dec., 1802.

EPPES, JOHN,
enl. 24 May, 1775, sergt., Capt. Barnes' Co., Col. Hutchinson's Reg.; return dated 1 Aug., 1775.
prob. son of Daniel Eppes of Danvers, who d. 1764.

FAIRFIELD, JOHN,
enl. 20 Feb., 1777, for Bennington Expedition, Capt. Page's Co., Col. Francis's Reg.: enl. 1777, for 3 yrs. Capt. Page's Co., 11th Reg., Continental Army; served 36 mos.
prob. b. in Wenham. John Fairfield, of New Boston, N. H., m. at Danvers, 9 Dec., 1799, to Hitty Baker of Wenham.

FELTON, ANTHONY,
enl. 25 Aug., 1777; dis. 14 Dec., 1777; Capt. Samuel Flint's Co., Col. Johnson's Reg.
bap. 1736; d. Danvers, 26 Apr., 1789; son of Jonathan and Rebecca (Needham) Felton; m. (pub. 11 Dec., 1763) Elizb. Pickard of Boxford, who d. 2 Aug., 1781. Ch.: Jedidiah, b. 17 May, 1768; m. Mary Proctor. He m. 2d, 2 Dec., 1781, Elizb. Nichols who d. 2 Aug., 1808.

FELTON, DAVID,
enl. 1776, Capt. Gray's Co., Col. Marshall's Reg.; 15 July, 1776.
b. 20 Apr., 1757; d. M'lr'd 15 Oct., 1818; son of Samuel and Mary (Smith) Felton; m. 1784, Hannah Swinton who d. 25 Feb., 1825, æt. 66. Ch.: John Swinton, b. 2 Oct., 1787. David, b. 3 Feb., 1794, d. 5 Nov., 1796. Andrew, b. 17 Dec., 1797; d. 9 July, 1798. Hannah, b. 30 Oct., 1800, m Jas. Sleeper.

FELTON, FORTUNE, negro,
recruit for Continental Army at Fishkill, Dec., 1778.

FISK, JOHN,
  enl. 6 Sept., 1781, for 3 yrs., Continental Army.
  m. 23 Jan., 1791. Huldah Woodbury of Beverly.

FLINT, JOSEPH,
  enl. 1775 or '76, Capt. Gay's Co., Col. Francis' Reg.: 2 days service: marched 31 miles.
  b. 21 Apr., 1759; d. 19 July, 1787, son of William and Ruth (Newman) Flint; m. July, 1780, Elizabeth Whittredge. Ch.: Ruth, b. 29 Jan., 1782. Joseph, b. 19 Apr., 1784. Ebenezer, b. 17 Nov., 1786.

FLINT, SAMUEL,
  enl. 1775; served 8 mos.; enl. 15 Aug., 1777, as Capt.: dis. 7 Oct., 1777, Col. Johnson's Reg.; killed at battle of Stillwater, 7 Oct., 1777.
  b. 9 Apr., 1733; son of Samuel (b. 29 Sept., 1693) and Ruth (Putnam, dau. of John and Hannah, b. 13 Feb., 1703) Flint; m. 12 Jan., 1758, Ede, dau. of Jos. and Mary Upton. b. 1739; d. 6 July, 1812. Ch.: Ruth, b. 17 Oct., 1758; m. Jona Sheldon. Samuel, b. 23 Aug., 1760; d. Oct., 1769. Elijah, b. 16 July, 1762. Ede, b. 18 Apr., 1764; m. Daniel Needham. Hezekiah, b 31 Jan., 1766. John, b. 16 Feb., 1768. Polly, b. 5 May, 1770; m. Sam'l Aborn. Samuel, b. 9 June, 1772. Benj., b. 25 Nov., 1774. Nancy b. 16 Sept., 1777; m. 4 July, 1788, Enoch Abbott.

FLINT, WILLIAM,
  Capt. Jona Procter's Co., Col. Jacob Gerrish's Reg., enl. 12 Nov., 1777; dis. 3 Feb. 1778: no residence. Received pension as of Danvers, 1836.

FOSTER, GIDEON,
  2d Lieut., Samuel Epes' Co., Lexington Alarm; also served in Mass. Militia in the war. Chosen Major General by the Legislature, 1801. Revolutionary pensioner in 1836.

(*Foster Continued.*)
  born So. Danvers, 13 Feb., 1748-49; d. 1 Nov., 1845; son of Gideon Foster; m. 18 June, 1771, Mercy Jacobs; m. 2d, 23 Nov., 1828, Mary Tapley.

FOSTER, JOSEPH,
  enl. 12 Mar., 1781, for 3 yrs., Continental Army.
  b. 6 Nov., 1752; adm. on estate of Joseph Foster, baker, of Danvers, to Henry Rust, 19 Apr., 1809; m. Sarah, (b. 4 Nov., 1750). Ch.: Joseph, b. 4 Aug., 1775. Sarah, b. 27 Mar., 1777. Elizb., b. 25 Dec., 1780; d. 25 Apr., 1793. John, b. 11 Dec., 1782; d. 21 Feb., 1785. Mary, b. 31 Mar., 1784. Polly, b. 13 Mar., 1786. Sukey, b. 29 Dec., 1788. Hannah, b. 26 Oct., 1791. Elizb., b. 5 Oct., 1794.

FOWLER, WILLIAM, of Boston,
  enl. 1777 for 3 years, Continental Army.

FOWLS, BENJAMIN,
  enl. 1775, Capt. Prince's Co., 19th Reg.: 6 Oct., 1775; enl. 20 Jan., 1777, for war, Capt. Page's Co., 11th Reg., Continental Army.
  As *Fowle*, enl. 27 Oct. 1779, for 3 yrs., Capt. Hunt's Co., 10th Mass. Reg.
  prob. son of Joseph, of Salem and (m. 6 Feb., 1733) Hannah Porter. Joseph m. 2d, 9 Sept., 1741, Hannah Swinnerton. Benj. d. Danvers, 14 Mar., 1814; m. (published 30 Mar., 1767) Mehitable Hayward. Ch.: Holten, b. 21 Feb., 1775, who m. Nancy and had Chas. Porter, b. Beverly, 3 Mar., 1802.

FRANCIS, JOHN,
  enl. 3 May, 1775, sergt.: Capt. Francis' Co., Col. Mansfield's Reg.: 1 Aug., 1775.
  Capt. John Francis, d. 30 July, 1822. He was pensioned 11 July, 1836. Capt. John was a brother of Col. Ebenezer Francis.

FRETO, WILLIAM,
  enl. 1775, corp., Capt. Putnam's Co., 19th Reg.: 6 Oct., 1775. Sergt., 15 July, 1776, Capt. Gray's Co., Col. Mar-

(*Freto Continued.*)
shall's Reg.; enl. 26 Mar., 1777, for 3 yrs.. Capt. Page's Co., Col. Francis' (11th) Reg., Continental Army.: enl. 5 July, 1780, sergt.; dis. 10 Oct., 1780.
m. Danvers, 13 July, 1769. Elizabeth Coose (b. Danvers, 31 Oct., 1750). Ch.: James, b. 14 Oct., 1763. Wm., b. 4 Dec., 1771.

FRIENE, NATHANIEL,
enl. 28 Mar., 1781, for 3 yrs., Continental Army.

GEORGE, TRUFTON.
enl. Capt. Baker's Co., 19th Reg.: 1 Oct., 1775.

GILE, BENJ., not on rolls. Received pension 1836.

GILFORD, BENJAMIN,
enl. 1775, sergt.; Capt. Gallusha's Co., Col. Ruggle's (25th) Reg.; Oct., 1775.
m. 17 Mar., 1755. Lydia Goodale. Ch.: Moses, b. 25 Apr., 1756. Lydia, b. 8 Dec., 1759. Aaron, b. 28 July, 1762. Simeon, b. 1 Aug., 1761; d. 11 Sept., 1765. Simeon, b. 17 Sept., 1766. Lucy, b. 26 Oct., 1768. Sarah, b. 25 Dec., 1770. Betty, b. 30 Jan., 1773.

GOODALE, ASA,
enl. 1775, Capt. Prince's Co., 19th Reg., 6 Oct., 1775.

GOODELL, ASA,
enl. 25 Aug., 1777, Capt. Flint's Co. Col. Johnson's Reg.: dis. 14 Dec., 1777.

GOODHUE, SAMUEL,
enl. Capt. Baker's Co., 19th Reg.; 1 Oct., 1775.

GOUDY, JAMES,
enl. 1775, Capt. Putnam's Co., 19th Reg.; 6 Oct., 1775.
prob. b. Marblehead.

GOULD, SIMEON,
enl. 1777, for 3 yrs., Continental Army.

GREY, ANDREW,
enl. 1775, Capt. Prince's Co., 19th Reg.; 6 Oct., 1775.

GREEN, SAMUEL,
enl. 1775, Capt. Winship's Co., Col. Nixon's Reg.; 30 Sept., 1775.
b. 3 Mar., 1755; m. at Danvers to Sarah (b. 29 July, 1754).

GREY, JOHN,
enl. 3 Aug., 1781, for 3 yrs., Continental Army.

GUILFORD, WILLIAM.
recruit for Capt. Town's Co., Continental Army at Fishkill, Dec., 1778. See French War Soldiers.
m. 6 Sept., 1763; m. Jane Bryers.

HARROWOOD, JONATHAN,
enl. 1775, Capt. Gallusha's Co., 25th Reg.; Oct., 1775; enl. as "Harwood" 1777 for 3 yrs., Continental Army.
Jona. Harwood, pub. to Ennice Briggs, 16 Nov., 1781. Ch.: Jacob, 16 Dec., 1781. Eunice, b. 15 Mar., 1783. Timothy, b. 1 Feb., 1785. Elice, b. 5 June, 1789. A Jona. Harwood, pensioner, d. æt. 73, 24 Oct., 1822. Adm. on estate of Jona. Harwood, 4 Jan., 1825. Jona. Harwood m. 21 Feb., 1775. Hannah Nurse and perhaps had a son Jona. who m. Thauful Dole, 1798, and d. 1 Aug., 1833, æt. 58.

HARWOOD, EZRA,
enl. 1777, for 3 years, Continental Army.
b. 19 May, 1752; d. 31 Jan., 1813; m. 13 April, 1786, Nancy Moulton, (b. 22 Mar., 1764). Ch.: Desire, b. 22 Nov., 1786. Nancy, b. 11 Feb., 1789. Betsey, b. 30 May, 1791. Zenith, b. 17 April, 1794. Mehitable, b. 14 Sept., 1796. John, b. 14 Aug., 1799. Ezra, b. 1803.

HARROD, EZRA, (Harwood),
enl. 22 Mar., 1779, for 3 yrs., Capt. Hitchcock's Co., 3d Mass. Reg.

HARROWOOD, URIAH,
  enl. 1775, Capt. Galusha's Co., 25th Reg.: Oct., 1775; enl. as "Uriah Harwood" 1777, for 3 years, Continental Army.

HAYWARD, ISRAEL,
  enl. 25 Aug., 1777; dis. 14 Dec., 1777; Capt. Flint's Co., Col. Johnson's Reg.

HAYWARD, LEVI,
  enl. 1775, Capt. Prince's Co., 19th Reg.; 6 Oct., 1775.
  d. Danvers, 9 May, 1810; m. Danvers, 7 Oct., 1776, Elizabeth Tucker, (d. 13 July, 1818). Ch.: Huldah, b. 17 Mar., 1778; m. —— Cheever. Samuel, b. 21 June, 1780. Jesse, b. 11 Mar., 1783. Jonathan, b. 6 Aug., 1786; d. 21 June, 1787. Jona, b. 5 Mar., 1788.

HELAND, JOHN, "a transient,"
  enl. 1777 for 3 years, Continental Army.

HENDERSON, WILLIAM,
  enl. 14 June, 1782, for 3 years, Continental Army. £60 bounty.

HILBERT, JOSEPH,
  enl. 1776, Capt. Gray's Co., Col. Marshall's Reg.; 15 July, 1776.

HILBURN, NATHAN,
  enl. 1777, for 3 years, Continental Army.
  Prob. son of Wm. below; m. (pub. 22 Feb., 1800) to Susanna Quinn of Salem.

HILBURN, WILLIAM, See Hilbort,
  enl. 1776, for 3 yrs., Continental Army.
  William Hilburt, b. 12 Aug., 1752; d. 24 May, 1841; m. Aug., 1778, Betsey Dickinson. (b. Woburn, Mar., 1753; d. 26 July, 1829). Ch.: Nathan, Sarah. Wm. Hilborn, jr., m. 17 Aug., 1777, Betty Richardson.

HIBBORT, JOSEPH,
  enl. 1775, Capt. Putnam's Co., 19th Reg.; 6 Oct., 1775.

HILBORT, WILLIAM, See Hilburn,
  enl. 7 Feb., 1777, for 3 years, Capt. Page's Co., 11th Reg., Continental Army.
  There was a Wm. Hilbert, revol. pensioner, æt. 82, in 1818. Living in Essex Co. in 1834.

HILBERT, WILLIAM,
  enl. 1775 or 6, Capt. Gay's Co., Col. Francis' Reg.; 2 days service: marched 31 miles.

HIBBORT, NATHAN, See Hilburn,
  enl. 1775, Capt. Putnam's Co., 19th Reg.; 6 Oct., 1775.
  The spellings above shown, Hibbort, Hilbort, Hilburn, Hilburt, Hibbort, seem to be variations of the same name, of which the correct form was Hilbert.

HOLT, WILLIAM,
  enl. July, 1780 for 6 mos.; æt. 16, 5 ft., 3 in., dark complexion; dis. 19 Dec., 1780.

HUNT, NOAH,
  enl. 10 July, 1781, for 3 yrs., Continental Army.

HUTCHINSON, ELISHA,
  enl. 7 May, 1775, Capt. Francis' Co., Col. Mansfield's Reg.; 1 Aug., 1775. Qt.-sergt.

HUTCHINSON, ELISHA,
  captured by British while serving on a privateer and d. 1777 in Halifax prison.
  b. 25 May, 1755; son of Col. Israel Hutchinson, q. v.

HUTCHINSON, ISRAEL,
  enl. 1775, Capt. Putnam's Co., 19th Reg.; 6 Oct., 1775.
  Received a pension 1833, then æt. 74, for service in Continental Line and militia; son of Col. Israel Hutchinson, q. v.

HUTCHINSON, ISRAEL,
Capt. of Co. of Minute Men, 19 Apr., 1775. Lt. Col. in Col. Mansfield's Reg. Com. Col., Sept., 1775.
See French War Soldiers.
His company at Lexington were in the thick of the fight. He was with Washington at the crossing of the Delaware. He served in the legislature 21 years. He was a housewright and mill owner, etc.

HUTCHINSON, JOHN,
enl. 1776, Capt. Gray's Co., Col. Marshall's Reg.; 15 July, 1776.

JACOBS, PRIMUS, negro,
enl. 21 Mar., 1777, for 3 yrs., Capt. Page's Co., 11th Reg., Continental Army; enl. 3 July, 1781, during war, in Cont. army.
m. 20 Mar., 1776, Dinah Smith (negro).

JOHNSON, JAMES,
enl. 1775, Capt. Prince's Co., 19th Reg.; 6 Oct., 1775.
Prob. son of James, (a cooper, d. 5 Sept., 1774, adm. on his estate to widow Anna who gave surety with Ezra Johnson, of Salem) who m. 8 May, 1754, Anna Curtis: published 30 Aug., 1785, to Lydia Whittredge.

JOHNSON, SILAS,
recruit for Cont. Army, Capt. Town's company at Fishkill, Dec., 1778; reported at Springfield, 18 Aug., 1779, as a recruit (9 mos.) for Capt. Town's Co., Col. Thorndike's Reg.; æt. 54; 5 ft. 10 in. in height, light complexion. Enl. 7 Mar., 1781, for three years, Cont. Army.
Published to Tabitha Beverly, 7 Oct., 1780.

JOSELYN, JOHN,
Occurs on list of pensioners residing in Danvers, 1836. Not on state archives.

KELLEY, LONGLEY, of Methuen,
m. 9 Aug., 1778, at Fishkill, for 9 mos., Cont. Army.

KELLEY, WILLIAM,
enl. 1775; Capt. Gallusha's Co., 25th Reg., Oct., 1775.
Son of George and Margaret (Scott, pub. 22 Sept., 1758) Kelley; b. 9 June, 1759.

KENNEY, JOSIAH,
enl. July, 1780, for 6 mos.; æt. 17, 5 ft., 3 in., dark complexion; dis. 19 Dec., 1780. Enl. 27 June, 1781, for 3 years, Cont. Army.
Pub. 17 Nov., 1759 to Mary Case of Middleton.

KIMBALL, BENJAMIN,
enl. 1775; Capt. Putnam's Co., 19th Reg., 6 Oct., 1775.
There was a revolutionary pensioner by this name, aged 66 in 1819, who d. 29 June, 1822. He was a sergeant in the Massachusetts Line. There was also a pensioner of same name, whose service was in the Mass Continental Line, U. S. Navy, and N. H. militia, who was æt. 73 in 1833.

LAKEMAN, DANIEL,
enl. 3 May, 1775, Capt. Francis's Co., Col. Mansfield's Reg.; 1 Aug., 1775.

LARRIBEE, BENJAMIN,
enl. 1777, for 3 years, Continental Army.
Perhaps the Benj. Larribee who d. Dec., 1782; m. 24 Feb., 1778, Anne Harriss. Ch.: Benj. b. 22 Oct., 1778. John, b. 20 Aug., 1782.

LATHERBEE, JAMES,
enl. 25 Aug., 1777; dis. 14 Dec., 1777. Capt. Flint's Co., Col. Johnson's Reg.

LISCOMB, EBENEZER,
enl. 1777, for 3 years, Continental Army.

LISCOMB, SAMUEL,
  enl. 1777, for 3 years, Continental Army.
  Samuel, jr., of Salem, published to Anna Hilbert of Danvers, 27 Feb., 1774.

LOVETT, ISRAEL,
  enl. 1775; Capt. Putnam's Co., 19th Reg., 6 Oct., 1775.
  m. 1 Jan., 1777, Deliverance Whittemore.

LUNT, JOSEPH,
  enl. 17 June, 1782, for 3 yrs., Cont. Army. Bounty £66.

MACINTIRE, NATHANIEL,
  enl. 2 Mar., 1777, for 3 years, Capt. Page's Co., 11th Reg., Continental Army; served 36 mos.

MALEY, JOHN,
  enl. 1776; sergt., Capt. Gray's Co., Col. Marshall's Reg., 15 July, 1776.

MANWELL, SAMUEL, of Bow,
  m. Fishkill, 9 Aug., 1778, 9 mos., Continental Army.

MAYBERRY, RICHARD,
  enl. 1777, during war, Lt. Col.'s Co., 3d Reg., Continental Army; served 12 mos.

MAYHUE, DANIEL,
  enl. 1777, for 3 years, Capt. Whipple's Co., 5th Reg., Continental Army; served 36 mos. (Mayo,) enl. 5 July, 1780, for 6 mos.; dis. 19 Dec., 1780; æt. 50 yrs.; 5 ft., 6 in., dark complexion; prob. member of Lt. Eleazer Lindsey's company in French War, 1756, q. v.

MAYO, DANIEL, see Mayhew.

MCCARRICK, JAMES, of Falmouth,
  enl. 1777, for 3 years, Continental Army.

MCCOY, BARNABAS,
  enl. 9 Apr., 1781, for 3 years, Continental Army.

MCKOY, JOHN, JR.
  enl. 1778; m. at Fishkill, 9 mos., Continental Army.

MONROE, ANDREW,
  Of Danvers in 1836, when he was on the pension rolls.

MORRIS, ADAM, "residence unknown,"
  enl. 1777, for 3 years; Continental Army.

MULCAHY, HUGH,
  enl. 25 July, 1780, for 6 mos.; dis. 9 Jan., 1781.

MURPHY, MILANDO,
  enl. 22 Feb., 1781, for 3 yrs., Continental Army.
  Æt. 69 in 1818 when he was placed on the pension list; d. Danvers, 11 Feb., 1827; pub. 8 Oct., 1784 to Betty Mitchel; pub. 23 Jan., 1802, to Hiphzi Johnson of Andover.

NASE, JUSTIN, of Boston,
  enl. 1777, for 3 years, Continental Army.

NICHOLS, JOHN,
  enl. 25 Aug., 1777; sergt.; Capt. Flint's Co., Col. Johnson's Reg.; dis. 14 Dec., 1777.

NURSE, EBENEZER,
  enl. 1777, for 3 years, Continental Army.

NURSE, ELY,
  enl. 1775; Capt. Prince's Co., 19th Reg., 6 Oct., 1775.
  b. Danvers, 31 Dec., 1755; son of Ebenezer (d. 23 April, 1787) and Hannah (d. 9 Mar., 1823) Nurse.

NURSE, JAMES,
  enl. 1777; during war, Capt. Cushing's Co., 1st Reg., Continental Army; served 33 mos., 20 days invalid.

NURSE, MICHAEL,

enl. 25 Aug., 1777; dis. 14 Dec., 1777, Capt. Flint's Co., Col. Johnson's Reg., m. at Fishkill, 1778, 9 mos., Continental Army.

b. 14 Nov., 1759; son of Ebenezer and Hannah; bro. of Eli, q. v.

NURSE, ROGERS,

enl. 12 Nov., 1777; dis. 3 Feb., 1778; as guard at Charlestown and Cambridge, Capt. Jona. Proctor's Co., Col. Jacob Gerrish's Reg.; re-enl. 3 Feb., 1778; dis. 3 April, 1778.

b. Danvers, 3 Nov., 1761; d. 2 Oct., 1839; m. 30 Oct., 1788, Mrs. Molly James, (b. 3 Nov., 1761; widow of Wm. James, by whom she had Polly, b. 27 July, 1782). Ch.: Hanna Rea, b. 28 Jan., 1789. Sally, b. 1 Dec., 1790. Lydia, b. 3 Nov., 1795; d. 30 Sept., 1840. Nancy, b. 19 June, 1798. Samuel, b. 27 Sept., 1800. Eli, b. 25 Oct., 1803; d. 2 July, 1807.

NURSE, SAMUEL,

enl. 1775; Capt. Francis's Co., 19th Reg., 6 Oct., 1775.

b. 25 Dec., 1757; a bro. of Eli and Michael, q. v.

OAKMAN, JOHN,

enl. 1778; m. at Fishkill, 9 mos., Continental Army.

b. 1759; d. Danvers, 1 Jan., 1808; pub. 22 May, 1778, Lydia Gilford; prob. son of John of Salem, a soldier in the French War of 1756.

OAKS, CALEB,

enl. 1775, Capt. Putnam's Co., 19th Reg.; 6 Oct., 1775.

Caleb Oaks of Medford, m. to Rebecca Putnam of Danvers, 12 Jan., 1757; perhaps the parents of Caleb of Danvers who m. 9 Nov., 1797, Mehitable Pope, b. 3 Apr., 1768.

OLIVER, THOMAS,

1775, surgeon's mate; Col. Mansfield's Reg.

PAGE, JEREMIAH,

Commissioned Capt., March,

(*Page Continued.*)

1773, in Col. Wm. Brown's Essex Reg; and on 4 Oct., 1774, in common with the commissioned officers of the 1st Essex Reg., resigned, refusing to serve under Col. Brown, who was a Mandamus Councillor. This action was taken 17 days before the Provincial Congress called upon the Mandamus Councillors to resign. On the 27 Oct., 1774, the 3d Company of Danvers, which belonged to the 1st Essex Reg., met and chose Jere. Page chairman, and afterward captain, 7 Nov., 1774; the company was ordered to meet at Capt. Page's house, "it is expected that all true sons of liberty will meet at the time and place aforesaid." Capt. of Company at Lexington. In December, 1775, on duty in camp, in Cambridge and Roxbury. Com. Lt. Col. 8th Essex Reg., 8 Feb., 1776; Lt. Col. of Col. Cogswell's jr., Reg.. Gen. Farley's Brigade, drafted for the relief of New York, Sept., 1776, and ordered to Horse Neck: was in battle of White Plains, 18 October, 1776. Resigned 9 Oct., 1777. His three commissions are in possession of Miss Sarah E. Hunt.

b. Danvers, 1722; d. 6 June, 1806.

PAGE, SAMUEL,

Capt. Col. Tupper's Reg.; was engaged in the battles of Lexington, Monmouth and Stony Point. Was at Valley Forge in 1777.

b. Danvers, 1 Aug., 1753; d. there Sept., 1814; son of Col. Jeremiah and Sarah (Andrews) Page; m. Rebecca dau. of Wm. Putnam.

PEDLEY, WILLIAM,
  enl. 28 July, 1781, for 3 yrs.: Continental Army.

PEPPERAL, EDWARD,
(Pepper on one roll).
  enl 1777, for 3 years: Capt. Whipple's Co., 5th Reg., Continental Army; served 35 mos., 29 days.
  A member of the Pepper family of Peabody, perhaps one of the first to add to their name. There is no connection between the Pepperrells of Danvers, Peabody and Lynn, and the family of Sir Wm. Pepperell of Kittery, now extinct.

PERKINS, WILLIAM,
  enl. 2 May, 1775, æt. 19; Capt. Baker's Co., Col. Little's Reg., 8 Oct., 1775; probably Quebec expedition.

PERLEY, ELIPHALET,
  enl. 3 May, 1775, sergt.; Capt. Francis's Co., Col. Mansfield's Reg.; 6 October, 1775.
  b. Boxford; son of Major Asa (a member of the Provincial Congress) and Susanna (Low) Perley; m. 24 Mar., 1774, Anna, dau. of John and Affia Porter.

PORTER, BENJAMIN,
  enl. 1777, during war, Colonel's company, 5th Continental; served 47 mos.; enl. 11 Dec., 1779, for 3 years, Lt. in Inf. Co., 5th Mass. Reg.
  b. 28 Oct., 1740; son of Benjamin (said to have served with 5 sons in the war); and Eunice (dau. of Samuel Nurse) Porter.

PORTER, JAMES,
  enl. 4 May, 1775, Capt. Francis's Co., Col. Mansfield's Reg., 6 Oct., 1775.
  b. 13 Jan., 1755; bro. of Benj. above.

PORTER, JONATHAN,
  fifer in Capt. Jeremiah Putnam's Co., Col. Nathan Tyler's Reg., 31 Jan., 1783. There was also a Jona. who was 1st Lt. in Capt. Jere.

(Porter Continued.)
  Page's Co., 19 Apr., 1775; 2 days service.

PORTER, JOSEPH,
  enl. 15 Aug., 1777, Lieut.; killed 7 Oct., 1775, Capt. Flint's Co., Col. Johnson's Reg.; another roll states he was dis. 12 Dec.
  b. 4 Apr., 1740; d. 12 Feb., 1805; son of Joseph and Mary Porter; m. 1st, Sarah, dau. Benj. and Sarah Putnam, who d. 10 Sept., 1766; m. 2d, 1767, Elizb. Herrick who d. 1816. Ch.: Joseph, b. 22 June, 1763; d. 3 June, 1820. Sarah, b. 5 Feb., 1765; m. Daniel Putnam. Elizb., b. 10 Jan., 1768. Phebe, b. 10 Aug., 1769. Polly, b. 20 Jan., 1771. Lydia, b. 7 June, 1772. Ruth, b. 12 May, 1774. Jona., b. 24 May, 1776; m. Eunice Boardman.

PORTER, MOSES (General),
  Helped work one of the guns at Bunker Hill. Enl. in Gridley's Artillery, Capt. Thos. Foster's Co.; and served during the siege of Boston, was promoted Lt. in 1780, and through various grades in the Artillery, until he was head of that arm of the service. He was wounded during the Revolution. After the war he served with Wayne in the Indian campaign, and commanded the artillery during the war of 1812. Breveted for distinguished service, 10 Sept., 1813. He died while still in the service at Cambridge, in 1822, and is buried in Danvers.
  b. 20 Mar., 1756; son of Benj. and Sarah (Rea) Porter.

PORTER, NATHAN,
  enl. 4 May, 1775, Capt. Francis's Co., Col. Mansfield's Reg., 6 Oct., 1775. See also Lexington Alarm.
  A cooper and mariner, son of John and Apphia Porter; b. about 1745; m. 25 Mar., 1773, Lydia Goodridge.

PORTER, PETER,

enl. 4 May, 1775, Capt. Francis's Co., Col. Mansfield's Reg.; 6 Oct., 1775.

b. 9 May, 1757, bro. of Benj. q. v.

PORTER, TITUS,

enl. 1777, for 3 yrs., 11th Reg., Continental Army; served 36 mos.

PRESTON, LEVI,

In Capt. Samuel Flint's Co., Lexington Alarm. Enl. 12 Nov., 1777, Capt. Jona. Proctor's Co., Col. Jacob Gerrish's Reg. of Guards, for service at Charlestown; dis. 3 Feb., 1778. Com. Capt. May, 1794.

b. 21 Oct., 1756; d. 5 Jan., 1850; son of Lt. John and Hannah (Putnam) Preston; m. 4 May, 1779, Mehitable, dau. of John and Elizb. (Prince) Nichols. His son Daniel was com. Capt. in 1813, Lt. Col. in 1817, and Col., 1818.

PRESTON, MOSES,

enl. 10 Oct.: dis. 10 Nov., 1779, Essex Co. Reg., Capt. James Mallons' Co.; stationed at Castle Island.

b. 20 Apr., 1758, d. 26 Feb., 1824; son of Lt. John and Hannah (Putnam) Preston; m. 1785, Sarah Berry of Middleton. Lived in South Danvers. Ch.: Sally, b. 25 Feb , 1787. Moses, b. 6 July, 1789.

PRINCE, ASA,

commanded company at Lexington. Enl. Col. Mansfield's Reg., 25 Apr., 1775; Com. Capt., 27 May, 1775. Resigned 6 May, 1778, as Capt. of 2d Company in 8th Essex Reg., to which he was Com., 6 Sept.: 1776; at Providence, July, 1777.

b. 22 Feb., 1747; son of Dr. Jonathan (b. 1707; d. 1753) and Mary, dau. of Joseph Porter) Prince; m. 15 June,

(*Prince Continued.*)

1769, Elizb. Nichols. Ch.: Jonathan, b. 29 Apr., 1771. Elizabeth, b. 15 Jan., 1774. Capt. Prince was noted for his coolness in the face of danger. He was at Lexington, Bunker Hill and Fort George. The only officer from Danvers, killed, during the war, was Capt. Samuel Flint.

PRINCE, JAMES,

two days' service Lexington Alarm, in Capt. John Putnam's Co.; enl. 5 July, 1780, to reenforce Continental Army; dis. 10 Oct., 1780, Capt. Benj. Peabody's Co., Col. Wade's Reg.

b. 28 Aug., 1763; d. 24 July, 1796; nephew of Capt. Asa and son of James (b. 1731) and Elizb. (Preston, d. 1822, aet. 86,) Prince; m. 3 June, 1787, Phebe Parker (b. Reading; d. 12 Nov., 1836). Ch.: Betsey, b. 9 Aug., 1788; d. Salem, Apr., 1831. Moses, b. 18 Aug., 1790; d. Havana, Aug., 1812. James, b. 22 Mar., 1792. Elzaphan, b. 22 Oct., 1794. Nathan, b. 16 Jan., 1797. Joseph, b. 1 Aug., 1799; d. Boston, 27 July, 1835.

PRINCE, MOSES,

Corp. in Capt. Asa Prince's Co., Lexington Alarm; Lt. in Capt. Stephen Wilkin's Co., Col. Wigglesworth's Reg.; allowed travel from Albany and Danvers, 1776.

b. 14 Feb., 1756, brother of James, q. v. There was a Moses Prince, steward of the Eagle, Capt. Wm. Grover, 17 June, 1780; 5 ft., 10 in., light complexion.

PROCTOR, WILLIAM,

enl. 30 Aug., 1781, for 3 yrs.; Continental Army.

PROCTOR, TITUS,

(Proiter, on rolls).

enl. 13 Mar., 1777, for Bennington Expedition; Capt. Page's Co., Col. Francis's Reg.

See under Porter.

PUTNAM, AARON,
enl. 1 Feb., 1777, for 3 years, Capt. Porter's Co., 11th Reg.. Continental Army; served 36 mos. See also Lexington Alarm lists.

PUTNAM, ALLEN,
enl. 18 May, 1775, for 8 mos., Capt. Enoch Putnam's Co., 19th Reg.; enl. 1 Aug., 1777, dis. 1 Sept., 1777. Capt. Asa Prince's Co., Col. Danforth Keyes' Reg. Served at Providence; reenl. and dis., 3 Jan., 1778. Enl. 25 July, 1780, (æt. 18, 5 ft., 6 in., light;) for 6 mos.; dis. 7 Dec., 1780.
b. 25 Oct., 1762; son of Henry and Sarah (Putnam) Putnam. He settled at Marietta, Ohio.

PUTNAM, ANDREW, (no residence),
Com. Capt. 7th Co., 8th Essex (Col. Thorndike's) Reg., 24 Apr., 1778.
It is not plain that the above was of Danvers, but he is probably the son of Edmund Putnam, who m. Mary, dau. of Col. Jeremiah Page.

PUTNAM, BENJAMIN, of Wilton, N. H. Credited to Danvers.
enl. 14 Dec., 1777, for 3 yrs.; Continental Army, Capt. Fox's Co., Col. Henry Jackson's Reg. Re-enl. 1 Jan., 1780; dis. 14 Dec., 1780.

PUTNAM, BENJAMIN,
enl. in Capt. Scott's Co., Col. David Henley's Reg., for 3 years. On returns dated 14 Feb., 1778 and 1 Dec., 1778. See also Lexington Alarm.

PUTNAM, DANIEL,
Com. 1st Lt., Capt. Sam'l Flint's (2d) Co., 8th Essex (Col. Henry Herrick's) Reg.,

(*Putnam Continued.*)
5 June, 1776. See also Lexington Alarm.

PUTNAM, ENOCH,
2d Lt. Capt. Israel Hutchinson's Co., Lexington Alarm. Enl. 6 Apr., 1775, Com. Capt. 27 May, 1775; Col. Mansfield's (19th) Reg., 6 Oct., 1775; Com. Lt. Col. 8th Essex Reg., 4 March, 1778. Com. as Lt. Col. for R. I. service, Col. Nathan Tyler's Reg., 18 June, 1778; and served till Jan. 1, 1780. Lt. Col. Comd't at West Point, of Reg. raised for three mos. under resolves of 30 June, 1781, engaged from 7 July, to 8 Dec., 1781. Appt. Col. 13 or 14 Nov., 1782.
b. 18 Feb., 1731-2; d. 1796; son of Jethro and Annie (Putnam) Putnam; m. 1st, 12 Apr., 1754, Hannah, dau. of Stephen Putnam, who died 18 Dec., 1776. He m. 2d, Elizabeth Stratton. Ch.: (Col.) Jethro, b. 22 Dec., 1753; d. May, 1815. Anna, Fanny, b. 7 Aug., 1764; d. 28 June, 1858; m. Joseph Putnam. Hannah, b. 24 May, 1771; d. 20 June, 1830; m. Timothy Putnam.

PUTNAM, EZRA,
enl. 3 May, 1775, major, 27th foot, (Col. Hutchinson). See French War Soldiers; also Lexington Alarm.
b. 1729; d. Marietta, O., 19 Mar., 1811; son of Ezra; m. 21 June, 1750, Lucy Putnam (d. Marietta, 20 July, 1818). Ch.: Betty, b. 18 Mar., 1751; m. Archelaus Batchelder. Nehemiah, b. 14 Oct., 1753. Lucy, b. 4 Jan., 1757; d. 19 May, 1802; m. Samuel Small. *Ezra, b. 5 July, 1759; killed by Indians in Ohio, 1791-92. Deborah, b. 19 Jan., 1761; m. David Fuller. David, b. 10 July, 1767. John, killed by Indians, in Ohio, 1791-92.

―――――――――――
*Was a drummer of a Middleton company, during siege of Boston. Also served 6 mos. in Continental Army.

PUTNAM, HENRY,
Sergt., in Capt. Addison Richardson's Co., Col. Mansfield's Reg.: enl. 12 May, 1775, for 8 mos. service. In service on 1 Aug., and 6 Oct., 1775. See also Lexington Alarm.

PUTNAM, ISRAEL, (General),
Served in French and Indian Wars, 1755 to 1763. Arrived at Cambridge 21 April, 1775 and commanded the 2d Conn. Reg. Commanded the Americans at the battle of Bunker Hill, 17 June, 1775. Commissioned Major General by the Continental Congress, June, 1775, and later was in command at New York and on the Hudson, and at West Point. Attacked with paralysis in 1780, he was obliged to relinquish his command. (See "A Sketch of Gen. Israel Putnam, by Rev. A. P. Putnam.")

b. Danvers, 7 Jan., 1717-18, son of Joseph and Mary (Veren) Putnam; d. Brooklyn, Conn., 29 May, 1790; m. at Danvers, 19 July, 1739, Hannah, dau. of Joseph and Mehitable (Putnam) Pope, who d. 6 Sept., 1765; m. 2d, 3 June, 1767, Mrs Deborah (Lothrop) Gardener, who died at Fishkill, 14 Oct., 1777. For descendants see History of the Putnam family by Eben Putnam.

PUTNAM, ISRAEL,
enl. 4 May, 1775, for 8 mos. in Capt. Asa Prince's Co., 19th Reg., 6 Oct., 1775. Enl. 5 Sept., 1775; dis. 3 Jan., 1778. R. I. service in Capt. Asa Prince's Co., Col. Keyes Reg. Israel Putnam of Danvers, drafted to join Capt. Poole's Co., and march to Horse Neck, but failed to appear. Enl. 8 July, 1779; dis.

(*Putnam Continued.*)
1 Jan., 1780, R. I. service, Capt. Jeremiah Putnam's Co., Col. Nathan Tayler's Reg. See also Lexington Alarm.

The above may relate to one man or several. It is impossible to always distinguish between two or more persons of the same name.

PUTNAM, ISRAEL,
enl. 5 July, 1780, æt. 19, 5 ft., 5 in., dark complexion; 6 mos., dis. 9 Jan., 1781.

PUTNAM, JEREMIAH,
Served two days in Capt. Jere. Page's Co., Lexington Alarm. Enl. 11 May, 1775, as sergt. in Capt. Addison Richardson's Co., Col. John Mansfield's Reg. Prom. ensign, Col. Hutchinson's Reg.; taken prisoner at Long Island; pay account allowed from 1 Jan., 1777 to 24 Jan., 1778. Ensign in Artillery Artificer Reg. Prom. Captain, detached as Capt. from Essex Co. Reg., 8 June, 1779, to proceed to Providence, under command of Col. Tyler. Mustered 1 July, 1779; dis. 1 Jan., 1780. In service as Capt. in Col. Wade's Reg., from 1 Jan., 1778, a part of the time stationed at East Greenwich. His orderly book for the R. I. campaign, is among the Archives of Essex Institute at Salem. Captain on roll dated 1 Jan., 1783, Col. Nat'l Wade's Reg.

b. 31 Oct., 1737; d. 16 Sept., 1799; son of Jonathan and Sarah (Perley) Putnam; m. 3 Feb., 1763, Rachel Fuller. Ch.: Thomas, b. 8 Oct., 1763. Eunice; b. 3 Jan., 1766; m. Israel Hutchinson, jr. Jeremiah. b. 21 Nov., 1769. Apphia, b. 23 May, 1772. Elijah. Levi. Rachel.

PUTNAM, JOSEPH, Jr.,
Com. 2d Lt., 5 June, 1776, 2d (Capt. Sam'l Flint's) Co., 8 Essex Reg.

PUTNAM, JOSEPH,
A Revolutionary Pensioner in 1836.

PUTNAM, NATHAN,
enl. 1775; Capt. Putnam's Co., 19th Reg.; 6 Oct., 1775.
b. 8 Sept., 1749; d. 10 April, 1823; brother of Jere. Putnam; m. 23 Oct., 1771 Hannah, dau. of Dr. Amos Putnam. Ch.: Nathan, b. 18 Mar., 1773. Perley, b. 16 Sept., 1778. (Gen.) David, b. 23 Dec., 1780. Amos, b. 10 Feb., 1785. Hannah P., b. 23 Nov., 1786; d. unm. John, b. 20 May, 1791.

PUTNAM, PHINEHAS,
Lexington Alarm, 2 days' service: Capt. Asa Prince's Co. Enl. 4 May, 1775, sergt.; Capt. Prince's Co., 19th Reg. In service 19th Reg., 21 Dec., 1775.
Either a son or grandson of Stephen Putnam.

PUTNAM, RUFUS,
enl. 5 July, 1780; Continental Army.

PUTNAM, TARRANT,
enl. 4 May, 1775, as Adj., Col. Mansfield's 19th Reg.; Oct., 1775. Also Lexington Alarm, 2 days service, Capt. Edmund Putnam's Co.

PUTNAM, THOMAS,
Enl. in Capt. Jere. Putnam's Co., Col. Wade's Reg.; 1 Jan., 1778, for one year, musician. Drummer, Capt. Jere. Putnam's Co., Col. Nathan Tyler's Reg., in R. I. campaign; enl. 25 July, 1779: dis. 1 Jan., 1780. Enl. 25 July, 1780, for 6 mos.; æt. 18, 5 ft., 3 in., light complexion: dis. 7 Dec., 1781.

PUTNAM, TIMOTHY,
enl. 5 July, 1780, Capt. Benj. Peabody's Co., Col. Wade's Reg., Continental Army; dis. 10 Oct., 1780. Rev. pensioner, 1836. He may have been the man who enl. in Capt. Jeremiah Putnam's Co., Col. Wade's Reg., 1 Sept., 1779, for R. I. service; dis. 1 Jan., 1780.

PUTNEY, JONATHAN,
enl. 1775, sergt.; Capt. Gallusha's Co., 25th Reg.; Oct., 1775.

QUIN, JAMES,
enl. 25 Sept., 1781, for 3 yrs., Continental Army.

REA, BENJAMIN,
enl. 1775, Capt. Prince's Co., 19th Reg.; 6 Oct., 1775.
m. 22 Nov., 1774, Lydia Putnam. Ch.: Benj., b. 8 Aug., 1775.

REA, CALEB, surgeon,
enl. 27 May, 1775, Capt. Barnes' Co., Col. Hutchinson's Reg.; 1 Aug., 1775.
b. 8 Mar., 1758; d. 29 Dec., 1796; son of Dr. Caleb (a soldier in French War) and Ruth (Porter) Rea, m. 4 Oct., 1781, Sarah, dau. of Capt. John White, of Salem. 6 ch.

REED, ABIJAH,
enl. Capt. Baker's Co., 19th Reg.; 1 Oct., 1775.
m. 9 July, 1778, Margaret Hill. Will prov. 12 Nov., 1794.

REED, JACOB,
enl. Capt. Baker's Co., 19th Reg.; 1 Oct., 1775.
m. 16 Nov., 1777, Hannah Whittaker.

RICE, WILLIAM,
enl. 1775, Capt. Winship's Co., Col. Nixon's Reg.; 30 Sept., 1775.

RICHARDSON, JAMES,
enl. 1777, for 3 years, Continental Army.
b. Woburn, 12 Mar., 1716; m. 17 July, 1783, at Danvers, Mary Crisfield (b. 24 May, 1749). Ch.: Hannah, b. 25 Apr., 1784. Asa, b. 18 Nov., 1785. Mary, b. 13 Jan., 1789.

RICHARDSON, JOSES,
enl. 4 May, 1775, Capt. Francis's Co., Col. Mansfield's Reg.; 1 Aug., 1775.

RICHARDSON, SETH,
enl. 1776, Capt. Gray's Co., Col. Marshall's Reg.; 15 July, 1776; enl. 1777 for 3 years, Continental Army.
b. 8 Feb., 1761; d. 27 Feb., 1831; m. 19 Sept., 1776, Hannah Waters. Ch.: Sally, b. 21 June, 1787. Edw., b. 15 July, 1789. Hannah, b. 1 Dec., 1793. Abel, b. 15 Dec., 1797. Lydia Waters, b. 18 Aug., 1800. Nancy, b. 8 Oct., 1802. Seth, b. 29 Nov., 1804; d. 1824.

RUSSELL, DANIEL,
enl. 1777 for 3 years, Continental Army.
pub. 26 Dec., 1767 to Lydia MacIntire, guardianship of minor son, Daniel, and Wm., son of Daniel Russell, æt. 14, to Eli Upton, 25 Sept., 1782.

RUSSELL, JONATHAN,
enl. 1775, Capt. Putnam's Co., 19th Reg.; 6 Oct., 1775; enl. July, 1780, for 6 mos; æt. 34; 5 ft., 8 in., dark complexion; dis. 9 Dec., 1780; enl. 7 Aug., 1781, for 3 years, Continental Army.
Jonathan Russell, jr., of Danvers; pub. 1 April, 1769 to Huldah Wilkins of Middleton.

RUSSELL, STEPHEN,
enl. 1775, Capt. Putnam's Co., 19th Reg.; 6 Oct., 1775.
b. 8 Oct., 1751; son of Benj. (jr.), (b. 15 Jan., 1718; d. 24 Feb., 1811) and Hannah Russell; m. (pub 14 Aug., 1773) 1774 Sarah Hayward of Andover.

RUSSELL, STEPHEN,
enl. Capt. Baker's Co., 19th Reg.; deserted 1 July, 1775.

SAWYER, EBENEZER,
m. at Fishkill, 1778, 9 mos., Continental Army.
Ebenezer Sawyer of Middleton m. to Sarah Russell (prob. sister of Stephen) of Danvers, 23 Feb., 1775.

SHAW, JESSE,
enl. 1775, Capt. King's Co., 25th Reg.; 29 Sept., 1775.

SHAW, SCIPIO,
enl. 25 Aug., 1777; dis. 14 Dec., 1777; Capt. Flint's Co., Col. Johnson's Reg.
Negro servant of Mrs. Hannah Shaw, widow. He m. 22 Aug., 1777, Filis, negro servant of widow Elizb. Buxton.

SERGEANT, AMOS,
enl. 10 Jan., 1780, sergeant, 3 years, Capt. Hunt's Co., 10th Mass. Reg., Continental Army.

SHELDON, DANIEL,
enl. 1775, Capt. Putnam's Co., 19th Reg.; 6 Oct., 1775.

SHELDON, JEREMIAH,
enl. 1775, Capt. Putnam's Co., 19th Reg.; 6 Oct., 1775; enl. 25 Aug., 1777, sergt.; dis. 14 Dec., 1777; Capt. Flint's Co., Col. Johnson's Reg.
m. 11 June, 1781, Elizb. Goodale, living 1804; adm. on estate to Elbridge Gerry Sheldon, 11 Jan., 1804.

SHELDON, JOHN,
enl. 1776, Capt. Gray's Co., Col. Marshall's Reg.; 15 July, 1776.
Ch of John and Susanna Sheldon; a child, stillborn. Sarah, b. 1 Feb., 1751. Susanna, b. 7 Jan., 1753. Betty, b. 7 Oct., 1755. Esther, b. 14 June, 1757. John, b. 1 May, 1759. James, b. 30 July, 1765. Jona, b. 5 Sept., 1767. Amos, b. 1 Feb., 1769.

SHELDON, JONATHAN,
  enl. 25 Aug., 1777; dis. 14 Dec., 1777; Capt. Flint's Co., Col. Johnson's Reg.
  m. Danvers, 10 June, 1779, Ruth Flint. Ch.: Betsey, b. 27 Feb., 1780. Fanna, b. 12 Dec., 1781. Polly, b. 16 Dec., 1783. Heze Flint, b. 27 Feb., 1787.

SKIDMORE, RICHARD,
  sergt in Capt. Jere. Page's Co., Alarm of 19 Apr., 1775. Served two days. Pensioned 13 Apr., 1818, then aged 86. He was a noted character and had served in the Spanish and French wars. q. v.

SMITH, AMOS,
  enl. 1777 for during war, Capt. Page's Co., 11th Reg., Continental Army; served 43 mos., 13 days.
  b. 29 Oct., 1748; son of Amos and Mary (d. 1 May, 1764) Smith who had also Asa, b. 15 Mar., 1756 (see below) and Nathan. b. 23 Nov., 1759. An Amos Smith m. 20 Aug., 1764 Abigail Hart; also Amos Smith m. 4 Apr., 1771, Mary Ranuff.

SMITH, ASA,
  enl. 10 Jan., 1780, for 3 yrs., Capt. Francis's Co., 10th Mass. Reg., Continental Army.
  see Amos Smith.

SMITH, ISRAEL,
  enl. 1776, Capt. Gray's Co., Col. Melville's Reg.; 15 July, 1776; enl. 15 July, 1780, æt. 36, 5 ft., 9 in., dark complexion, for 6 mos.; dis. 15 Dec., 1780. He reported at Springfield, 8 July, 1780.
  m. (pub 29 June, 1766 to Sarah Cooper of Rowley) Sarah Downing. Ch.: Israel, b. 16 Mar., 1769. Sally, b. 25 Sept., 1775; d. 26 Oct., 1776. Sally, b. 16 Oct., 1776. James, b. 30 June, 1783. Betsey, b. 16 Dec., 1785. Huldah, b. 25 Sept., 1790. Nathaniel, b. 9 Sept., 1792.

SMITH, JOHN,
  enl. 30 Aug., 1781 for 3 yrs., Continental Army.
  b. 18 Nov., 1761; d. 6 Feb., 1798; son of Nathan (d. 1770) and Mary Smith; m. 28 June, 1781, Susanna Newhall, (d. 19 Mar., 1835). Ch.: Nathan, b. 11 May, 1782; in war 1812; d. at Plattsburg, 2 April, 1815. Susa, b. 18 Mar., 1784. Lucy, b. 23 Nov., 1785. Molly, b. 22 Oct., 1787. John, b. 15 June, 1789. Ruth, b. 28 May, 1791. Sally, b. 28 Mar., 1793. Betsey, b. 27 Jan., 1795. Tabby, b. 16 Aug., 1796. Jos. Newhall, b. 24 April, 1798.

SMITH, JOB,
  enl. 1777, for 3 yrs., Continental service.

SOUTHWICK, NATHANIEL,
  Boy on ship Rhodes, commanded by Capt. Nehemiah Buffington; æt. 16, 5 ft., 3 in., light complexion.
  There were others of this name from Danvers, i. e. John, 3d, and John, 4th. George Southwick, jr., was a Revolutionary pensioner in 1836.

SPRING, JOSIAH, of Conway,
  enl. 1777 for 3 yrs., Continental Army.

STACY, JOHN,
  enl. 6 July, 1780, Lt.; dis. 10 Oct., 1780; Capt. Peabody's Co., Col. Wade's Reg.
  Prob. b. Ipswich, 1736; in 1756 was a resident of Danvers and a member of Capt. Andrew Fuller's Co. in Crown Point Expedition.

STEVENS, THOMAS,
  enl. 20 Nov., 1779; corp. for 3 yrs., Capt. Hunt's Co., 10th Mass. Reg., Continental Army.

STEVENS, THOMAS,
  enl. 1776, Capt. Gray's Co., Col. Marshall's Reg.; 15 July, 1776; enl. 15 Feb., 1777, for the war, Capt. Page's Co., 11th Reg., Continental Army.

STEVENS, WILLIAM,
enl. 1777, for 3 yrs., Continental Army.

STONE, ROBERT,
enl. 1775, Capt. Putnam's Co., 19th Reg.; 6 Oct., 1775; enl. 15 July, 1780, for 6 mos.; dis. 15 Aug., 1780, æt. 40; 5 ft., 8 in., "red" complexion.

b. 17 Sept., 1765; d. 10 Aug., 1811; son of ? Robert who m. Mary Aborn of Salem 20 Dec., 1752; m. 8 May, 1782, Hannah Southwick, b. 16 Nov., 1756; d. 17 May, 1806. Ch.: Joseph Southwick, b. 7 July, 1786. Robert, b. 22 Aug., 1788. Wm., b. 1 April, 1790; d. 29 Dec., 1835 at Danvers. Nathan Holt, b. 31 Oct., 1793; d. 2 Feb., 1838, at Danvers. Jonathan, b. Apr., 1797; d. May, 1797.

STONE, SAMUEL,
enl. Capt. Baker's Co., 19th Reg.; 6 Oct., 1775.

There was a pensioner by this name in 1834, a resident of Essex Co. He was aged 76 in 1818.

STONE, SHUBAEL,
enl. 3 June, 1782 for 3 years, Continental Army. £60 bounty.

SYMONDS, JOHN,
enl. 1777, for 3 yrs., Capt. Will's Co., Col. Crane's Reg.: served 36 mos.

m. Ruth. Ch.: Ruth, b. 4 May, 1760. Thos., b. 28 Sept., 1761. Francis, b. 29 Aug., 1762. Abigail, b. 6 Oct., 1763. Nathaniel, b. 28 Oct., 1764. Hannah, b. 4 Jan., 1766. Huldy, b. 28 Aug., 1767.

SYMONDS, POMP,
enl. 1 Mar., 1777, during war, Capt. Whipple's Co., 5th Reg., Continental Army.

TAPLEY, ASA,
enl. 14 Oct., 1779; dis. 22 Nov., 1779, Capt. Benj. Peabody's Co., Col. Jacob Gerrish's Reg.

Rev. pensioner in 1830.

TAPLEY, AMOS,
2 days service as sergt., Capt. Sam'l Flint's Co., 19 Apr., 1775; 2d Lt., in Capt. John Pool's Co., Col. Jona. Cogswell's Reg.; ordered to march to Horse Neck, 12 Sept., 1776. Drafted from 1st Co., 8th Essex Reg.; Com. 6 Sept., 1776, 2d Lt., 2d Co., (Capt. Asa Prince's Co.), 8th Essex Reg.: prom. 1st Lt. of same organization: resigned 4 May, 1778.

TAPLEY, BENJ., (no residence.)
reported prisoner. taken at Ft. Washington, belonging to Capt. Baker's Co., Col. Israel Hutchinson's Reg.: 16 Nov., 1776.

TARR, DAVID,
enl. 1777, 3 years, Col. Scammell's Reg., Continental Army: enl. 5 Mar., 1781, for 3 years: Continental Army.

b. Danvers, aged 58 in 1818, when he was placed on the pension list, pub. 12 Jan., 1786, to Abigail Stevens (b. Andover). Adm. on his estate 20 Nov., 1820, to wid. Abigail. Ch.: David, b. 4 Apr., 1786. Samuel, b. 25 May, 1788. Abigail, b. 25 May, 1790. Jacob, b. 23 Apr., 1792. Louisa, b. 5 Sept., 1795. John, b. 23 Sept., 1798. Francis Kidder, b. 22 July, 1801.

TARDERIC, ⎫ RICHARD, "a tran-
? TARDEN, ⎭ sient,"
enl. 1777, for 3 yrs., Continental Army. Tarden, enl. 12 Dec., 1779, during war, ditto; Capt. Whipple's Co., 5th Mass. Reg.

TAYLOR, ELIPHALET,
enl. 1775: Capt. Galusha's Co., 25th Reg.; Oct., 1775.

d. 19 June, 1782; pub. to Eliz'b Sibley, 22 Nov., 1758.

TOWN OF DANVERS.   133

TAYLOR, WILLIAM,
  enl. 9 Mar., 1781, during war;
  Continental Army.

TITUS, TIMOTHY,
  enl. 23 Mar., 1781, for 3 yrs.;
  Continental Army.

TOLMAN, THOMAS,
  m. 9 Aug., 1778, Fishkill, 9
  mos., Continental Army.

TORLA, JANE, "of Boston,"
  enl. 1777, for 3 yrs.; Continental Army.

TOWN, DANIEL,
  enl. 25 Aug., 1777; dis. 14
  Dec., 1777; Capt. Flint's Co.,
  Col. Johnson's Reg.
  b. 9 July, 1760; son of Thos. and Anna Town.

TOWNE, WILLIAM,
  Capt. of a company of militia
  in Danvers; also of a company
  in Col. Thorndike's Reg.

TRASKE, JONATHAN,
  enl. 25 Aug., 1775; dis. 14
  Dec., 1777, Capt. Flint's Co.,
  Col. Johnson's Reg.
  m. (pub. 20 Feb., 1767) Hannah Gowing of Lynn. Ch.: Patty, b. 27 July, 1773. Nehemiah, b. 25 Aug., 1775. John, b. 12 Dec., 1777. Sally, b. 25 Nov., 1780. Zadoc, b. 6 July, 1783. Levi, b. 12 Jan., 1788.

TRASKE, PRIAM,
  enl. 25 Aug., 1777; dis. 14
  Dec., 1777, Capt. Flint's Co.,
  Col. Johnson's Reg.

TRUELL, DAVID, of Bow,
  m. at Fishkill, 1778, 9 mos.;
  Continental Army.

TUCKER, GEORGE, of New Gloucester,
  enl. 1777, for 3 years, Capt.
  Turner's Co., 16th Reg., Continental Army; served 26
  mos., 3 days.

TUCKER, LEMUEL, of New Gloucester,
  enl. 1777, for 3 yrs., Continental Army.

TUFTS, EBENEZER,
  enl. 6 Aug., 1781, for 3 years,
  Continental Army.

TURNER, JAMES, a "transient,"
  enl. 1777, for three years, Continental Army.
  James Turner of Andover, and Mary Shepard of Danvers, m. 20 Feb., 1755.

TURNER, JAMES,
  enl. 13 Mar., 1777, for Bennington Expedition; Capt.
  Page's Co., Col. Francis's Reg.

TWIST, DANIEL,
  enl. 1775, Capt. Francis's Co.
  19th Reg.; 6 Oct., 1775.

UPTON, JUBA,
  enl. 22 Feb. 1781, for 3 years,
  Continental Army.

VERRY, BENJAMIN,
  enl. 1777, for during war,
  Capt. Burbeck's Co., Col.
  Crane's Reg., Continental
  Army; served 32 mos., 26 dys.
  prob. son of John and Eliz'h Verry, and b. 5 May, 1760.

VERRY, DAVID,
  enl. 1776, Capt. Gray's Co.
  Col. Marshall's Reg.; 15 July,
  1776; m. at Fishkill, 1778, 9
  mos., Continental Army.
  b. 15 May, 1755; son of John and Elizb. Verry, bro. of Benj., q. v.; m. 30 July, 1782, Jermima Skidmore.

VERRY, DANIEL,
  enl. 1775, Capt. Putnam's Co.,
  19th Reg.; 6 Oct., 1775.
  b. 5 April, 1750; d. Danvers, 2 Nov., 1817, brother of Benj., q. v.; m. 16 Dec., 1778, Hannah Larrabee of Lynn; prob. father of Dan'l who was b. 2 Nov., 1779, and m. Sarah Osborn.

VERRY, GEORGE,
 enl. 1777, for 3 yrs., Continental Army.
 Received pension, 1819, then æt. 78; died 26 Feb., 1825, son of Samuel (a son of Benj. Verry, Sr.).

VERRY, JOSEPH,
 enl. 1775, Capt. Gallusha's Co., 25th Reg.; Oct. 1775.
 m. 16 Nov., 1763, Abigail Philips.

VERRY, WILLIAM,
 enl. 1775, Capt. Gallusha's Co., 25th Reg.; Oct. 1775; enl. 1777 for 3 years, Capt. Whipple's Co., 5th Reg., Continental Army; served 36 mos.

VERY, BELA,
 enl. 1777 for during war, Capt. Burbeck's Co., Col. Crane's Reg., Continental Army; served 5 mos., 6 days; killed.

VERY, WILLIAM,
 enl. 1775, Capt. Prince's Co., 19th Reg.; 6 Oct., 1775.
 Received pension 1819, æt. 71; d. 2 Jan., 1824; prob. son of Sam'l and brother of George, q. v. Wm. Very and Sarah Moulton, pub. 27 Dec., 1783.

WAITE, JONATHAN,
 enl. 26 Feb., 1781 for 3 yrs., Continental Army.
 He was a pensioner, æt. 61 in 1818; d. 12 Jan., 1821.

WAIT, PETER,
 enl. 1776, Capt. Gray's Co., Col. Marshall's Reg.; 15 July, 1776; enl. 1777 for 3 years, Continental Army.

WAIT, SAMUEL,
 enl. 25 Aug., 1777, sergt.; dis. 14 Dec., 1777, Capt. Flint's Co., Col. Johnson's Reg.

WARDELL, JOHN,
 enl. 1776, Capt. Melville's Co., Col. Craft's Artillery; 8 June, 1776.

WASHBURN, ELIJAH,
 enl. 1775, Capt. Putnam's Co., 19th Reg.; 6 Oct., 1775.

WEATHERLY, JOHN, of Chelmsford,
 recruit 1778, sent to Fishkill, 9 mos., Continental Army.

WEBB, MICHAEL,
 enl. 1775, Capt. Putnam's Co., 19th Reg.; 6 Oct. 1775.

WEBBER, RICHARD, "transient,"
 enl. 1777, for 3 yrs., Continental Army.

WELCH, PETER,
 enl. 1775, corp.; Capt. Prince's Co., 19th Reg.; 6 Oct., 1775.

WHIPPLE, BENJAMIN,
 enl. 1775, Capt. Putnam's Co., 19th Reg.; 6 Oct., 1775.

WHIPPLE, DAVID,
 enl. 1775, Capt. Putnam's Co., 19th Reg.; 6 Oct., 1775; enl. 1777, for 3 years, Continental Army.
 prob. a bro. of Capt. Job, q. v.

WHIPPLE, JOB,
 enl. 1775, Lt.; Capt. Putnam's Co., 19th Reg.; 6 Oct. 1775. See also French War soldiers. Capt. Job Whipple was wounded at Bennington.
 b. 28 May, 1739; son of Deacon Joseph (b. 2 Feb., 1702; d. 1740) and Sarah (dau. of Joseph and Mary Swinnerton) Whipple. Ch.: (Capt.) John, b. 1776; d. 1857.

WHIPPLE, SAMUEL,
 enl. sergt., Capt. Putnam's Co., 19th Reg.; 6 Oct., 1775; enl. 1777, during war, Capt. Page's Co., 11th Reg.; served 44 mos., 3 days.

WHITE, HAFFIELD,
 enl. 13 Apr., 1781, for 3 yrs., Continental Army.
 Son of Haffield and Lydia (Masters) White of Wenham, born there 4

(*White Continued.*)
Apr., 1764; d. unm. 1793. He was a mariner and lived in Danvers, and a nephew of Thomas White below.

WHITE, JOSIAH,
enl. 26 Mar., 1781 for 3 yrs., Continental Army.

WHITE, JOHN,
enl. 1775, Capt. Prince's Co., 19th Reg.; 6 Oct., 1775.

WHITE, JOSEPH,
enl. 10 Oct., dis. 10 Nov.. 1779; Capt. Mallon's Co., Essex Co. Reg. Stationed at Castle Island.

WHITE, THOMAS,
enl. 2 May. 1775, Capt. Eben'r Francis's Co., Col. Mansfield's Reg. In service 27 Oct., 1775. He was probably of Wenham.

WHITE, THOMAS,
enl. 4 May. 1775, as sergeant in Capt. Enoch Putnam's Co., 19th Reg. In service 26 Oct., 1775.
The two above are probably father and son, the father a son of Josiah White.

WIAT, JOSEPH,
enl. 25 Aug., 1777, drummer; dis. 14 Dec., 1777; Capt. Flint's Co., Col. Johnson's Reg.

WIET, SAMUEL,
enl. 1775, corp.; Capt. Prince's Co., 19th Reg.; 6 Oct., 1775.

WILKINS, AQUILA,
recruit for Capt. Foster's Co., at Fishkill, Continental Army, Dec., 1778.

WILKINS, DAVID,
enl. 1775, corp., Capt. Prince's Co., 19th Reg.; 6 Oct., 1775.

WILLIAMS, EBENEZER,
enl. 1775, Capt. Gallusha's Co., 25th Reg.; Oct., 1775; enl. 1 Jan., 1777, during war,

(*Williams Continued.*)
Capt. Hitchcock's Co., 1st Reg., Continental Army, served 48 mos.

WILLIS, EBENEZER, JR.,
enl. 1777, for 3 years, Continental Army.

WILSON, JOSEPH, of Billerica,
enl. 1777, during war, Capt. Fox's Co., 16th Reg.; Continental Army; served 38 mos., 23 days.

WINES, THOMAS,
enl. 1775, Capt. Putnam's Co., 19th Reg.; 6 Oct., 1775.

WITT, JOHN,
enl. 7 May, 1782 for 3 yrs., Continental Army. £84 bounty.

WOOD, JONATHAN,
enl. 1775, Capt. Putnam's Co., 19th Reg.; 6 Oct, 1775.

WOOD, THOMAS,
enl. 11 Sept., 1781, for 3 yrs., Continental Army.

WOODMAN, BENJAMIN,
Capt. Low's Co., 19th Reg.; 6 Oct., 1775.

WOODMAN, BENJAMIN, "residence unknown,"
enl. 1777, for 3 yrs., Continental Army.

WOTEMORE, GEORGE,
enl. 1777, for 3 yrs. Continental Army.

WYATT, JOSHUA, see Wiat,
recruit for Capt. Town's company at Fishkill, Continental Army, Dec., 1778. Reported at Springfield, 10 July, 1779 as a recruit (9 mos.) for Capt. Towne's Co., Col. Thorndike's Reg.; æt. 22, 5 ft. 9 in. in height, light complexion.
b. 5 Dec., 1757; son of George, jr. and Sarah Wiat.

Hanson gives a list of names of men from Danvers engaged in the Revolution. As the list printed above is not and cannot, from the imperfect nature of the existing records, be absolutely correct, it is thought advisable to add such names given by Hanson which will not be found elsewhere in this report. As the list was compiled in the forties, doubtless many of the names were obtained from elderly people then living.

Barker, Benj.
Berry, William
Clinton, John
Colley, William
Dale, John E.
Deadman, William
Downs, Nathaniel
Elwell, David
Endicott, John
Eppes, Samuel
Larrabee, David
Larrabee, Jona.
Le Count, Samuel
Leeds, Nathaniel
Lewis, Elijah
Loring, Benj.
Nichols, Joseph
Osborne, Sylvester
Pillsbury, Joseph
Porter, John
Proctor, Johnson
Rano, Thomas
Reed, Benjamin
Reed, William
Rue, William
Setchel, Jonathan
Setchel, John
Shaw, Benj.
Shaw, Joseph
Smith, Ephraim
Stone, James
Symonds, Francis
Symonds, Sip
Symonds, Thomas
Tanner, David
Towne, George
Tufts, Joseph
Twiss, Joseph
Twist, Samuel
Waite, Jonathan
Whipple, Matthew
Wilson, Jonathan
Wilson, Newhall
Wood, Moses
Wyman, Solomon

There are many evident errors in this list of Hanson's both in Christian and surnames. Perhaps some of these were privateersmen, of whom no other list exists.

MILITIA OFFICERS.

During the twenty years following the Revolution many of the veterans of that war obtained commissions in the militia and thus a list of the officers commissioned from Danvers is of especial interest.

Gideon Foster was commissioned Colonel of the 6th regiment, 13 Sept., 1792, Brigadier General, 30 April, 1796 and Major General, 17 June, 1801, was discharged 1806.

Ebenezer Goodale commissioned Captain, 20 Dec., 1796, Major, 1 Dec. 1800, Lieutenant-Colonel, 12 April 1804, Major General, 7 Feb., 1812, placed under arrest 8 Aug., 1812, and cashiered 13 Oct., 1812.

Jethro Putnam commissioned Major, 13 Sept., 1792, Lieutenant-Colonel, 4 April 1796, Colonel commanding, 20 Oct., 1796.

Jacob B. Winchester commissioned Adjutant, 12 Sept., 1793.

Ebenezer Shillaber commissioned Quartermaster, 17 Sept., 1793.

The following were commissioned Lieutenants at the dates set after their names:

Amos King, 10 Oct., 1791.
Andrew Nichols, 10 Oct., 1792, promoted Captain 5 April, 1796, promoted Major 20 Oct., 1796.
Daniel Reed, jr., 3 June. 1794.
Jonathan Walcutt, 25 Sept , 1794.
Jonathan Procter, jr., 3 May, 1796.
Daniel King, 31 Aug., 1796, promoted Captain 9 Dec., 1796.
Richard Osborne, 9 Dec., 1796.
Nathaniel Felton, 19 Dec., 1796, promoted Captain 26 Jan., 1801.
Samuel Flint, 2 May, 1797, promoted captain 26 Jan., 1801.
John Gardner, 26 Jan., 1801.
William Cross, 26 Jan., 1801, promoted Captain 22 May, 1804.
Thomas Emerson, 20 May, 1802, promoted Captain 3 April, 1804.
John Fowler, 19 July, 1802.
Andrew Monroe, 3 Feb. 1803, promoted Captain 14 March, 1803, promoted Major, 24 May, 1804.
Ebenezer Moulton, jr., 14 March, 1804.
Jonathan Porter, 3d, 26 Sept., 1803, promoted Captain.
John Sanders, 3 April, 1804.
Elijah Flint, 22 May, 1804.
James Proctor, 7 May, 1805.
Wm. Goodale, 27 June, 1806.
The following were commissioned captains on the date set against their names:
James Foster, 10 Oct., 1791.
Benjamin Putnam, 18 Oct., 1792.
Zechariah King, 15 April, 1792, promoted Major 18 April, 1796.
Levi Preston, 6 May, 1794.
Johnson Procter, 25 April, 1796 (he was ensign, 10 Oct., 1791).
Sylvester Osborne, 3 May, 1796, promoted Brigade Major.
Daniel Usher, 22 Nov., 1796.
Fitch Pool, 12 April, 1802.
David Putnam, 28 July, 1803, promoted Major.
John Felton, 2 July, 1804, promoted Major.
Daniel Preston, 31 Aug., 1813; promoted Lt. Col. 19 Sept., 1813; promoted Colonel 5 Aug., 1818.

From a return of the sixth regiment, first brigade, second division, 1797, it appears that Jethro Putnam was colonel and Johnson Proctor, Daniel Usher, Daniel Ring, Solomon Wilkins, Ebenezer Goodale were captains. Adjutant, Daniel Osborn.

SHAY'S REBELLION.

There were fourteen men from Danvers in Capt. John Frances' company, in Col. Wade's Essex County regiment, which marched to help subdue the so-called Shay's rebellion. The names of four of these are as follows, Daniel Needham, lieutenant; Josiah White, sergeant; Moses Thomas, corporal; Daniel Bell, drummer.

SOLDIERS OF THE WAR OF 1812.

LIST OF SOLDIERS BORN IN DANVERS, WHO SERVED IN THE REGULAR ARMY AS SHOWN BY RECORDS IN THE ADJUTANT-GENERAL'S OFFICE, WAR DEPARTMENT, WASHINGTON.

Dodge, Joseph, was enlisted by Captain John Leonard, February 5, 1814, at Concord, Mass., and served in Colonel Joseph Loring's 40th U. S. Infantry. He was discharged at Portland, April 10, 1815.

Gowan, Daniel W., artificer was enlisted at Boston, January 5, 1814, and served in Captains A. Larrabee's, Francis Stribling's and Nathan Towson's companies. He was discharged January 4, 1819.

Hammond, Samuel H., was enlisted by Lieutenant Peckham, May 20, 1814, at Boston, and served in the 4th U. S. Art'y, Capt. Burton's Co., and in the 5th U. S. Infty, Captain George Gooding's company. He was discharged at Williamsville, N. Y., June 1, 1815.

Harwood, Timothy, was enlisted by Captain James Green, jr., at Salem, Mass., November 8, 1814. He was at Ft. Pickering and Ft. Defiance, and was discharged at Boston, April 20, 1815.

Hall, John, was enlisted at Boston, November 17, 1812, by Lieutenant Clark, and served under Captains O. G. Burton, Geo. Gooding, E. Childs, and J. H. Vose. He was discharged at Ft. Wayne, November 17, 1817.

Harwood, Jacob, was enlisted at Salem, November 5, 1814, by Captain Green, for the U. S. Art'y, and was discharged at Boston, April 20, 1815.

Moulton, John, was enlisted November 3, 1814, at Salem, by Captain James Green, jr., for the U. S. Art'y, and discharged at Boston, April 20, 1815.

Melburn (also Milburn), Thomas, was enlisted March 29, 1814, at Boston by Lieutenant Hight for the U. S. Art'y. He served in Captain T. Ketchum's company and was discharged at Plattsburgh, June 6, 1815.

Pettingale, Ephraim, was enlisted May 30, 1811, at Boston by Lieutenant Hanham for the U. S. Art'y. He served under Lieut. George E. Wells and Captain Alexander S. Brooks, and was discharged May 29, 1816.

Reed (also Read), Isaac, was enlisted Mar. 30, 1813, at Salem, by Captain Ropes. He served in the 21st U. S. Inf't'y under Captain Joseph Treat and was discharged May 24, 1815.

Small, Jonathan, was enlisted November 26, 1814, by Captain James Green, jr. He served in the 15th U. S. Inf't'y, and was discharged April 20, 1815.

Smith, Nathan, was enlisted April 14, 1814, at Salem by Captain T. Ketchum. The "Daily Report" at Plattsburgh, of April 3, 1815, shows him reported as "died since last report."

Southwick, Nathaniel, was enlisted January (or June) 14, 1814, at Newburyport by Lieutenant Hight. He served under Captains F. Stribling and Thomas Ketchum, and was discharged May 25, 1815, at Sackett's Harbor.

Thompson, John, was enlisted May 16, 1814, at Concord, N. H., by Captain Way for the 4th U. S. Inf't'y. He deserted May 22, 1814.

Wyman, Ebenezer, was enlisted March 24, 1814, at Boston by Lieutenant D. Chandler, for the 9th U. S. Inf't'y. He served also under Captain E. Childs, and was discharged May 17, 1815, at Sackett's Harbor.

FROM STATE ARCHIVES.

Putnam, Elbridge, on guard at Fort Lee, Salem, 13 Sept. to 7 Nov., a private in a company of which Asa Tapley and Amos King were lieutenants.

He was born 4 Sept., 1794, and was the son of Timothy and Hannah, dau. of Col. Enoch Putnam. He died 2 Nov., 1839. His wife was Sally, dau. of William Goodale (b. Danvers, 15 May, 1796; d. 9 Nov., 1843); they were married 13 Nov., 1825. Ch.: Sarah A., b. 25 June, 1826; m. 31 Dec., 1848, Daniel Baker of Danvers. Harriet A., b. 12 Sept., 1829; d. June, 1878. Hannah V., b. 4 Jan., 1832.

Without doubt there were other men from Danvers but the residence is not given on many of the rolls.

Roll of company commanded by Capt. Jesse Putnam of Danvers, stationed at Salem from 22 Sept., 1814 to 31 Oct., 1814. This was an artillery company raised in Danvers.

Jesse Putnam, captain, David Foster, lieutenant.

SERGEANTS.

Warren Porter, Amarial Prince, George Abbott, Aaron Tapley.

CORPORALS

WARREN PORTER, given as Sergeant in Capt. Jesse Putnam's company, was promoted Lieutenant after said company was stationed at Beverly, and later was Lieut.-Colonel and Colonel of Artillery. The star was by error affixed to Corporal Alfred Porter (page 139), a brother of Warren Porter.

Charles Foster	Nathaniel Reed	Abel Lincoln
David Wilkins	Ephraim Flagg	Edward Hooper
Thomas Chadborn	Richard Butler	Eben Fry
Isaac Monroe	Benjamin Nichols	George Floyd
Eliphalet Taylor	Nathaniel Smith	

*He was promoted Lieutenant and later was Lt. Col., and Col. of Artillery.

The uniform of the Danvers Artillery was a chapeau brass cap with long white plume, tipped with red, a long skirted red coat with white trimmings, white waistecoat, buff breeches with buckles at the knees and long boots. A sword was worn in a belt over the shoulder, and the hair was powdered and made up in a queue, which hung over the coat collar.

ALARM LIST AT NEW MILLS.

Samuel Page, captain.   Thomas Putnam, lieutenant.

SERGEANTS.

Caleb Oakes,   John Endicott.

John Page, clerk.

PRIVATES.

Thomas Cheever, Edward Richardson, Hooper Stimpson, Stephen Brown, Samuel Pindar, John Fowler, Samuel Trickey, William Francis, Samuel Fowler, Benjamin Kent, Moses Black, Daniel Putnam, Joseph Stearns, Jonas Warren, Eben Dale, George Waitt, Nathaniel Putnam, John W. Osgood, Allen Gould, Ebenezer Jacobs, Moses Waitt, Andrew Gould, William Trask, Israel Hutchinson, George Osgood, Henry Brown, Ebenezer Berry, William Cutler, Daniel Hardy, Jonathan Sheldon, Seth Stetson, Michael Saunders, Ezra Batchelder, Thomas Symonds, Richard Skidmire, Ephraim Smith, Hercules Josselyn, Jeremiah Page, Benj. Wellington, Moses Putnam, Israel Andrew, Nathaniel Mayhew, John Wheeler, David Tarr, John Russell, John Kenny, Jacob Allen, Daniel Usher, Israel Endicott, James F. Putnam.

ALARM LIST IN SOUTH DANVERS.

Gideon Foster, captain, Johnson Procter, Nathan Felton, lieutenants; Daniel King, ensign; John Upton, orderly-sergeant.

PRIVATES.

William Pool, Eben S. Upton, Rufus Wyman, Eben King, Amos King, John Goldthwaite, John Osborn, Oliver Saunders, Joseph Griffin, Stephen Procter, Asa Bushby, Asa Tapley, James Wilson, John Needham, Jonathan Osborn, Amos Osborn, W. W. Little, James Southwick, Joseph Shaw, George Southwick, Sylvester Osborn, jr., Benj. Stephens, Benj. Gile, Elisha Gunnison, Eben Osborn, Solomon McIntire, William Sutton, Samuel Buxton and others.

Soldiers in Mexican War.

FROM RECORDS IN THE ADJUTANT-GENERAL'S OFFICE, WASHINGTON, D. C.

Putnam, John J. (sailor), was enlisted by Captain Duprene, in July, 1847, at Vera Cruz, for " G," Third Dragoons, and discharged (no date) for disability at New Orleans.

Tucker, John, was enlisted at Boston (no date) by Lieutenant Archer for the 9th Infantry. He deserted June 15, 1847.

Very, Benjamin F., was enlisted at New Orleans, Dec. 11, 1844, by Captain Holmes, and served in " K," Seventh Infantry; wounded Aug. 20, 1847, in battle at Contreras; died Aug. 24, 1847, in hospital at San Angel, Mexico.

b. N. H.

Wilson, Douglas R., served in the navy. See Rebellion Record.

ENLISTMENTS IN THE FIRST REGIMENT MASS. VOLUNTEERS, CALEB CUSHING, COLONEL, CHARLES B. CROWNINSHIELD, CAPTAIN. ALL OF COMPANY E. STATE ARCHIVES.

Prime, Hiram, enl. 3 Feb., 1847, æt. 23, born in Danvers.

Twiss, Joshua, enl. 8 Feb., 1847, æt. 20, born in Danvers.

Twiss, William H., enl. 8 Feb., 1847, æt. 18, born in Danvers, died in the army.

Hanson in his History of Danvers, states that five Danvers men (not named) were in the Mexican War.

MILITIA COMPANIES OF DANVERS.
1796 – 1817.

Subsequent to the Revolution and prior to 1800 there were two or more organizations in Danvers. One of these was commanded by Capt. King, commissioned, 1791, and succeeded by Capt. Proctor, 1796. The roll of the company in 1796 is appended.

Roll of Capt. Levi Amos King's Company, 1796.*

LIEUTENANTS.
Amos King, Johnson Proctor.

SERGEANTS.
Nathan Felton, Jona. Proctor, jr., John Gardner, jr., David Taylor, jr.

PRIVATES.

Joseph Brown	Daniel Marsh	Daniel Proctor
Daniel Brown	Ezekiel Marsh, 3d	Francis Proctor
Allen Curtice	Thos. H. Marsh	James Proctor
Nath'l Davis	Aaron Marsh	Amos Putnam, jr.
Joseph Doutey	John Mansfield	Rufus Putnam
Nath'l Felton	Joseph Mansfield	Stephen Putney
Asa Felton	Eben'r Moulton, jr.	Geo. Southwick, jr.
Ebenezer Felton	Andrew Munroe	Nathan Southwick
Aaron Foster	Nathaniel Nurse	Oliver Taylor
Daniel Goodale	Jasper Needham	Eben'r Twiss
John Gardner, 3d	John Needham, jr.	John Thorrington
John King	Nathaniel Newhall, jr.	Amos Verry
Eben'r Larrabee, jr.	Joseph Newhall, jr.*	Henry William
Enoch Marble	David Newhall, jr.*	Samuel Taylor
Bartholemew Moulton	Moses Preston	

The book of the company in the sixth regiment, first brigade, second division commanded by Captain Johnson Proctor (appointed 25 April, 1796) until 16 Jan., 1801, preserved among the records in the Adj. Gen. Dept. is evidently the record of King's company subsequent to his retirement from command. It furnishes the names of a few of the enlisted men, of which the following occur from 1796 to 1817 ; Jona. Procter, Nathaniel Felton, John Gardner, Henry Williams, Aaron Marsh, Andrew Monroe, Ebenezer Moulton, John Felton, James Procter, Thomas H. Marsh, Daniel Brown, Amos King, 3d, Samuel Newel, Henry Douty, Solomon Arbin, Jonathan Small, John Nurse, John Hook, Thornedike Procter.

*Archives Danvers Historical Society.

Jonathan Danforth, Thornedike Felton, John Mansfield, jr., Ebenezer Putnam, David Putnam, John B. Fowler, Eben Felton, John Needham, jr., Charles Putnam, Jonathan Butterfield, David Center, Joshua Putnam, John Williams, jr., Silas Winchester, Amos Flint, jr., Aaron Marsh, Nathan Southwick, Ebenezer Twiss, John Needham, 3d, John Twiss, Daniel Taylor, jr., David Newhall, jr., Joseph Douty, Asa Gardner, Aaron Foster, Nathaniel Felton, jr., John Carr, Edmund Monroe, Moses Preston, jr., Benj. Herrick, Daniel Galusha, John Jacobs, 3d, Temple Roberts, Stephen Needham, Aaron Wood, Henry Preston, Daniel Felton, Richard Crowninshield, William Patterson, David Wood, John Tarbox, Jonathan Barrett, Stephen Procter, Daniel Moore, Timothy Harwood, Asa Goodale, Uriah Monroe, Benj. Hoyt, Moody Morse, Joseph Newhall, Nathan Parker, Jeremiah Sheldon.

There were usually about fifty men enlisted in the company.

Fines for neglect of equipment and absence from parade are frequent matters of record.

THE DANVERS LIGHT INFANTRY, M. M.

ORGANIZED 1818.   DISBANDED ABOUT 1850.

The first officers of the company were Robert S. Daniels, captain, Abner Sanger, lieutenant, Allen Gould, ensign.

The uniform consisted of a blue swallow tail coat with gold buttons, a white or buff waistcoat and pantaloons, high, stiff hat, larger at the top than base, with gold trimming and a tall plume.

The company was disbanded about 1850, but on the 10 Sept., 1862, over 100 of the past members of the organization escorted a company of volunteers departing for the scene of war. This was the last appearance of the Danvers Light Infantry under the old regime.

DANVERS LIGHT INFANTRY, M. V. M.—ORGANIZED 1891.

A sketch of the Danvers Light Infantry. Co. K. Eighth Regiment, M. V. M., would be incomplete without a word of reference to its immediate predecessor.

The Mechanic Light Infantry of Salem, also known as Co. K, Eighth Regiment, was disbanded by order of the commander-in-chief, issued by Adj't Gen'l Dalton, Nov. 30, 1889, after a continuous existence of 82 years, having been organized Feb. 2, 1807. The officers at the time of disbandment were William H. Dunney, captain; Horace Durgin, first lieutenant; William H. Tweed, second lieutenant. It bore upon its rolls at the time 5 enlisted men, the full quota.

The place thus made vacant in the Eighth Regiment was sought after by many companies. A petition from Salem was denied in 1889. Finally, in 1891, it was given out that a petition from Danvers would be favorably received by the governor (William E. Russell) and the paper was accordingly drawn up by Lieut. Col. (subsequently Colonel) Charles L. Dodge, of the Eighth, and circulated among the young men of the town by F. Pierce Tebbetts. John T. Carroll was the first signer.

March 9, 1891, Col. J. Albert Mills of the Eighth came to Danvers and met the signers of the petition at the skating rink on Maple street, which building was subsequently remodeled for an armory for the company.

A few days later, the colonel's impressions having been favorably reported to the governor, the petition was sent in, and Adj't Gen. Samuel Dalton was directed by the commander-in-chief to inspect the would-be soldiers, which he did on the evening of March 17, at Town hall, assisted by Col. George A. Keeler.

Upon receipt of the general's report, the governor caused an order to be issued, directing the muster-in of the company at Danvers, on March 25. On that date the men gathered at the Old Berry Tavern, where the old time militia-men were wont to assemble years ago, and Col. Mills then and there mustered into the state service 51 men. Assisting Col. Mills were Lieut. Col. Dodge, Maj. Pew, Surgeon Hersey, Assistant Surgeon Galloupe and Paymaster Warner. Lieut. G. N. B. Cousens of I Company, Lynn, who was detailed to act as instructor to the new company, was also present.

On the same evening a special town meeting had been called, and upon a presentation of the matter by Frank C. Damon and Col. Mills, $100 was appropriated to heat and light the armory of the company for a year. Later the selectmen leased the skating rink for a period of five years, and the company, assisted by the honorary members, and skating rink association, remodeled and furnished the structure at an expense of some $3,000.

The first drills were held at Town hall, under the instruction of Lieut. Cousens. Here, April 7, the members of the company assembled for the election of officers. Lieut. Col. Dodge presided, and the result was as follows: Frank C. Damon was elected captain, receiving all of the 45 votes cast. F. Pierce Tebbetts was elected first lieutenant, receiving on the second ballot 42 of the 49 votes cast. Fred U. French was elected second lieutenant on the second ballot, receiving 25 votes, while A. Preston Chase received 24.

On the 22d of April the above named officers appeared before the military examining board, of which Brig. Gen. Peach was president, at the State House, Boston, and were commissioned and assigned to duty.

The new armory was opened in due form, Aug. 26, 1891, and drills have since been held there weekly.

In May, 1892, Lieut. Tebbetts resigned, and Lieut. French was promoted to first lieutenant, while Sergt. A. Preston Chase was elected second lieutenant.

There have been many changes in the membership of the command in the three years that it has been in existence, but most of the officers remain the same. The original members of the company are given herewith, those marked with an asterisk being mustered in at various times between March 25 and the first encampment in July, 1891.

Muster Roll of Company as It Went to Its First Camp, July, 1891.

Frank C. Damon, Captain.

F. Pierce Tebbets, First Lieut.   Fred U. French, Second Lieut.

Sergeants.

Alfred H. Cook, First Sergt.

A. Preston Chase, John T. Carroll, George W. Battye, Herbert E. Hall.

Corporals.

Thorndike P. Hawkes, George B. Moulton, Henry W. French, Michael H. Barry.

Privates.

J. Allen Atwood	Albert F. Learoyd	Francis L. Parker
Alfred E. Ayers	Orrin F. Legro	George O. Rundlett
Elmer J. Ayers	William P. Levy	William A. Sillars
Lewis E. Blanchard	George S. Lawson	Walter T. Stone
*John D. Brummitt	Arthur W. Lake	George H. Scampton
*William L. Burns	James Means	George F. Sutherland
Henry C. Crosby	Charles F. Mackenzie	*John Smiley
Herbert E. Dole	John J. Macauley	*William F. Searle
*Daniel J. Doyle	*E. Eugene Mitchell	*Orrin E. Swain
Charles L. Elliott	Frank D. Nimblett	*Fred E. Swain
Harvey W. Eaton	Eugene E. O'Neil	*Charles E. Stuart
Edwin Flye	Austin H. Putnam	Herbert B. Tibbetts
George H. Flint	Fred C. Patterson	Justin A. Towne
L. W. Goldthwaite	James A. Perry	William S. Walcott
Samuel B. Hoar	George H. Poor	Laforest W. Watson
Edwin L. Jacques	Edwin W. Palmer	*John Lowery
Alonzo G. Kimball		

58 men and 3 officers—61.

1775 – April 19, – 1891.

The Danvers Historical Society celebrated the 116th anniversary of the Battle of Lexington, Apr. 20, 1891, by exercises afternoon and evening at the Town Hall, with an intermission of a couple of hours, pleasantly spent at the supper table, which was spread in Gothic Hall, and at which nearly two hundred covers were laid.

The Town Hall was gracefully and appropriately decorated under the personal supervision of Dr. Warren Porter. Upon the platform were portraits of Gen. Gideon Foster and Gen. Moses Porter, the rapier once owned by Capt. Jeremiah Page, and memorials of Capt. Samuel Flint. Upon the platform were seated many invited guests; there being a large delegation headed by their President, from the Lexington Historical Society. The hall was taxed to its utmost seating capacity, nearly five hundred people being present.

Shortly after half-past three, after the singing of a hymn written by Rev. James Flint and prayer by Rev. E. C. Ewing, President A. P. Putnam addressed the meeting, saying:

"*Ladies and Gentlemen:* Other towns which were represented prominently in the battle of April 19, 1775, have from time to time very worthily commemorated the event. Lexington has done so this year; Concord is now doing so. I am not aware that Danvers has celebrated the day except as the old, undivided town commemorated it at the dedication of the monument to the men who fell in the engagement. That act of dedication was fifty-six years ago today. It is proper, we think, that the good old town should follow the example of her sister towns, and it has seemed meet that the Danvers Historical Society should take the initiation. That is why we are here today, for Danvers, as well as other towns, took an honorable part in that day's strife and warfare, a part which it has seemed to us should be told as it has not been before. Her citizens had long considered the course of affairs before April 19, 1775; had discussed in shop and store and tavern and town meeting the oppressive measures of the mother country, and had more and more entered into a determination to be free and not slaves. They organized militia and minute companies, trained them on their own Common in the town and on the Village Green, and more and more prepared themselves for action in case the hour of emergency should arrive. That hour arrived and not less than eight companies rushed forth to the scene of action.

The story will be told by those who are to follow me. I shall not take up their precious time. It is enough for me simply to announce the character of the meeting, the purposes of it and what we trust will be the lesson of it, and to welcome those who have been invited to join us as special guests of the occasion. They come, I might well say, from many a battlefield of that day, for the battlefield extended all the way from Lexington and Concord back to Lexington and on to Charlestown. It was one continuous day's work. And we have to greet friends here and now from Lexington, Concord, Acton and elsewhere, from Boston, from Salem and towns immediately around us, as well as invited guests from the town of Danvers. It is with great pleasure that we welcome Rev. Dr. George W. Porter, a native of Beverly, the President of the Lexington Historical Society, the nephew of General Moses Porter, one of the most illustrious soldiers of his time, whose portrait you see before you. We welcome Charles Parker of Lexington, the great grandson of the Capt. Parker who commanded the militia on Lexington Common. We welcome Luther Monroe. Ensign Robert Monroe, sixty-three years old, the first man killed at Lexington, was his grandfather's uncle."

Dr. Putnam then introduced Mr. Ezra D. Hines, the historiographer of the Danvers Historical Society who delivered the following interesting sketch of the part the Danvers men took in the battle, many of the facts being freshly collated and more fully given than in any other historical account on record:

WHAT THE DANVERS MEN DID.

"We meet today and in the language of the poet say—

'Backward, turn backward! O Time in thy flight,'

—so that we may in imagination believe the wheels of time actually turned back, and that we stand face to face with the men and the events of long ago.

What are we here to celebrate? We assemble near the anniversary of that great day, April 19, 1775, that day dear to all true American hearts, to celebrate events which have become historic, and which have become noted the world over. We are here to call to remembrance that day when the first blood of the revolution was shed by our townsmen and our countrymen in defence of their lives, their liberties and their homes.

We come also to commemorate that day which has been made glorious, and which is and shall be renowned as the day on which were begun those events which finally culminated in the emancipation of the American colonies from the yoke of England, and which resulted in the establishment of a new nation and the beginning of a career of future usefulness and glory. But more especially do we come to recount the deeds and to rehearse the brave actions of the men of Danvers, our ancestors, who took part in that first bloody resistance to the British authorities, and in which some of them gave their lives in defence of their country.

The storm which on the 19th day of April, 1775, burst upon this neighborhood was neither sudden nor unexpected: it had been brewing for a long time, and as we are told in Holy Writ of the wise man who built his house upon a strong foundation, so that when the rain descended and the floods came and the winds blew and beat upon that house, it fell not, because that man had builded wisely, with the solid rock for a foundation: so, when this April Revolutionary storm beat upon our ancestors, upon men wise in judgment, and with principles and convictions firm and enduring as the solid rock, they were not surprised, and this occurrence did not take them unawares, for, like the wise man, they were prepared and ready when the emergency came.

Governor Gage issued writs Sept. 1, 1774, convening the General Court at Salem on the 5th of October, but dissolved it by proclamation dated Sept. 28, 1774. The members, however, who were elected to it, pursuant to the course agreed upon, resolved themselves into a Provincial Congress. One of the members of this Congress was Dr. Samuel Holten, a man honored and beloved in Danvers. This body, on the 26th of October, adopted a plan for organizing the militia, maintaining it and calling it out when circumstances should render it necessary. It provided that one-quarter of the number enrolled should be held in readiness to muster at the shortest notice, who were called by the popular name of Minute Men. An executive authority—the Committee of Safety—was created, clothed with large discretionary powers, and another called the Committee of Supplies. Another very important act of this Congress was the authorizing of the collection of military stores.

The several towns also formed alarm-list companies. These were stirring times, but men were found equal to the occasion; men who had the courage of their convictions and who dared to declare that 'no danger shall affright, no difficulties shall intimidate us: and, if in support of our rights we are called to encounter even death, we are yet undaunted, sensible that he can never die too soon who lays down his life in support of the laws and liberties of his country.'

How soon some of them were to lay down their lives we shall presently see.

The town of Danvers had at that time some regular militia companies, and new companies were now formed to carry out the wishes of the late Congress, so that when the 19th of April arrived we find there were eight companies in the town.

Before I speak of the Danvers men and the part they took in this first battle, let me briefly relate what happened on the night of the 18th of April, and the early morning of the 19th.

As before stated, the Congress of which I have spoken authorized the collection of military stores, and one of the places where such stores had been collected was at Concord.

To seize these stores was an objective point on the part of the British General Gage: so on the night of the 18th of April, about 10.30 o'clock, the British troops, consisting of grenadiers, light infantry and marines, about 800 in all (the flower of the British army), under the command of Lieut. Colonel Smith, leave Boston and get across in boats to the Cambridge side, landing at Lechmere's Point, East Cambridge; they remain here awhile, and then march along and reach Menotomy (what is now Arlington) about 2 A. M. of the 19th, and then continue their march to Lexington, where they arrive in the early morning, and where the colonists are drawn up in arms to meet them, having been warned of the approach of the British, as you are all well aware, by Paul Revere in his midnight ride. And here in Lexington was the first resistance offered to the British on their march.

The question has often arisen, Who fired the first shot on that eventful morning? But no one has ever doubted that the first shot was fired and that it was heard around the world. And now let us leave the British troops at Lexington and come back to our own town of Danvers.

Wednesday the 19th day of April, 1775, has arrived. The glorious orb of day in his course through the heavens casts his beams aslant on the villages of our town, in which peace and harmony and intense loyalty dwell. He looks down upon our pastures green with grass, upon the peach trees in full bloom, upon the barley waving in the fields. His hot rays presage a warm and sultry day. This describes the early morning. It is now near nine o'clock. The hurried hoof-beats of a messenger's horse are heard in our streets, where so recently all was quiet. He announces in a loud, strong and vigorous voice: 'The British have marched to Lexington, our brothers there have met them, and a battle has ensued. Rise, brothers, and without delay hasten to their relief!'

No sooner is the message given than the men of Danvers prepare to depart for the scene of carnage. Let us bear in mind that the Danvers of 1775 was a very large town, including besides the present town of Danvers the town now known as Peabody. The messenger had undoubtedly first aroused the people of the south part of the town, which is now Peabody; and now, from field and mill, from farm and shop, from parsonage and humbler dwelling, do the men of Danvers rush forth to their country's defence. Truly can it be said of them:

> 'Swift as the summons came they left
> The plow, mid furrow, standing still,
> The half-ground corn grist in the mill,
> The spade in earth, the axe in cleft.
>
> They went where duty seemed to call.
> They scarcely asked the reason why;
> They only knew they could but die,
> And death was not the worst of all.'

Eight companies marched from Danvers on that eventful day.

Three of the companies belonged to the Essex Regiment, commanded by Col. Timothy Pickering of Salem. One of these companies was under the command of Capt. Samuel Flint. It numbered about forty-five officers and men, and from their names it would seem that it came from what is now West Peabody and Danvers Centre.

Another was Capt. Samuel Epes's company, consisting of eighty-two officers and men. This company was from the south part of the town, now Peabody. The late Gen. Gideon Foster was an officer of this company.

I should remark here that upon the lists at the State house, Gen. Foster is not named as commander of a company ; but, at the dedication of the monument in 1835, in his remarks he alluded to the fact that about ten days previous to the battle, he raised a company of minute men, and had command of them on that day. The men were taken from Capt. Epes' company.

On the morning of the 19th of April, Capt. Epes, after the alarm was given, hastened to Salem and saw his Colonel (Pickering) in his office, the Registry of Deeds, and obtained permission from him to march in advance of the regiment.

The third company belonging to this regiment was under the command of Capt. Jeremiah Page and consisted of thirty-seven officers and men.

A company of minute men commanded by Capt. Israel Hutchinson included fifty-three officers and men from the north part of Danvers, mostly, perhaps, from what is now Danversport, and many from Beverly.

Capt. Caleb Lowe's company, in all twenty-three officers and men, were evidently from the south part of the town. The sixth company was that of Capt. Asa Prince, and numbered thirty-seven officers and men from what is now Danvers Centre. The seventh company was an 'alarm company,' commanded by Capt. John Putnam, and had thirty-five officers and men from the north part of the town. The eighth organization was also an 'alarm company' of seventeen officers and men, commanded by Deacon Edmund Putnam and Rev. Benjamin Balch as first lieutenant. This company was evidently from Putnamville and Beaver Brook.

These were the companies that marched on the 19th. The day was exceedingly warm. They marched and ran to the scene of the conflict over fences, through fields, scaling stone walls, and now on the roads they travelled on, the feeling uppermost in their minds being how to get there the soonest. They probably could not have started much before 10 o'clock, and they must have reached Menotomy (now Arlington) in the neighborhood of half-past two or three. What a march, or run ! What brave fellows they were, and what an heroic spirit they displayed ! They did not go together, the men from the south part of the town going one way and those from the north part another. The cry was, On! on! any way to get there! The goal was finally reached. They arrived at Menotomy, and here with others they prepared to attack the British on their retreat into Charlestown.

While they are waiting let us go back to the early morn at Lexington. The British, after their encounter with the Lexington men, march on to Concord to carry out the purpose for which they started, to wit, to seize the stores already accumulated there. Here, too, as well as at Lexington, they meet with resistance, and finally are obliged to beat a retreat. Their ammunition having given out, they were in great danger of being captured had not Lord Percy's reinforcements met them near Lexington. The number of the colonists constantly increasing, and the firing continuing incessant, the British had nothing to do but to stand and fight or retreat. They begin a retreat, which is continued until they reach Charlestown. In the vicinity of 5 P. M., they reach Menotomy, where our men from Danvers and others are impatiently awaiting them that they may give them battle.

And now the British come in sight, and soon our Danvers men with others will engage them here. From the entrance of the British army into Menotomy until they leave the place, they are beset behind and before. Both sides fight with great vigor. Paige, the historian, says that the carnage was greater here than in any other town on that day. Greater, indeed, than in all others combined, if it be true, as has been stated by a diligent investigator, that at least twenty-two of the Americans and probably more than twice that number of the British fell in West Cambridge.

It seems that the Danvers men, or many of them, had stationed themselves in the yard of Jason Russell, not far from the centre of Menotomy. I understand the house is still standing. In this yard there were many bundles of shingles, looking as though the proprietor was about to shingle his house. Here a sort of barricade was made with these shingles, and inside of this enclosure they stationed themselves and attacked the British soldiers. Near this place is a hill, around which the road wound in such a manner as to conceal the British.

King, in his address at the dedication of the monument to the memory of the Danvers men who fell on that day, states that 'rumor had deceived our men as to the force of the British ; it was their expectation here to have intercepted their retreat. But they had little space of preparation : they soon saw the British in solid column descending the hill on their right, and at the same moment discovered a large flank guard advancing on their left.'

The men here in this enclosure (our Danvers men forming a part), finding themselves in this fearful and trying position, fought desperately and gallantly. The British, too, were desperate. They were mad clear through. They had been harassed all the way thus far on their retreat, but most of the way the provincials had attacked them from under cover. Now to have surrounded them, they were determined to show no quarter.

In this trap our Danvers men were caught; they were pressed so furiously by the British that some of the men—possibly some of our Danvers men—were driven into the cellar of a neighboring house, where they were inhumanly treated.

In this yard of Jason Russell's, or in the cellar of the house above referred to, perished the men whom we are proud to call the Danvers martyrs. As in the past, so now, let us rewrite in letters of living light upon the scroll of the fair record of our good old town the names of those heroes who fell at Menotomy—Benjamin Daland, jr., Henry Jacobs, jr., George Southwick, jr., Samuel Cook, jr., Eben Goldthwait, Perley Putnam, Jotham Webb—who died fighting for their homes and against oppression.

Nor would we forget the wounded of that day, Dennison Wallis and Nathan Putnam, nor the others, officers and men, who survived the fearful fight and lived many years after, but who have all long since passed away. But I must hasten on. The remainder of the story is soon told. The British go on in their retreat, and at dusk have neared the haven they longed for—Charlestown— where they remain for the night. The day is over, the sun has now disappeared from view and soon the darkness of night will cover the scene. What a day it has been! What scenes have been enacted! The dead are tenderly and reverently cared for by the survivors, who know that they have nobly and gloriously fallen, and that—

> ' No more on life's parade shall meet
> That brave and fallen few;
> On fame's eternal camping ground
> Their silent tents are spread,
> And glory guards, with solemn round,
> The bivouac of the dead.'

The troops remain over night accommodating themselves as best they can to the circumstances in which they are placed. The British have been beaten and have been driven back to the place from which they started on the 18th and 19th of April. The war has begun in earnest. There being no immediate prospect of another battle our Danvers men return to their homes, bearing with them their dead and wounded, and on Friday, the 21st, these men, who two days before started for the battle with their comrades, full of life and hope, are now laid to rest in the soil of their own homes and among their kindred. Brave souls! ye gave up your lives for others. Greater love hath no man than this that he lay down his life for his country and his friends.

I was to give a general sketch of the events of the 19th. To other hands is left the task of filling in the details as to individuals, who and what they were and the part they took on that eventful day.

But for the brave men of this and succeeding battles of the Revolution, we should not today have a country to love. Let us remember the debt we owe to these brave heroes and tell it to our children, that they in turn may tell it to their children, and to their children's children, and thus may we keep their memory fresh and green—both now and in all time to come."

Hon. Alden P. White of Danvers read the following letter from John G. Whittier:

OAK KNOLL, APRIL 16, 1891.

Dear Miss Hunt:

I fear that I shall not be able to be present at the meeting of the Danvers Historical Society on the 20th inst. I am sure that the occasion will not be lacking interest, as it will recall the heroism and self-sacrifice of the old historic town a century ago. Your society is doing a good and needed work, and it deserves the hearty support of all our citizens.

I am very truly thy friend,
JOHN G. WHITTIER.

D. Webster King of Boston, a native of Peabody, read a paper concerning Capt. Samuel Flint and General Gideon Foster, both of whom led companies to Lexington. Mr. King is a descendant of these two heroes. A brief abstract is here presented:

"Of the Flints who served in the Revolution, history records but two who were residents of Danvers, Samuel and William; these were descendants respectively of two brothers, Thomas and William, who emigrated to Salem probably previous to 1640. They were evidently in favor of Free Trade; surely they were not High Protectionists; whatever may have been the degree of loyalty of the English ancestors, it is evident that their descendants, in 1775, held slight respect for British rule.

I have no record of Wm. Flint's connection with the battle of Lexington, but he was one of the soldiers from Danvers engaged in the Revolutionary War.

Captain Samuel Flint was in command of one of the seven companies from Danvers which answered to their country's call in the hour of peril, April 19, 1775. It was rumored that Capt. Flint was among the slain, and his return to his family and friends was a joyous surprise. He was, however, destined to die a soldier's death for on the seventh of October, 1777, at Stillwater, he was slain at the head of his company. An officer once asked him where he should find him on a certain occasion; his reply was worthy the proudest days of Sparta: 'Where the enemy is, there will you find me.' Capt. Flint was probably the only commissioned officer from Danvers killed in the Revolution.

Gen. Gideon Foster was born Feb. 13, 1748, in a house formerly standing at the corner of Foster and Lowell streets, Peabody. His father was Gideon Foster, a native of Ipswich, who had married

Lydia Goldthwait of Danvers. Gideon Foster married Marcia, daughter of Daniel Jacobs, Oct. 6, 1750; their children were Gideon, John, Marcia and Lydia, none of whom married, so the family is now extinct.

Gen. Foster was of a commanding and impressive bearing as I well remember. Of the company drafted here he was chosen commander and the first time he led them to face the enemy was on Sunday, the twenty-sixth of Feb., 1775, when Col. Leslie attempted to destroy the stores at Salem and Danvers. I quote Gen. Foster's own words from his address fifty-six years ago: 'About ten days before, I had been chosen to command a company of minute men. They all assembled on this very spot where we are now assembled and in about four hours from the time of meeting, they travelled on foot (full half the way upon the run) sixteen miles, and saluted the enemy. Three of them were slain upon that day. I alone remain to tell their story.'

In 1792, Capt. Foster was promoted to the rank of Colonel; in 1796, he was chosen Brigadier-General and in 1801 he was elected Major General by the Legislature.

Gen. Foster was probably the last surviving commissioned officer of the Revolution."

Mr. Eben Putnam spoke as follows:

The Putnams at Lexington Fight.

" I have been asked to tell you something of ' Captains Edmund and John Putnam and others.' I shall confine myself to the Putnams, but were I to include amongst the 'others' all of that name who were present at the Retreat of the British from Concord, or even those there from Danvers, I should be taking the time allotted to the more eloquent and interesting speakers yet to follow.

Before I pass to a more extended notice of those to whom such is due, it is meet that I indulge in a brief résumé of the part which the Putnam family took on that memorable 19th of April.

Unfortunately the tax lists of Danvers for 1775 are missing, but from those of 1773 I find that thirty-six by the name of Putnam, most of whom were heads of families, were taxed at that date; and in 1775 I find that thirty-four Putnams marched from this town to Lexington. Probably there were at that period capable of bearing arms, about forty of this name in Danvers, so it is evident that the martial spirit of the family was thoroughly aroused.

Upon the Lexington Alarm Lists at the State House may be seen the names of eighty-six Putnams, all of the Danvers family, who hastened to Lexington from various Massachusetts towns upon the alarm. Not all reached that place in time to get a shot at the retreating British, but those from Danvers, Beverly, Chelmsford, Reading, Medford and Sudbury did; and of our Danvers men, you have already heard how, in that fatal walled enclosure, Perley Putnam was killed and his brother Nathan severely wounded.

These two young men were sons of Jonathan Putnam, a great-great-grandson of my emigrant ancestor. Perley was born on the 17th of March, 1754, and had but reached his 21st year.

Nathan was his senior by not quite five years. These young men were in the Company of Israel Hutchinson, which had for its second lieutenant Enoch, son of Jethro Putnam, a member of the same younger branch of the family, and who afterward rose by successive steps in the service to the grade of colonel. With them was also Tarrant Putnam, a second cousin of Enoch, and whose widow married Captain Robert Foster of Revolutionary fame.

Nathan Putnam had in 1771, married the daughter of Dr. Amos Putnam, whose portrait hangs upon our walls.

I find but little mention of Nathan in after years except that he continued in the service during the siege of Boston and at one time enjoyed the office of constable. He died in 1783.

Still another brother was Jeremiah Putnam, afterward a captain in the 27th Foot Regiment, who served long and honorably in the war. A sister of these three brothers married Henry Putnam, the son of another martyr to Liberty on that eventful day. The father of this Henry bore the same name as his son, and was at this time living in Medford, in that part near Charlestown, where at one time he kept school. He was a veteran of Louisburg, a man of experience in military matters and had earned the commission of lieutenant which he held during the Louisburg Expedition. Although exempt from military duty he accompanied the troops to Lexington and fell in action. His sword which he carried at Louisburg and other military trappings are in the possession of his descendants. The son Henry had marched as a first lieutenant in Jeremiah Page's company and was quite badly wounded (a fact not mentioned in any of the chronicles of the fight) and remained at Medford, where his wife joined him. Upon the morning of the 17th of June, she drove him to the foot of Bunker Hill, and he did good service on that and other occasions, as he served throughout the siege.

Deacon Edmund Putnam, who so gallantly led his band of minute men, or more properly speaking, Alarm List, was the son of John Putnam and a great-great-grandson of the first John, through his second son Nathaniel, and was born 27 June, 1725. Deacon Edmund was a man of great strength, both mentally and physically, and his character was highly esteemed. Rev. Benjamin Balch acted as lieutenant of this company.

---

¹LOST in the battle of Menotomy by Nathan Putnam, of Capt. Hutchinson's Company, who was then badly wounded, a French Firelock, marked D, No. 6, with a marking Iron, on the breech. Said Putnam carried it to a crofs Road near a mill. Whoever has faid Gun in l'offeffion, is defired to return it to Col. Manffield of Lynn, or to the Selectmen of Danvers, and they fhall be rewarded for their Trouble.
Danvers, May 16th, 1775. From *New England Chronicle* or *The Essex Gazette,* May 25, 1775.

At the time of the Lexington Alarm, Deacon Edmund was living in the old Daniel Rea house, still standing on the road to Putnamville, although at one time he lived over the line in Topsfield.

In his company were Ensign Tarrant Putnam, Sergeant Benjamin Putnam, and Private Aaron Putnam, all of the tribe of Nathaniel and near neighbors of their captain.

Benjamin and Aaron were credited with but one day's service. How this is, I do not understand, as it seems improbable that they would have gone to Cambridge and back on the same day, to say nothing of having taken part in the battle. Sergeant Benjamin had a son in Captain Jeremiah Page's company and Aaron's brother Phineas served in the company of Captain John Putnam, the half-brother of Edmund. Captain John Putnam was born in 1720 and died in 1786. He was a man of great influence among his neighbors and was, I imagine, of a more pugnacious disposition than Edmund. John Putnam as well as his brother Edmund, served the town in many capacities having often been selectman and on various important committees. His title of captain adhered to him through life, while that of his brother Edmund speedily gave way to his older, more dignified, and sober title of deacon. While Captain Edmund's company was one of the smallest of our Danvers companies, that of John's was much larger. Among Captain John's men were Corporal Asa, likewise a deacon in the First Church, Phineas, Enos, Joseph, and James Phillips, a son of Dr. Amos Putnam.

Deacon Edmund Putnam was one of the first to adopt the Universalist faith in the vicinity and among his descendants may be reckoned one of the most prominent Unitarian divines.

We must not forget, that there were equally true and brave men among the Loyalists of those days. A Danvers man, James Putnam, had, previous to the Revolution, risen to high honor in the legal profession. He was born just below the present home of the poet Whittier, and there his brother Archelaus still lived at the outbreak of the Revolution.

Another brother, Dr. Eben Putnam, lived in Salem and was a member of the Committee of Safety. All of these brothers were unjustly accused by the mob of being tories, and suffered considerable annoyance.

The battle of Lexington lost James Putnam his extensive properties in Worcester, sent him a refugee to England and lost to Massachusetts the best lawyer of the time, one to whom the patriot Adams owed much of his legal ability. His letters in my possession tell of the most sincere love for his country. Both of his brothers regained the confidence of their fellow-citizens, and each in his own way served his country.

Another Danvers man has been deeply wronged by tradition and I cannot close without correcting the mistake. Timothy Putnam is said, in the History of Essex County, to have left his native hillside and fled, a tory, to Nova Scotia.

In *fact*, Timothy Putnam died here in 1756, and his widow, who had previously been the wife of Caleb Putnam, married Richard Upham and in 1761, with her family of young sons removed to Truro, Nova Scotia and there the sons founded a flourishing branch of the Putnam family, who mistakenly pride themselves upon being descended from refugees.

I have not told you of the young son of Major Ezra Putnam, who, aged 16, went as a drummer to Lexington and served throughout the siege, nor of the boy Amos Putnam, son of a Danvers man, who had settled in New Salem. This boy who died of exhaustion on the rapid march to Lexington, is to be honored as much as his more fortunate cousin, Perley, who fell by British bullets.

The martial spirit of the family did not die away with the evacuation of Boston, for over one hundred of its members served in the Continental Army, and in the second great war of Liberty, there were at least three hundred bearing the name amongst the ' Boys in Blue,' and the record is not yet complete."

Doctor Putnam then introduced Hon. Robert S. Rantoul, Mayor of Salem, who spoke as follows:

" Many of the acts of our lives are well enough forgotten, not that they are in themselves bad or mean, or necessarily selfish, but that they are trivial and have no ultimate results. They produce no ripple upon the current of human events. But now and then a great historic event occurs, and when that happens, such an event as we are here today to commemorate, it is a thing not to be forgotten, but to be perpetuated and kept in memory to the remotest time. Therefore it is not only a pleasure but a solemn duty to attend an occasion like this, and to help in every way in our power to hand down to our posterity the recollections of the virtues and excellences of our ancestry. Had there been time, I should have tried to emphasize this single view of the extraordinary transactions of the day which we are now celebrating—a view of the extremely homely, domestic, personal character of this encounter at Lexington. It always seems to me to be a hand-to-hand fight of the nations. The relations of the colonists to the representatives of the British government were so peculiar, so intimate, the colonists were such thorough-going law and order men, conservative in every fibre, respecting the law, desiring to obey the law, respecting the emissaries of the law who had been sent here to govern them, that the colonists who stood on Lexington Common had a terrible task to bring their minds to the position in which they found themselves that day. The very muskets which they took to defend themselves with were known as 'King's arms.' They were fighting at their own thresholds, behind their own stone fences, in presence of their own families and children ; they were fighting at Concord Bridge with their own venerated pastor looking from his own study window upon his own parishioners to see them quit themselves like men, as they did on that glorious occasion. There was none of the flaunting of banners and the blare of trumpets and the excitement and chivalry and romance which carries young men off on a march with an army to attack a distant or foreign enemy. If there was any of it, it was on the British side. I think the feeling those men had in their minds was not so much aggressive as conservative. I think they felt they were driven to the wall, that they were cornered, that there was no escape consistent with self-respect and the preservation of the rights of Englishmen from the dilemma in which the British government had placed them. Therefore they resolved that the last price—the price of blood—was not too great a price to pay for the liberties of Englishmen. It is not reasonable to suppose that they saw very clearly the vast dimensions of the struggle which was before them or the results which were to follow. It is idle to think that they were fighting for a nation as wide as a continent, spanning from one ocean to another, or anything of that sort. I think that they studied out from Blackstone their legal rights as Englishmen, and I think that 'they knew their rights, and knowing, dare maintain.'"

The afternoon exercises came to a close with the singing of "America."

The exercises were continued during the evening: among the speakers was Hon. M. Chamberlain who said:

"What actuated the men of the Revolution in the course which they took? Was it actual taxation? No. Not a penny was ever paid by them on an ounce of tea, not a penny was ever paid for a stamp under the stamp act. From Maine to Georgia, never was a cent taken out of the pockets of the colonists by reason of the taxation of the British Government. What was it, then, against which they took up arms? It was against the principle of the right to tax as expressed in the stamp act and kindred measures. The marvel of all this matter to me is that 3,000,000 of people should take up arms, not in consequence of what they suffered, but in consequence of what they apprehended; not because it bore heavily upon them, but because of the right. There was a principle at stake which touched their patriotism, and a principle which touched their religion; and for that they went to war, for that they suffered hardships. Who were they? They were men of clear intelligence and right thinking, of determined perseverance. They had thought this thing out, and they knew what their rights were. Those were the men to whom we are so much indebted.

What was the course of instruction which so impressed those men of New England with a desire to vindicate their rights and to withstand and confront and finally to conquer the most colossal power of modern times? Patriotism was then, as it ought to be today and forever, a religious sentiment with them. It was a part of their religion not to submit false principles in civil government any more than in religion or in church government. That lay at the foundation of their action."

At the close of Mr. Chamberlain's address, the Grand Army Post entered the hall. They were greeted with applause, the entire audience standing. After they had stacked their arms and colors in front of the platform, President Putnam extended to them an eloquent welcome.

President Capen of Tufts College spoke in part as follows:

"I have been wondering what my own connection is with all that has been said. I was not born in Essex County. I was not born in Middlesex county. I was born on the other side of the Neponset river, beyond the Blue Hills. And though I have a Revolutionary ancestry on both sides, so far as I know, I have no relationship, no kindred with any of the men who fought at Lexington and Concord. But it is enough for one to be an American citizen to have contact with the day and the events that you celebrate. It is true that for sixteen years now I have had my residence in that most historic spot in Massachusetts, in the new world. Every morning I may look out of my chamber window before I rise from my bed and see that granite shaft rising to greet the sun in his coming, which commemorates one of the grandest and most historic acts in the history of mankind. And from another window I may survey the road over which the British soldiers tramped on their way to Lexington, and see some of the points where the men of Essex County intercepted them on their return at nightfall. No man can live there without breathing that atmosphere, without catching its inspiration, without having some of its glorious memories stir within him, and without having the lessons of this noble past burned into his soul.

What are some of those lessons? First, those men, though subjects of the British crown, had developed an independence which was entirely different from Englishmen. They were thoroughly American. That is the lesson we want to learn here—to be thoroughly American. We welcome here the oppressed of all nations, but we want them to come leaving the old-world associations and memories behind them, to come here to fight under the flag, to educate their children here; we want them to come here prepared to enter into our ideas and institutions, and to help perpetuate them.

The second lesson is the lesson of patriotism and love of country as distinguished from the spirit of commercialism. The spirit in our politics that would make business interests of more importance than the principles on which this Government was founded —the principles of humanity, liberty and justice—that spirit is the danger that besets us, was the peril that surrounded us before the War of the Rebellion and that compelled these brave men whom I see before me belonging to this Grand Army post to go to the war.

We want to put into the foreground the spirit of patriotism that was so admirably illustrated by these men of the Revolution."

Dr. A. P. Putnam read the following poem, which he had written expressly for the occasion:

Our Heroes of 1775 and our "Boys in Blue."

By Rev. A. P. Putnam. D. D.

One April morn fleet tidings came,
   That, out New England's dear old town,
The *Red coats*, proud and gay, had marched
   To serve by guilty deeds the Crown.

Our fathers heard the warning cry,
   Seized sword and gun with eager hand,
Quick left the plough and bench and hearth,
   And flew like lightning o'er the land.

No storied past, of Greece or Rome,
   Can tell the tale of nobler braves
Than Danvers men, who "ran" that day,
   To *fight*; nor feared untimely graves.

Stern, dauntless Captain Flint, he said:—
   "*Where face the foe, there I am found;*"
Dyed with their blood you Cambridge heights,
   And, with his own, Stillwater's ground.

See here the battered steel he flashed,
   The gory belt that girt him fast,
As there he led his comrades on,
   And gave his precious life at last.

A gallant hero, too, was Webb,
   Nor deemed his nuptial suit too fine,
In which to act a soldier's part,
   And pour his gifts at Freedom's shrine;

But donned his best, and kissed his bride,
   And sped to make the sacrifice,—
The wedding garb his glory shroud,
   The fatal ball his pearl of price.

And Spartan mothers still were here,
   Who counted not the loss or pain,
But bade their fair and valiant sons,
   "Come with the shield or on it slain."

Dame Quaker Southwick scorned to share
   With "men of war" her basket store;
Yet swift her heart outran her creed,
   And gave them all they asked, and more.

For when dread hours that peril all,
   Arrive as there at Lexington,—
Our discords vanish into air,
   And love of country maketh one.

Oh! Beauty of our Israel,
   Whose bloom so early suffered blight,
And ye who from the victor's chase
   Returned to prosper still the Right,—

No tongue of ours just meed can give,
   Nor granite shaft that art can raise;
The Nation is your monument,
   And Liberty shall sing your praise.

Say, did ye bend from heaven and see
   The faith that armed our "boys in blue,"
Who, when Rebellion struck the flag,
   And storm and darkness hid the view,

Sprang to their feet and rushed to save
  The starry Union of their sires,
Till impious and colossal wrongs
  Went down amidst consuming fires:

Till smoke and cloud had cleared away,
  And stilled was cannon's thunderous roar,
While high the banner of our joy
  In splendid triumph waved once more?

The wine press of our woe they trod,
  In winter cold and summer heat;
The broad expanse, the mountain pass,
  They tracked with sore, but patient feet.

The weary toil, the sleepless watch,
  The midnight damp, the fevered brain,
The furious charge, the awful strife,
  And shot and sabre's quivering pain;

Torn limbs whose comfort was the sod,
  Sad hearts that pined in dungeons drear,
And crowded wards that dreamed of home,
  Nor saw its pitying angels near:—

Here, too, the stripes that healed our hurt,
  The Rock from which was hewn the State;
And here, as there, forever shine
  The names that now we celebrate.

God give us grace to know full well,
  Who sowed the seed that we might reap;
And, while eternal harvests grow,
  Let Memory her jewels keep.

NOTE.—The above abstract of the proceedings 20 Apr., 1891, is taken from a more lengthy account in the Apr., 1891, issue of the Salem Press Historical and Genealogical Record.

The Old Training Field.

The piece of land at the Centre known as the common or the training field is inseparably connected with the military history of Danvers, for according to the bequest of Nathaniel Ingersoll, it is " for a training place for ever." Last year, 1894, on June 30, the boulder, with its noble inscription was dedicated in the presence of many hundreds of people of our own and neighboring towns.*

Regarding the training field, Upham is more than usually eloquent. In his description of the place and its former owner he says " it was probably used as a training field at the first settlement of the village. From the slaughter of Bloody Brook, the storming of the Narragansett Fort, and all the early Indian wars ; from the Heights of Abraham, Lake George, Lexington, Bunker Hill, Brandywine, Pea Ridge, and a hundred other battle fields, a lustre is reflected back upon this village parade ground. It is associated with all the military traditions of the country, down to the late rebellion. Lothrop, Davenport, Gardners, Dodges, Raymonds, Putnams, Porters, Hutchinsons, Herricks, Flints, and others, who have taught or learned the manual or drill, are names inscribed on the rolls of history for deeds of heroism and prowess."

The illustration made from a photograph by Mr. D. E. Woodward, of Danvers Centre is remarkably clear. The boulder was found in one of the quarries situated in a part of the old town, a section which anciently contributed her quota to the training band of Danvers, and many of the men whose records are enrolled in this volume came from that part of the town.

Of Nathaniel Ingersoll, the donor of the land it may be said that he was an upright, God fearing man. He was the son of Richard Ingersoll who was the lessee of the Townsend Bishop farm, now better known as the Nurse farm. Richard Ingersoll died when Nathaniel was but about eleven years old and the young man went to live on the Orchard farm of Gov. Endicott, that he might the better learn how to carry on the farm left him by his father. At an early age he married Hannah Collins of Lynn and built on a spot a little in the rear of the parsonage at the Centre. There he resided for seventy years. Near by stood the block house where a watch was continually kept in the years when Indian raids were

---

*Among those present was Genville M. Dodge, a native of Danvers, whose gallantry at Pea Ridge and on other fields won him the highest rank. He has been a major-general in the army and a member of Congress and had charge of the surveys of the Union Pacific R. R.

feared. He commanded the respect of all, and rarely was his judgment at fault. At his house were held the parish and church meetings and when the church was organized we find that he was one of the two deacons. As he had no children to provide for he seems to have made no attempt to accumulate property and during his life was always liberal. He gave land for the church in which he had a deep interest. He died in 1719 and lies in an unmarked grave.

The cost of the boulder and expenses connected with its preparation and erection were met from an appropriation of $125 by the town and the subscriptions of a few public spirited citizens. The names of the committee having the matter in charge were Alden P. White, chairman; John W. Porter, Charles B. Rice, Charles H. Preston and Eben Putnam.

THE LEXINGTON MONUMENT.

This shaft imposing from its very simplicity is built of hewn sienite and was erected according to the tablet on the monument on the 60th anniversary, 1835. On the easterly side is a slab of white marble with the names of the Danvers men who fell at Lexington, 19 April, 1775, as follows:

Samuel Cook, æt. 33; Benjamin Daland, æt. 25; George Southwick, æt. 25; Jotham Webb, æt. 22; Henry Jacobs, æt. 22; Eben'r Goldthwaite, æt. 22; Perley Putnam, æt. 21.

Gen. Gideon Foster placed the corner stone and delivered a brief address. The Danvers Light Infantry did escort duty. On that day nineteen survivors of the Revolutionary soldiers were present. For Gen. Foster's account of the battle and organization of the Danvers companies, see page 106 *et seq.* of Hanson's Danvers.

Names of Soldiers and Sailors Buried in Danvers.

From Records of Ward Post 90, G. A. R.

In Walnut Grove.

Angus Ward
Gorham P. Dunn
John Rosenthal
Nathan Rosenthal
N. P. Fuller
C. N. Ingalls
Joseph F. Wiggin
Edwin Hull
John Moore
George Ingraham
William H. Mosher
Edgar M. Riggs
Moses G. Colomy
Florence H. Crowley
William H. Chadwick
William Metzger
Daniel Asquith
Henry Buckminster
William Brown
William E. Shelden
Andrew Mullen
Joseph E. Barnes
James A. Green
Darling Lowe
A. M. Hill
Charles H. Adams
Timothy Hawkes
Timothy Hawkes, jr.
Edwin Beckford
Samuel M. Porter
Samuel P. Richardson
Henry Proctor
William S. Evens
Alphonzo Sanford
John H. Williams
William H. Shirley
Charles F. Kelly
Ezra D. Kimball
Daniel J. Preston
John H. Perkins

George H. Jones
T. C. Taylor
Jacob Rosenthall
George F. Young
Stephen A. Hall
Ezra Watson
Franklin Perkins
N. P. Fish
Samuel P. Nourse
Jonathan Whitehouse
Amos Pearson
Eben Day
J. Albert Giles
William Goodwin
John G. Weeden
John Merrill
Thaddeus Osgood
Albert Kimball
Alonzo Gray
James Kelly
Charles H. Young
William Goodwin
John Withey
Richard Hood
William W. Jessup
Robert W. Jessup
Edwin Fuller
Elbridge Kennedy
George W. Kenney
Charles W. Peart
John B. Hanson
William F. Twiss
Isaac Cross
Charles Cross
Asa Lakeman
Pulaski Galucia
Joseph G. Whitehouse
George A. Wiggin
J L. Fish
George Pitman

Joseph Walworth
Samuel Page, War of 1812.
Albert A. Fowler
Daniel Smith
Patrick Traynor
Thomas Musgrave
Alphonzo Howard
James Hobbs
William C. Dale
Charles Colomy
John Goodwin
E. J. Getchell
Ephraim Getchell
Albert T. Cressy
Brig. Gen. Moses Porter, Revolution
Alfred Porter
Henry Dockham
Thomas Barnett
George Elliott
Gilman Andrews
Watson Williams
William S. Inman
William H. Ogden
Elbridge Guilford
Samuel P. Trask
John B. Putnam
Charles Putnam
Albert Henderson
George H. Dwinell
Dr. E. Hunt
Frank P. Reed
Daniel Eaton
David M. Seates
Eben Cressy
Augustus Putnam
Warren Porter
Wm. H. Wood
George Pettingell

Catholic Cemetery.

John J. Hurley
John W. Kelly
David Coleman
Thomas McKeigue
Patrick Collins
Patrick Toomey

William O'Brien
William Reynolds
Daniel A. Caskin
Owen Murphy
Edward Murphy
James Reynolds

James McCarthy
John Carrol
Michael Kirby
William O'Neil
Richard D. Poor
Timothy O'Brien

HOLTEN CEMETERY.

Hugh Cuthbertson	James Battye	Freeman A. Chase
Thomas Hartman	John Shackley	John Q. Welch
Frank Scampton	Donald Sillars	George M. Morrison
George Wylie	William Sillars	Douglass R. Wilson
James Hill	C. E. M. Welch	Abraham North
Fred Woodman	Alonzo Rogers	Robert Ferrell
Andrew Paton	William F. Guilford	Joseph G. Martin

SWAN'S CROSSING.

Major Wallace Putnam	Robert Putnam	Samuel Glover

WADSWORTH CEMETERY.

Milford Tedford	Charles A. Shepard	Albert Woodbury
	Lewis A. Verry	

HIGH ST. CEMETERY.

Frank Batchelder	Ruben Ellis	Jeremiah Page, Revolution
Moses Kent		

PUTNAMVILLE CEMETERY.

Joseph E. Annis

EAST DANVERS.

Henry Wiggin	Reuben Kenniston, Revolution

DANVERS CENTRE.

James Martin

PINES AT DANVERSPORT.

George A. Wilson

At the annual town meeting of 1895, the town voted to place markers over the graves of Revolutionary soldiers and appointed a committee to locate such graves. It is hoped that the next annual town meeting will appropriate a sum of money to print a list of the names of Revolutionary soldiers buried in town and the location of the graves.

www.ingramcontent.com/pod-product-compliance
Lightning Source LLC
Chambersburg PA
CBHW020254170426
43202CB00008B/369